T0301170

# THE LAST YAKUZA

# THE
# LAST
# YAKUZA

## JAKE ADELSTEIN

## A Life in the
## Japanese Underworld

corsair

CORSAIR

First published in Australia in 2023 by Scribe
First published in the United Kingdom in 2024 by Corsair

1 3 5 7 9 10 8 6 4 2

A CIP catalogue record for this book
is available from the British Library.

HB ISBN: 978-1-4721-5831-4
TPB ISBN: 978-1-4721-0915-6

Printed and bound in Great Britain by Clays Ltd, Elcograf S.p.A.

Papers used by Corsair are from well-managed forests
and other responsible sources.

Corsair
An imprint of
Little, Brown Book Group
Carmelite House
50 Victoria Embankment
London EC4Y 0DZ

An Hachette UK Company
www.hachette.co.uk

www.littlebrown.co.uk

# CONTENTS

**Part II: Merit Badges** (貫目)

**Part III: The Broken Gate** (破門)

# Author's note

This book is based on the lives of several yakuza bosses and is meant to tell the history of the yakuza in the last century in Japan: why they came to power, why they were tolerated, how they began, and how they have changed over time. Many people involved in the writing of this book—including lawyers, yakuza, police officers, prosecutors, and journalists—shared with me details of their lives, above and beyond the call of duty, and sometimes against their own self-interest. They told me about the history of themselves, their organization, and their friends in great detail. They talked with me about crimes they had committed or investigated, and regrets they had, gave me access to confidential information about their work, and some turned over their private videos, photographs, letters, documents, faxes, *hamonjo*, and emails. In doing this, they took incredible risks. Many of them violated codes set up by their organization that forbade them from speaking to the press without permission; and possibly, in speaking to me, they broke the law. If they had been caught cooperating with me, or the full contents of what they disclosed was known, they could have faced not only the loss of their jobs but possibly their lives or liberty.

In 2010, Japan repealed the statute of limitations on all capital crimes (death penalty offenses), and extended the statute of limitations for other felonies by up to twenty-five years. The civil servants' laws are strict in Japan, and leaking information can result in criminal prosecution. The State Secrets Law, which came into effect on December 10, 2014, punishes those who leak information with up to ten years in prison. The vagueness of those laws also theoretically allows journalists to be sentenced to up to five years in prison for "instigating leaks."

When I began researching this book, the statute of limitations revisions and the State Secrets Law were not even on the horizon. The ideal for me would have been to use only real names and not to alter any descriptions or chronologies, but in consideration of the risk that my sources face, I have done the best I could.

In exchange for my informants' cooperation, most made only one request: that I not use their real names as long as they were alive, and that details be obscured so they would not face criminal prosecution. Individuals who went on the record and said they would allow their real names to be used later recanted and asked to become anonymous.

Consequently, most names in this book have been changed, and many personal details have been altered or obscured, to protect the innocent and the not-so-innocent. A few events have been reordered chronologically or tweaked to make them less discernible to the people involved. This was not done for "narrative momentum," but to ensure the safety of everyone involved, including myself. Saigo is primarily based on the life of one yakuza, but his personal details were merged with others to protect him and them.

No one likes to deal with angry yakuza or pissed-off cops. And also, despite those who say, "It's all on the record unless the person says otherwise at the start," most sources spoke to me in good faith or in the mistaken assumption that they could no longer be held criminally responsible for their actions. Accordingly, I have decided to protect their identities as much as possible.

Covering the yakuza and writing about them is always a challenge. First of all, many of them are pathological liars, and if even they're not lying, they greatly embellish their tales to make themselves or their organization look better. Triangulating something they tell you is an arduous task. I've used biographies, court records, newspaper articles, hundreds of hours of interviews, yakuza fanzines, and police materials to do so. If I were an academic, this book would have footnotes galore. As it is, I've kept the footnotes to a minimum.

The nature of the yakuza is to pick a fight and then to demand compensation. It's one of their primary money-making methods. In Japanese, this is called *innen wo tsukeru*. It is one of the practices prohibited by the organized crime-control ordinances that were passed nationwide on October 1, 2011, and was also banned in the first anti-organized crime laws that came into effect in 1992. The laws initially had little effect.

Dealing with the yakuza and former yakuza is always like walking through a field of land mines after imbibing too many cups of sake. The only thing worse than cranky, lying yakuza are disgruntled entertainment journalists with a chip on their shoulders and too much booze in their gut. I fully expect that if this book is successful, at least one or two of the people I spoke with will try to shake me down. That's how the yakuza work—that's their nature. If you were to say "Good morning" to the wrong yakuza, in fifteen minutes he would be making you apologize for saying you were glad his mother had died that morning—on this so-called good morning—and you'd be paying him a few hundred dollars to show your repentance and sincerity. A few weeks later, another of his buddies would blackmail you for paying off the yakuza, which is now a crime. If you were very lucky, maybe it would end there.

As an investigative journalist, trouble is my business.

For yakuza, troublemaking is their business.

However, from over thirty years of reporting on organized crime in Japan, I have decided to take those risks in publishing this book because I feel the story of the yakuza in Japan and their ultimately negative influence on society is something that, even now, people should know about. There are some yakuza who have followed a rudimentary code of ethics, who, within the context of the underworld, are "admirable" people. There are few of them left, if any at all.

The influence and power of the yakuza has waned dramatically. There were nearly 80,000 in 2011, but, according to the National Police Agency, there were only around 24,000 or fewer active yakuza as of 2021. If you only include full-fledged members, that number drops to 12,300. Any way you look at it, the decline is steep, and shows no signs of slowing down.

The Yamaguchi-gumi split into two factions on August 26, 2015, marking the tenth anniversary of Shinobu Tsukasa taking the throne. The new faction was led by Kunio Inoue of the Yamaken-gumi, and called itself the Kobe-Yamaguchi-gumi. Retired gangster Tadamasa Goto put up the seed money. A third faction calling itself the Ninkyo aka Humanitarian Yamaguchi-Gumi emerged in 2017. The three groups have been engaged in a bloody battle for dominance for years now, but until there are civilian casualties the Japanese government is happy to just watch the war of attrition.

The Kobe-Yamaguchi-gumi has already lost the war, but refuses to surrender. The Yamaken-gumi split apart from them, and in 2022 the Takumi-gumi, led by its well-respected boss, Tadashi Irie, declared independence. By the time you read this, the Kobe-Yamaguchi-gumi may even be gone.

The yakuza were allowed to exist until the 2020 Olympics (held in 2021) were over. The criminal conspiracy bill that would have put them out of business never became law in a way that could dismantle them permanently. Additional laws are unlikely to pass so long as the major yakuza groups still have political capital and a few politicians in their pockets.

If you doubted that the yakuza still had power, the cherry blossom viewing parties held by prime minister Abe (when he was alive) and his henchman Yoshihide Suga, which yakuza bosses quietly attended, showed they were still pulling strings behind the scenes. The cabinet decision after that scandal, to declare that there was no actual definition of yakuza (anti-social forces), was a new low point in Japanese politics. I've come to feel that the only difference between Japan's Liberal Democratic Party and the yakuza are two things: the yakuza have different badges, and some of the yakuza have a code of ethics.

I write about the yakuza less and less. I can't say that this bothers me. In a few years, I think if I'm writing about the yakuza at all, it will be as history, not as news.

People ask me if there is anything good about them. Well, you can learn some valuable life lessons from the best of them. If there are any lessons to be learned from the Inagawa-kai, specifically the Yokosuka-ikka, they are these:

Pay back the kindnesses bestowed upon you.
Every promise matters.
It's good to have a code.
Be ready to be betrayed, but don't be the betrayer.

This book is dedicated to Coach; my father, Eddie Adelstein; and Takahiko Inoue, a yakuza boss and Buddhist priest, who tried his best to convince the yakuza around him that there is one law that can never be thwarted: the law of karma.

One would hope that is really the case.

# Timeline

1870s: Japan's oldest existent yakuza group, the Aizukotetsu-kai, is founded in Kyoto by an angry, deadly dwarf gambler.

1913: March 28: Kazuo Taoka, the godfather of godfathers, is born.

1915: The Yamaguchi-gumi, Japan's largest organized crime group, is founded in Kobe. After the war, Kazuo Taoka becomes the third-generation leader, only after setting up a corporation to expand the group's activities into the business world.

1948: The Inagawa-kai (at the time, Inagawa-gumi) is founded by Kakuji Inagawa aka Seijo Inagawa. It is still the third-most powerful yakuza group in Japan.

1963: Yoshio Kodama, right-winger, war-profiteer, former spy for the CIA, and co-founder of Japan's Liberal Democratic Party, creates a coalition of all yakuza groups in Japan, and begins to give orders to the government.

1964: The Japanese government, realizing the yakuza are too powerful, launches its first crackdown.

1976: Saigo enters a motorcycle gang and becomes the second-generation leader of a small group in the Inagawa-kai Yokosuka-Ikka.

1992: Yamaguchi-gumi Goto-gumi members assault film director Juzo Itami after he makes a film advocating resisting the yakuza, which also portrays them as greedy, petty thugs.

1993: The first anti-organized crime laws go into effect.

1995: Aum Shinrikyo, an apocalyptic cult, also connected to the yakuza, releases nerve gas on the Tokyo subway system, injuring over 1,000 people.

2002: Saigo rises to executive committee level in Inagawa-kai.

2005: Saigo is arrested and fined 300,000 yen for assault.

2007: A member of a rival gang shoots another yakuza and has a standoff with the police. Local police crack down on Saigo's organization.

2008: Saigo is expelled from the Inagawa-kai.

2011: Ordinances forbidding dealing with or paying off any yakuza member go into effect nationwide. Membership starts to rapidly decline.

2014: The Buddha of the Yakuza aka Takahiko Inoue dies mysteriously.

2015–2016: The Yamaguchi-gumi splits apart; the Kobe Yamaguchi-gumi is founded.

2017: The Yamaguchi-gumi and Kobe-Yamaguchi-gumi split, resulting in the formation of the Ninkyo-Yamaguchi-gumi.

2021: Kudo-kai bosses are sentenced to death for crimes committed by underlings—an unprecedentedly harsh punishment.

2022: The Takumi-gumi leaves the Kobe-Yamaguchi-gumi, effectively ending the group; the Yamaguchi-gumi is still in flux.

# Main characters and organizations

(in order of appearance)

Note: At the end of each entry is a letter indicating the yakuza group or social group that the individual is affiliated or associated with: I: Inagawa-kai; Y: Yamaguchi-gumi; S: Sumiyoshi-kai; K: Kyokuto-kai; and P: Police

## The yakuza

Inagawa-kai: founded in 1948. Japan's third-largest yakuza group, originally a federation of gamblers, once the ruling yakuza group in eastern Japan.

Yokosuka-Ikka: once one of the most powerful factions in the Inagawa-kai crime family.

Makoto Saigo (aka Tsunami): born after the war to a Japanese American woman. A juvenile delinquent, motorcycle gang member, and right-wing group leader, he rises up in the Inagawa-kai. (I)

Fujimori: Saigo's former band member during the days when they played rock and roll together. (I)

Takahiko Inoue (aka The Buddha): The former bodyguard of Susumu

Ishii and an executive of the Yokosuka-gumi faction. Also later a Zen Buddhist priest. (I)

Hideo Hishiyama: a crafty underboss in the Inagawa-kai, and Saigo's first *oyabun* (father figure). (I)

Susumu Ishii: The brilliant second-generation leader of the Inagawa-kai who took the group into the financial sector, sometimes called "The Father of the Economic Yakuza". (I)

Hiroshi Miyamoto: a loyal soldier to the Inagawa-kai second-generation boss Susumu Ishii. (I)

Kakuji Inagawa, also known as Seijo Inagawa: the wise founder of the Inagawa-kai who earned tremendous influence and respect in postwar Japan. (I)

Daisaku Hanzawa: a loose cannon under Saigo with serious drug problems. (I)

Coach: Nobuyuki Kanazawa, a former professional baseball player turned yakuza. A major executive in the Inagawa-kai who would later become the head of the Yokosuka-Ikka. (I)

Kenji Mizoguchi: one of Saigo's most loyal and dependable soldiers over the course of his criminal career. (I)

Kazuo Kawasaki aka Purple: The third-generation head of a *tekiya* (street merchant) yakuza group that became part of the Inagawa-kai. Eccentric, hypersexual, and Saigo's older brother in the yakuza world. (I)

The Preacher: a high-ranking Inagawa-kai yakuza boss who also claimed to be a Christian. (I)

Yoshio Tsunoda: a close friend of Coach and the fourth-generation leader of the Inagawa-kai. (I)

Chihio Inagawa: The son of the founder of the Inagawa-kai, Japan's third-largest organized crime family. He was the third-generation leader. (I)

Jo Yabe: A low-ranking Inagawa-kai member with a drug problem. (I)

Kyokuto-kai: a yakuza group, originally *tekiya*), founded before the war in Tokyo. Infamous for peddling methamphetamines. (K)

Kinbara: a bad-tempered boss in the Kyokuto-kai, head of the Kinbara-gumi, and rival for Saigo's turf. (K)

Tosei-kai, a predominantly Korean Japanese yakuza group that rose to power in postwar Tokyo. Now known as the Toa-kai.

Hisayuki Machii: aka The Bull. The leader of the Tosei-kai.

The Sumiyoshi-kai: a federation of Kanto yakuza groups, it is Japan's second-largest yakuza organization. (S)

The Yamaguchi-gumi: founded in 1915, Japan's largest organized crime group, and likened to Goldman Sachs with guns.

Kazuo Taoka: the charismatic third-generation leader of the Yamaguchi-gumi. Born March 28, 1913. (Shares the same birthday as the author.) (Y)

Masaru Takumi: a top leader of the Yamaguchi-gumi known for his financial wizardry and strong political and economic connections. (Y)

## Cops and colleagues

Detective Lucky: a reasonable and crafty organized crime control division police officer. (P)

Junichiro Koizumi: former prime minister of Japan whose grandfather had also been a yakuza and had friendly ties to the Inagawa-kai. (I)

Detective Midorigawa aka Greenriver: A rule-breaking cop in the organized crime control division who came to form a sort of friendship with Saigo. (P)

Barbarian: A rapper, former marijuana dealer, and eventual friend of Saigo. (I)

Yuriko: Saigo's second wife.

Takashi Muraki: a corrupt cop on the Kanagawa prefecture police force who would shake down yakuza when it suited him. (P)

Aum Shinrikyo: A doomsday cult that spread nerve gas on the Tokyo subway, killing several and injuring thousands. They earned money for their operations by producing methamphetamines and other drugs, and selling them wholesale to the Yamaguchi-gumi, especially to the Goto-Gumi.

Shoko Asahara: The leader of the doomsday cult, Aum Shinrikyo. (See above.)

# PROLOGUE

# July 2008

There were three of us in the room. Me, Makoto Saigo, and, having come along for the ride, Tomohiko Suzuki.

Saigo, pronounced like "sigh" of relief, and "go", as in get up and go, was a former yakuza who had once lorded over 150 soldiers as the boss of a subset of the Inagawa-kai, which is the third-largest organized crime group in Japan.

Tomohiko Suzuki was one of the best yakuza writers in Japan and a former editor of the yakuza fan magazine *Jitsuwa Bull*. Suzuki seemed more like yakuza than the people he wrote about. He sat on the floor; Saigo sat on the red faux-leather sofa; and I sat on the chair across from him. Between us was a small, round table, a *chabu-dai*, great for a tea ceremony and not bad as a coffee table or a place to put an ashtray.

The living room was silent. It felt like someone had turned down the sound on the whole world. It was cold for June. The rain had been pouring since morning, with a strong wind. It rattled the *amado* (rain shutters), and I could hear the rain splattering on the windowsill. And in that raindrop-punctuated silence, I thought about the circumstances that had brought us together.

I was in a bit of a tight spot. I'd managed to piss off one of the most vicious crime bosses in Japan, Tadamasa Goto, a Yamaguchi-gumi consigliore. The Yamaguchi-gumi is Japan's largest crime group, with 39,000 members. How I had pissed him off is a long story, and one I've told elsewhere.* Let's just say that I dug up some dirt about the man in question that proved he had traded favors with the feds in the United States, for his own benefit and to the detriment of his organization.

For the moment, I had the protection of the Tokyo Metropolitan Police Department, excluding one corrupt cop working for Goto. I had a tacit alliance with one member of the Yamaguchi-gumi. I didn't feel that the odds were in my favor. Still, I had an ace in the hole—I just needed to keep myself alive long enough play it.

I had to write an article that would get Goto off my back. Once the story was public, I would be a much harder target to hit.

I was stuck in Japan for two months trying to figure out a way to get the story out. I didn't want him following me home to the United States and having him use his connections to take me—and possibly my wife and two children—out.

To be honest, I was kind of hoping that if I could get the story written, his own people would kill him. It seemed like a reasonable bet. Nobody likes a rat, especially the yakuza. In Japan's case, the word for a rat is "dog." Either way, the yakuza took a dim view of one of their own cooperating with law enforcement.

I contacted Suzuki, because if anyone could help me get a detailed story into print, it would be him. I also needed him to put me in touch with Saigo, whom we both knew. I knew things hadn't gone well for him in recent years—he'd either left or been kicked out of the Inagawa-kai. I wasn't sure what had happened there. I did know he was looking for work and that he had a one-year-old son. I needed a bodyguard, and I wanted to hire him to protect me.

---

\*   In *Tokyo Vice: An American Reporter on the Police Beat in Japan.*

Before I asked Saigo to work for me or with me, I wanted to be absolutely sure I could trust him. I had known him casually for many years. His nickname was Tsunami. He was called Tsunami because he was like an unstoppable force of nature, relentless and violent, and nobody could predict when he would come and launch a rain of destruction. However, in the underworld, you never know someone entirely. That's just how it is.

I contacted the only man in the underworld I sort of trusted. It wasn't easy to reach him. I had to go to a pay phone and then call one of his front companies, leave a message, wait for the message to get to him, and then pick up the phone when he called. He would call from a public pay phone, and, thanks to the miracles of Japanese technology, my phone would tell me as much when he called.

He called just before midnight the same day I reached out to him. I explained the situation, and I gave him the name.

"Ah, Saigo. I knew him well. He's a *kyodai* [practically brother] to one of our own—not my faction, though. His *oyabun* is a stand-up guy. So is he."

He sounded perfect. But my "advisor" had a word of caution.

"He's very stubborn. Won't listen to reason, and when he decides he's in the right and loses his temper, he plows down anything in his way."

It sounded good to me. If Saigo really was a storm incarnate, that could make me a mini-*Raijin*, the Japanese god of thunder and lightning. It would be an improvement over feeling like a tangerine placed on a Buddhist altar for the dead.

Saigo had come to the house with Suzuki dressed in a black suit that had seen better days; it was a funeral suit, as best I could tell. He was huge for a Japanese man, his hair slicked back, and tattoos flashing past the cuff of his whitish shirt. He was polite and quiet. His eyes looked sunken, as though the sockets had been punched back and stayed there, but even in his late forties you could still feel a raw power coming from him.

I asked Saigo to protect me, and pulled the rough draft of the story out of my bag, ignoring Suzuki's unsubtle signals to put the thing back immediately. Saigo took a long time to read it, going over it word by word, his finger touching each character as though he was reading Braille.

The snake knows the way of the serpent. *Ja no michi wa hebi.*

That is one of my favorite Japanese proverbs. It is also like its counterpart: treat poison with poison. I figured the best way to get through this entire problem with the Goto-gumi was to hire another yakuza—even a former yakuza from an opposing group. It couldn't hurt, and it might help.

The big question was, would Saigo take the job.

He put down the manuscript and looked me in the eyes.

"I think you have a serious problem. I hope you've realized that yourself. You've pissed off Goto Tadamasa. Let me tell you something—I know Goto. He's not like other yakuza."

"How's he different?" I asked.

"He's an asshole; an arrogant, double-dealing asshole. He used to be one of ours, an Inagawa-kai member, but jumped ship to the Yamaguchi-gumi. I know him." Saigo pulled out his cell phone, flipped it open, and scrolled through the directory. There it was: Goto Tadamasa and his number.

Goto killed people, or had them killed—ordinary people, civilians — and he didn't flinch. "That's not how the yakuza are supposed to operate," Saigo said. *"Katagi ni meiwaku o kakenai."* ("Don't cause trouble to ordinary people.") That used to be the rule. Goto got to where he was, and had amassed the money he had made, because he never paid attention to that rule. Maybe he defined the future of the yakuza. It all seemed to come down to money these days.

"Jake-san, how much is this story worth to you? Because there's a good chance that, before you publish it or even after, I'll get killed protecting you, and then Goto will kill you."

I had thought about just getting the hell out of Japan, but I'd always be looking behind me. There was more to it than that. It wasn't just a story anymore. It had become personal. Maybe it was a vendetta. I hesitated to say such melodramatic crap, but I couldn't grasp better words.

"It's worth my entire life."

"Well," Saigo said, rolling the words out of his mouth, "then I guess it's worth my life as well."

With that, he agreed to be my bodyguard. He was willing to risk dying for me — but he wanted to know what I was willing to do for him in return. It wouldn't have mattered what I offered in return. He'd already made up his mind. His question to me was largely a formality.

"What would you like me to do?" I asked.

"Let me think about what I want for a second," he said, almost in a whisper.

He lit up his cigarettes, Short Hopes, inhaled, and closed his eyes, deep in thought. His huge hands made the cigarette look like a matchstick. He held his tobacco in a way that made it hard to notice he was missing the first two joints of his pinkie.

Actually, "missing" would be the wrong word. As I learned later, he'd amputated it in the yakuza tradition of paying penance. I didn't know why he'd done it, and I certainly wasn't going to ask. Not today.

He sat back on the couch, and I got a better look at his face. He had a crew cut and a beard that was speckled with gray hair. Not only his eye sockets, but his cheeks were sunken, and his skin had an unhealthy gray pallor. He looked like the living dead. That wouldn't be bad, I thought. You can't kill a zombie; they keep on coming. He would be the perfect bodyguard.

"When it's all done, you write my biography. I'm proud to have been a yakuza, and I want my son to know who I was and what I did. I don't think I'll live long enough to see him grow up."

I hesitated. I needed him to be my bodyguard, but I wasn't willing to become a yakuza cheerleader. It wasn't worth it.

"I'm not going to write something glorifying the yakuza," I said. "If I were to write it, it would have to cover everything."

His answer surprised me.

"I'd expect nothing less."

And, with that, our lives were bound together, but I wouldn't find out Saigo's real reasons for taking the job until much later.

# PART I

# LEARNING THE TRADE
## 修行

# CHAPTER ONE

# A half-American yakuza

Saigo's mother, Josephine Kato, grew up in Seattle in the 1920s and 1930s. By 1940, the United States and Japan seemed to be heading towards war. Anti-Japanese sentiment was tangible all around her, and as a *nisei* (a child born to Japanese parents in a different country), Josephine felt that, if war broke out, she and her family would be imprisoned. They decided to return to Japan, where they would be safe.

Her older brother, James Y. Kato, joined the U.S. Army, where he served as a code-breaker until the end of the war. For a few years, he even held a position at General Headquarters (GHQ), the offices of the occupation government in postwar Japan. GHQ included a staff of several hundred U.S. civil servants as well as the military personnel. Some of these staffers effectively wrote the first draft of the Japanese Constitution, which the Diet (Japan's parliament and the equivalent of the U.S. congress) then ratified after a few amendments. He never discussed what he really did at GHQ.

When she went back to Japan with her family, she did not renounce her American citizenship, which technically makes her son,

Makoto Saigo, the son of an American (though it's unlikely he would easily get American citizenship now).

After the war, which she doesn't like to talk about, Josephine met Saigo's father, Hitoshi Saigo. It wasn't an arranged marriage, which was usual at the time, but *ren-ai kekkon* — a marriage of love. It wasn't a match made in heaven because, at her core, Josephine was an American. Mr Saigo was by no means a typical Japanese man, but he wasn't quite internationalized either.

He was certainly not a rabid Japanese national.

Growing up, Mr Saigo wanted to become a police officer, partly because his father had been one, but also because, "I wanted to make the world a better place; a safer place. I wanted to do something good."

World War II interfered with that. He joined the army without much of a choice, and volunteered to be a "kamikaze" — technically known as *Tokotai,* "special attack forces." He didn't actually have a desire to die.

"I knew we couldn't win the war. America was going to crush us. Anyone could see that. When I'd hear my commander tell us that Japan would fight until every single Japanese died for the emperor, I thought it was crazy. How can you win a war if there is no one left alive to savor the victory?"

While there were a number of Japanese who believed the emperor was divine and were gung-ho about fighting to the death, he wasn't one of them.

Mr Saigo was a practical man. He had a stoic understanding of the world that he often succinctly expressed by quoting this Japanese proverb: "You can spend your whole life laughing, or spend your whole life crying. Either way, you only have one life."

"I figured I'd die in the war. So, if death is inevitable, isn't it a lot cooler to raise your hand and volunteer to die as a kamikaze rather than just be more cannon fodder?" When the time came to volunteer, he raised his hand and smiled. Perhaps some of that cheery fatalism was passed along to his son.

When the war ended, Mr Saigo was enrolled in the Navy Fighter Pilot Training Program in Tsuchiura. In another year, he would have been dead. He wasn't sorry that the war ended, or that Japan had been defeated.

He promptly enrolled in the postwar police force, where he received the training necessary to pursue his dream of becoming a police officer and possibly a detective. However, the specter of the military cast a shadow over his plans.

On the day of his graduation in the summer of 1950, after several years of training, he and a group of other would-be graduates were called to one side. Their commander told them they had a special mission for them. They were going to be a special kind of police officer in the newly formed National Police Reserve.

Everyone was puzzled. One cadet raised his hand and asked, "What's the 'National Police Reserve?'"

The commander sucked in air dramatically. "It's the army. The new army."

The cadets were floored. An army? Hadn't Japan's army been decimated? Japan wasn't supposed to have an army.

One cadet raised the issue. "MacArthur banned the army."

The commander replied, "Well, he changed his mind. That's the way it is. If any of you don't want to be part of it, you can quit now."

About 20 percent of them did. Mr Saigo did not. He had come too far to pull back now. Maybe things would change.

GHQ officially created the National Police Reserve on August 10, 1950. It would later become Japan's de facto army, the Japan Self-Defense Forces. According to documents uncovered by the *Sankei* newspaper in 2014, GHQ agreed to its creation due to fears of communism and the riots by Korean Japanese.

A large number of Koreans had moved to Japan during its colonial period (1895–1945) and stayed even after the war. Some of those who stayed had been dragged to Japan as forced labor for the war effort. In 1948, the ministry of education sent an official letter to the Osaka government to close down the Korean schools, which taught Korean language and culture. The Koreans responded with extreme anger and violent protests.

On April 24, 7,000 people, mostly Koreans, surrounded the Osaka prefectural headquarters. In Kobe, protesters swarmed the Hyogo headquarters and held the governor in virtual captivity, demanding he overturn the decision to close the schools. The occupying forces declared a state of emergency in the Kobe area. Lieutenant General Robert L. Eichelberger was dispatched from GHQ to deal with the problem, and issued an official condemnation of the riots. GHQ learned that some of the protestors were communists, giving some weight to Japan's request to have a stronger police force, which Prime Minister Yoshida had repeatedly requested.*

Mr Saigo knew none of this — all he knew was that he signed up to be a cop, and instead found he had somehow volunteered to be in the army again. He imagined that, since he had already escaped death on the battlefield once, he might not be able to escape it again in the foreseen war with Russia.

He was sent to Hokkaido. After four years of Spartan practice, learning military arts and strategy, it was clear that his division was going to become part of the new Japanese army. They would never be cops.

Yet, for all practical purposes, they were organized like the police force and dressed like the police force. The only difference was that they didn't have the right to arrest anyone.

---

* The Koreans in Japan were in some ways responsible for Japan rebuilding its army. They would later go on to power Japan's second army: the yakuza. Unlike the rest of Japan, which harbored racism towards Korea and Korean Japanese, and still does, the yakuza were very much a meritocracy.

The training was brutal. The climate was cold and hostile. He had to learn to fire shotguns and machine guns, scale walls, and do everything a SWAT team member had to do.

He managed to get transferred to Camp Fuji, where life was easier, and there, on his occasional R & R, he met Josephine.

At first, he thought she was a little crazy and intimidating. At a height of 174 centimeters, Josephine was a giant among the Japanese women at the time, but Mr Saigo decided to rise to the challenge.

He was still a civil servant, so, after pulling some strings and knocking on a few doors, he managed to leave the military and join the Bank of Japan. Shortly afterwards, Mr Saigo and Josephine decided to get married. Both of their families were opposed. Josephine's family wanted her to marry an American, and Saigo's family was puzzled that he was marrying this giant of a woman who was clearly more American than Japanese — and very far from being the ideal superficial, subservient Japanese wife.

It wasn't quite domestic bliss, but it wasn't bad. They were happy. They moved to Machida City, a large suburb within Tokyo. Josephine gave birth to three children. Makoto Saigo was the first. He was born two days after Christmas, on December 27, 1960.

Every morning, Josephine would make an American breakfast for the family. This didn't go over well with "Dad", who always wanted fish, rice, seaweed, and miso soup. "Mom" would only occasionally make a Japanese breakfast. As a result, young Saigo was bad at using his chopsticks. Seeing him make clumsy attempts to eat rice with chopsticks drove his father crazy.

"Makoto," he would say, "That is no way to eat rice. You have to hold the chopsticks like this." He'd then demonstrate.

Josephine would counter him, saying, "If you have a knife and a fork and a spoon, you don't need chopsticks."

Saigo would then agree with her retort. "Yeah, Dad, who needs chopsticks?"

Infuriated, Saigo's dad would then slap him on the head and say, "You're in Japan. We eat with chopsticks here and, if you're going to live here, you better learn to eat properly."

In Josephine's mind, however, eating "properly" was oatmeal, eggs, bacon, toast, and hamburgers. The quintessential American diet. Her son agreed with her on that. The typical Japanese breakfast: rice, fish, dried seaweed, and miso soup? Saigo didn't like that at all.

Well, it turned out that, by eating American-style, Saigo grew in leaps and bounds. He towered over his classmates like a bear among deer. And perhaps because of his height or the way his mother spoke to him in front of the neighbors, when Saigo went to elementary school, the other kids meanly called him *gaijin*, which means foreigner.

The long form of the word is *gaikokujin*, coming from the words for outside, country, and person. The abbreviated form was sometimes taken to mean "not human" (outside person), and was derogatory. It's certainly a word that makes an individual feel alienated in Japanese society. It's not a coincidence that over 30 percent of the yakuza are non-Japanese. Many of them are now third- or fourth-generation Korean Japanese. The current head of the Inagawa-kai, Jiro Kiyota , is a Korean Japanese man who has never been nationalized.

If you asked Saigo whether being treated as a foreigner in his younger years attracted him to the yakuza or made him a rebel, he would tell you that you were overthinking it. He insisted that the reason he became a yakuza was because he didn't like school, he didn't like straitlaced Japanese society, and it was much more fun to be an outlaw than it was to be a salaryman.

As he was growing up, he decided he liked being called an American. After all, his mother was an American, and America had won the war.

His father was surprisingly pro-American as well. His dad would often tell him, "America saved us from ourselves. They defeated us, but they showed us great mercy and helped rebuild this country. If we had been faster at building an atomic bomb, we might've won the war. I doubt we would've been this merciful."

Of course, Saigo did not understand what his father had meant about Japan building an atomic bomb. However, years later, when in prison, he read a newspaper article about Japan's secret atomic bomb program, and realized that his father was exceptionally well informed. He had great respect for his father.

But, like most Japanese children, his father was an absentee dad. At the time, that was the Japanese way of raising children for many households. While everyone had a mom and dad, the families were essentially single-mother households. Saigo saw much more of his mother than he ever did his father, and simply accepted that as the way things were. His father left the house early, came home late, and sometimes worked weekends. When Saigo saw him, it was usually at breakfast. His father didn't show him much affection or attention. His idea of educating Saigo was to pound sense into his son's head by using his fist or an open palm.

His parents fought often, but the fights were more comical than vicious. Josephine and Hitoshi would often quarrel during breakfast about any number of things. They quarreled about the war, school, Japan's place in the world, about the emperor, and about breakfast itself. They were both ethnically Japanese and had a common language; but, culturally, Josephine was a liberated American woman, and Hitoshi (Mr Saigo) was a staid Japanese man.

When they argued in Japanese, the stymied and flustered Josephine would always return to English mode, slam her hands on the table, and scream "*No!*"

Hitoshi, not being very good at English, would then usually give up.

Once he asked her what she thought of the emperor, and her reply was, "The U.S. president is greater." That wasn't really the question, and the answer didn't exactly charm her husband.

They argued over about what to call each other. Japanese people usually refer to one another by their family name, followed by an honorific. Japan is a vertical society in nature, and the language reflects that. To speak it properly, you have to determine where you and the person you are addressing are in relation to each other in the social power grid. The way you conjugate your verbs and adjectives is important for showing politeness, and how you address people is particularly important.

*San* is the most familiar honorific suffix to people in the West, and it's relatively neutral. *Sama* is more formal. Males will refer to their close friends, equals, or inferiors with *kun* and, sometimes, *chan*. *Chan* used to be a more feminine honorific. Women use *san*, *sama*, and *kun* as well, but *chan* is the term of endearment that women use to address each other. They sometimes use *chan* for men and boys, too. A mixture of *sama* and *chan*, which is pronounced "*chama*," can also be used by either gender, but only in a joking way. Within a company, the position of the supervisor can be used in place of a name. For example, "Toshiaki Kato, division head of tractor parts" might just be called *kacho* (division head) by his subordinates. If there was another division head from a different department present at meeting, Toshiaki Kato might be called Kato Kacho to clarify the situation. Some new recruits might even attach honorifics to the job title, resulting in phrases such as Kato Kacho-Sama, which older Japanese would tell you is being too polite, and thus rude.

In the world of the yakuza, the head of the group is often just called *Kumi-cho*. *Cho* means the top. The leader is also called *oyabun*, which literally means "father-figure." If you are on very friendly terms with your boss, you can even call him *oyaji* — which in English is close to "the old man" or "Pops."

One of the worst things you can do is call someone by their name with no honorific at all, which is known as *yobisute* aka "throwing away the honorific."

Josephine liked to be called "Josephine" and just that. No honorific needed. Hitoshi felt she should use her Japanese name, Kazuko. He wanted to call her Kazuko-chan. Josephine didn't like that. At first, she just called him Hitoshi, but over time this unusual term of endearment began to feel unnatural to him. They began to argue about it. Finally, they settled on Me and You. Josephine called him "You." He called her "Me." It didn't quite make sense, but it worked. And when it didn't work, they used first names. When they were very, very, very angry with each other, they'd politely refer to each other by their last names with a *sama* attached.

If the two started bandying about "Saigo-sama" and "Kato-sama," it meant the cold war had broken out.

At the height of one of their worst arguments, Josephine lost her cool and called her husband "Jap." This almost resulted in blows. He spat back, *"Hikokumin!"* — Japanese slang for a non-native national, but Josephine wasn't bothered in the least. She coldly replied, "Yes, I am. I'm an American. I may look Japanese, but inside I'm an American."

And so was her son. In spirit, at least.

Japan places a great deal of importance on the individual harmonizing with the group. Japanese people are bound by a countless number of rules about what is proper behavior.

To an American like Josephine, who was Japanese only in appearance, Japan seemed very uptight and rigid. Modes of speech changed depending on whether you were addressing a man or a woman; someone older or younger; a social inferior or superior;

or a close friend or an acquaintance. Even the prestigiousness of a profession had an influence over how you spoke and acted towards another. A doctor was given the title *sensei*, but a construction worker could simply be referred to as "You over there."

There was an informal dress code that came with one's place in society. White-collar workers wore white dress shirts, dark, unpatterned navy-blue suits, dark ties, and dark shoes. Construction workers dressed in special slacks, two-toed shoes, and often sported the same haircuts. School children all wore the same uniforms, making it impossible to distinguish who was wealthy and who was poor. From the first days of school, Japanese people were taught not to "go their own way," but to act as others did and to get along with their classmates; to share chores, responsibility, and the same values.

There was even a right way and a wrong way to bow, and the depth of the bow depended up on both the time and place of the bow and whom you were addressing.

Japan is all about *wa* — the ideal of social harmony. Everyone plays the roles they are assigned to on the great stage that is Japan. Everyone is a performer, and everyone is an audience member — each watching and performing for the other. It requires everyone to say their lines at the proper time and in the correct way.

Well, the spirit of *wa* also known as *Yamatodamashi* (the soul of a Japanese person), wasn't engrained in his mother, and it wasn't engrained in him. He couldn't see the point of shutting up and submitting for the greater peace of the group. In a society where you gotta have *wa*, he wasn't interested; but he wasn't interested in being an American either.*

Josephine tried to teach her son some English, but gave up when she realized he had no interest in learning the language. Maybe it

---

\*   On that note, Robert Whiting's book *You Gotta Have Wa*, while ostensibly about Japanese baseball, is a wonderful microcosm of Japanese society in general.

was because he was sometimes embarrassed to be called an American or being treated like a foreigner, or maybe he was just lazy. Even Saigo can't remember his reasons, but he does wish he'd paid more attention.

If he'd learned English, maybe he could have done other things. He might have excelled in at least one class, but he didn't. It turns out that his areas of expertise were less to do with school, and more to do with crime.

## CHAPTER TWO

# Driving past the point of no return at full speed

By April 1975, Saigo was a confirmed juvenile delinquent. His only skills were playing the guitar and winning fights. At the age of fourteen, he passed the exam to get into Tokyo Machida High School. By the third day of his first year, his troublemaking, frequent fights with classmates, bad attitude, and maybe even his bad-ass haircut resulted in him being given an ultimatum: leave on his own, or get kicked out within a week.

During this time, he had two loves: music and motorcycles. Gaido aka The Evil Path was a legendary rock band, and he was one of the original members.

In the 1970s, Gaido had a huge following of delinquent youth, young yakuza, and motorcycle gangs. Their songs and lyrics were extremely controversial for their day. Songs such as "Yellow Monkey" ridiculed modern Japan, and their neo-punk version of Japanese right-wing anthems inflamed conservatives as well. One of the songs that Saigo helped write, "Kaori," was a hidden ode to smoking pot. *Kaori,* in Japanese, is a woman's name, but it also means "scent." The lyrics noting that "Kaori will always give you away" referred to the strong smell of marijuana. Songs like this and their general attitude made them the rebel rockers of their time. At their best, they sounded like the Sex Pistols crossed with Kiss (although they existed way before the Sex Pistols). Saigo was a member by 1974, when he was just thirteen years old. In the original line-up, he played guitar and did some vocals. His senior, Shinji Maruyama also did vocals and played the drums. Although thin, Maruyama was as tall as Saigo. He had an extremely flat face and a wide smile that seemed to go from ear to ear.

Gaido took intense delight in pissing off the authorities. They wore deformed kimonos, put on make-up, and made liberal use of the Japanese flag. No one could tell whether they were right-wingers or left-wingers; everyone knew they were troublemakers.

Machida is sometimes called the Detroit of Japan — a surprising number of great Japanese rock bands such as Luna Sea have emerged from its bleak urban landscape. It was an industrial town when Saigo was growing up, with little to do, few parks, and a general atmosphere of urban decay. While part of Tokyo, it was a strangely lawless place. The term "urban jungle" wouldn't be simply a cliché, but a judicious description. The town was full of bars, brothels, and live-music venues. That was entertainment in the town: getting drunk, getting fucked, and/or listening to rock.

Today, Machida has two nicknames. The first is Nishi Kabukicho, which refers to its network of sleazy sex shops, love hotels, and massage parlors. The second is Machida Music City. However, being born in Machida alone was no guarantee of being a talented musician.

Saigo wasn't the best guitarist, and by the time the group made their first full-fledged live performance, he was relegated to the sidelines; he had roadie status. Gaido's early performances are captured in a two-record set, "The Crazy Passionate Machida Police 1974 (Live)." The two-record set consists of the band playing at the Machida Gymnasium in February 1974, and then again at the Machida Town Festival in September 1974. They played on a temporarily constructed stage right next to the Machida Police Station. In between songs, the band — clad in white kimonos, jeans, and torn clothing — taunt the cops by asking, "Mr Policeman, are you having fun?" and the cops and locals are heard asking them to get off the stage and stop playing. The Gaido groupies can be heard rowdily cheering the band and telling everyone who complains to shut up. A grainy videotape of the performance made its way onto YouTube a few years ago. If you look closely, you can see Saigo, in a red dress shirt with hair permed to look like an Afro, happily dancing near the stage. He appears almost giddy with delight.

The performance not only irritated the police, but because of the large numbers of motorcycle gang members attending, the media took notice. A portion of the performance was aired on national television, portraying Gaido as a corrupting influence on Japan's rebel youth. It was the best advertising the group could have hoped for.

Since Saigo had left school and was no longer a performer in the band, he had plenty of time on his hands and not much to do, so he bought a motorcycle. He rode it for a year, and then, as soon as he turned sixteen, he got a license and joined the local motorcycle gang, Mikaeri Bijin (Beautiful Girl Looking Back, BGLB). They were the two-wheeled kings of Machida City.

And they were feared.

During the 1960s, Japan was considered to be one of the world's most conformist nations. Groups of juvenile delinquents or those who had fallen through the cracks of the rigid educational system started to gather to form large motorcycle gangs. The gangs became a popular haven for them because many kids wanted to be different and to stick out from the rest of society. At first, the gangs were called *kaminari-zoku*, meaning "the thunder tribes," but that name didn't last long.

The Japanese media created the term *bosozoku*, which means "tribe that drives fast and violently" or "speed tribes," as they came to be known in the west. They would go to places where there were a lot of people — Enoshima, Hakone, Shinjuku, Shibuya.

Like many things in Japan, *bosozoku* started as a movement imitating American culture. In Japan's rapid-growth period, the Hells Angels became infamous in Japan, and Japanese youth began to emulate them. Staying true to his heritage, Saigo patched his jacket with the Japanese flag, also called the *Hinomaru*, but added the American flag as well.

There were several variations of speed tribes, and even motorcycle gangs with women riders as well.* They became well known for riding noisy customized motorcycles. A common trend was to cut a bike's muffler down so it made an ear-splitting howl. Saigo didn't agree with doing that. He thought that was a nuisance to the public.

*Bosozoku* also became known for their elaborate uniforms, which they called *tokkofuku* — a nod to the stylized outfits that Japan's *kamikaze* pilots wore to their deaths. BGLB made their own embroidered uniforms, stickers, and flags. They spent far more on their motorcycles than other groups did. Some of the men spent more than 500,000 yen on modifying their bikes.

The year that Saigo joined up, the speed tribes became a fully fledged "social problem" after the Shonan Shichirigahama incident.

In early June 1975, the Tokyo speed tribes and the Kanagawa prefecture speed tribes, after months of bitter battles, decided to duke it out on the coastal road in Kamakura City. The gangs, many with silly-sounding names such as The White Knuckled Clowns, armed themselves with *bokken* (wooden swords), nunchucks, lethally

---

\* A rarity in Japan's traditionally male-dominated delinquent world culture.

remodeled model guns, chunks of lumber, baseball bats, and other crude weapons.

The scene could have been the inspiration for the opening scene in the iconic film *Akira*.

The result was absolute mayhem. The groups came riding in on over 350 vehicles, resulting in a gang fight in which twenty-seven people, including five policemen were injured; four vehicles were set on fire, or alternatively, blew up; twenty-eight vehicles were destroyed; and 412 people were arrested or put under protective custody. The motorcycle gangs wanted to be noticed; the kids wanted attention, and they got it.

BGLB was an all-male gang. The group grew to include several hundred motorcycles. Saigo rose to become the second-generation leader of his BGLB Speed Tribe in 1976. By that time, the associated gang members had risen to 1,500 people.

The *bosozoku*, in many ways, resembled the lawless gangs, called *gurentai*, that wreaked havoc in Tokyo in the chaos after World War II. *Gu* meant "stupidity," and *rentai* was slang for a "regiment." Thus the translation for *gurentai* was "the regiment of the stupid," or "the stupid regiment." Nowadays, we call them gangs. They went around collecting protection money, terrorizing the locals, and constantly fighting with other speed tribes over real and imagined slights.

Among all of them, Saigo was the toughest, and he was huge for a Japanese man of his era. It was here that Saigo earned his nickname, Tsunami. "Saigo would show up without warning and swiftly decimate his enemies," said a fellow gang member. "He was a force of nature. He was overwhelmingly powerful, afraid of nothing, and, just like a tsunami, no one ever knew when he was coming or how much damage he would do when he showed up."

But Saigo wasn't just a young thug who had made his way to the top with sheer brute force — he also had a good business sense.

As the organization got bigger, he made every member who joined put a BGLB sticker on their bike, and forced them to pay 3,000 yen, which was quite a sum at the time, for a two-sticker set. He had spent 50,000 yen on creating the printing plate for the stickers, but with the membership increasing at a huge pace, he soon made back his money. The actual production cost per sticker was a mere 300 yen, giving him an almost ten-fold profit margin and more.

The gang would gather every Friday and Saturday at the Daikyo Gasoline stand on the edge of town. There would be hundreds of bikers. Most of them had illegally altered their bikes, with the mufflers removed, and their capacity for speed improved. Several helmets would be passed around, and all those attending would throw in some money for "gasoline costs." Saigo would pocket most of it.

Other times, he and his pals would call for donations in their various fundraising drives, which they called *kanpa*. The word itself was derived from the Russian word *kompaniya* (компания), which was used to refer to collecting funds for a political campaign. However, there was nothing political in what BGLB was doing; they stood for nothing and had nothing they wanted to accomplish, other than cause trouble.

Sometimes there was a reason for the *kanpa*. "We need to buy gifts for our buddy in the hospital." "We need to get some new baseball bats." "We gotta fix our bikes." However, often there was no reason given. Money was requested, and young punks who wanted to be cool and ride with the big boys turned in what cash they had. Some members of the gang began forcing their juniors still in school to buy stickers as well. "Sticker fees" became a synonym for low-level extortion in parts of Tokyo.

"It was a lot like what we'd do later in the yakuza," Saigo said. "The people at the top were always collecting money from the lower gangs at the various yakuza rituals, ceremonies, and special occasions."

The BLGB had some unspoken rules. If you violated them, you were out of the gang, and would be beaten severely as you were booted out:

1. No fooling around with another member's woman
2. No starting gang wars without executive approval
3. No snitching to the cops
4. No robbery, theft, or rape
5. No bothering women, children, and elderly people*
6. No disrespecting your seniors in the organization.

Saigo wasn't content with just running the biggest motorcycle gang in Machida; he wanted to run the biggest gang in Tokyo. Through fights and intimidation, BGLB began to absorb the other motorcycle gangs as well.

"It was like doing mergers and acquisitions. We'd pick a fight with a local gang, beat the crap out of their leaders, and offer them a choice: join us, or never ride again. Most of them joined us."

One by one, the local groups fell under the umbrella of the organization, even the dreaded *Gokuaku* (Ultimate Evil). Saigo enforced the basic rules that all gang members had to follow, but there was very little that could get you kicked out once you got in. In fact, leaving the gang was the hard part. It officially could cost you 10,000 yen, or a beating. Most people who left just chose to quietly fade or move away.

As a manager, he made sure to keep one step ahead of the law. When the traffic laws were changed to mandate all motorcycle riders wear helmets, all his members were made to get helmets. When the laws were changed raising the driving age for large motorbikes, he

---

\* Driving loudly through neighborhoods and disturbing the sleep of women, children, and elderly people was somehow exempt from this rule.

made sure that people were only riding bikes that they were properly licensed for. Saigo was starting to learn that to be a successful outlaw, you needed to keep up with the law. Just like the blind spot in a mirror, there was always a blind spot in the law you could work with, if you just stayed on top of things.

However, as the groups got bigger, reaching their peak around 1976, the conflicts between factions became increasingly violent. A mob mentality began to take over. It became standard to have two men per bike; they rode in teams. Before each run, the "executive members" would be assigned a role to perform.

Some groups would hold the rear, keeping police cars from breaking up the convoy; another group would be the scouts, checking for oncoming gangs or the authorities. Sometimes, a special patrol would be carrying extra weapons. On every bike, the team was divided into one man who carried a weapon, and the other guy who drove the vehicle.

When other gangs began to carry wooden baseball bats to knock over pursuing police and Saigo's people, he ordered all his members to get metal baseball bats. When the other guys got metal baseball bats, Saigo ordered his members to arm themselves with *tantō* (Japanese daggers). When baseball bats or daggers were in short supply, members would knock over "for sale" signs on property lots, pry the signs off their posts, and use the posts, with nails sticking out of them, as weapons. Saigo, through a friend whose father was a yakuza member, managed to acquire several Japanese swords, and armed his closet lieutenants.

His favorite sword had a curved blade. It was mass produced as an officer sword during World War II. The quality was dubious.

When a fight began, Saigo would stop his bike, jump off, and unsheathe his sword; brandishing it in the air, and daring anyone to come close to him. Even guys still riding their bikes, with baseball bat–wielding thugs sitting behind them, wouldn't dare lunge at him — one mistake, and they knew they might be skewered like chicken at a *yakitori* stand. He would glower at the assembled enemy, yelling, screaming, and behaving very much like a Japanese Conan the Barbarian.

He slashed up a few guys with the sword, but never stabbed anyone — that would surely kill them. And while the best-made Japanese swords are allegedly able to slice a man in half, his sword was more for show. It scared the hell out of people anyway. He knew enough to keep it shiny. The edged and tapered point was blunt and slightly rusted, but the ridges of the blade, called *shinogi*, were so polished that if he tilted the blade in the sun or in strong moonlight, it was like flashing a light in someone's eyes.

The original definition of *shinogi* was the edge of a blade. Back in the Edo period, samurai and *ronin* (masterless samurai) made their living as swordsmen in battle and as security guards. The more you worked, the more you used your sword. Over time, the edge would wear away.

Saigo's sword, however, had a sharp edge. He could have cut off someone's arm or leg with it. He wielded his sword with two hands. It was heavy. He always made sure to just cut the arm. If you slice with full power, you'd cut off the arm. So you hit, and then you pull, stopping in full swing. Saigo might have amputated someone, but he most likely didn't. His opponents would always run away, and he didn't stick around to check for spare limbs lying about either. He cut deep sometimes, but never cut all the way through. "I was really careful not to kill anyone. I'd say, 'This time, I'll let you live,' and I always did. It's bad to kill people. We were careful. We would never slice at a guy when he was riding with his woman, and never slice a woman — even when she'd slice us up with a razor or whatever she was carrying."

As the violence escalated, however, Saigo began to fear that what had started as good, violent fun might really turn deadly.

There came a point when things were too out of hand for him. There were too many people, too many fights, and the scale of gang warfare reached proportions that the police would not and could not ignore.

In 1977 and 1978, the news was filled with tales of terror caused by the speed tribes. In Osaka, motorcycle gangs attacked the police with two-by-fours spiked with nails. In the Fukushima prefecture, two gangs clashed, resulting in a fight between forty gang members in a junior high school courtyard. The kids armed themselves with *bokken* and glass bottles, and they fought until six of them were seriously injured. The Black Emperor gang raided a gas station in a guerrilla attack, laying siege to the police and taking over the pumps. The police arrested and/or detained 109 of them. Yakuza groups began incorporating the *bosozoku* into their ranks, using them to sell methamphetamines and to extort money from the local populace. The motorcycle gangs were becoming more and more like the yakuza.

The National Police Agency took a dim view of the speed tribes, and by October 1, 1978, a new law went on the books forbidding dangerous unified activities while driving. The law was designed to punish the speed tribes for running on the roads at high speeds in groups, racing each other, and even gathering their vehicles together to move in a convoy. The members were constantly being fined for driving over the speed limit, but the new changes in the law imposed a 50,000-yen penalty for dangerous driving — the kind of hefty fees that could put a teenage punk into serious debt.

Everyone thought the new laws would be the end of the speed tribes. The power of the groups was in their numbers. If they couldn't drive together, they had no power. The penalties were steep, and no one wanted to be the first person captured under the new laws. Many *bosozoku* were quitting the lifestyle completely.

One day, while riding, Saigo and his gang were caught by the police. The police threatened that they'd be arrested unless they broke up the group. Saigo was pretty much tired of the *bosozoku* scene at that point anyway, so he decided to give up life as a motorcycle gangster. He dissolved BGLB, and decided to go back to music.

By this time, he had become infamous in his hometown. The local paper even interviewed him and published a heartwarming feature on his retirement, wishing him a better, more creative, and useful life.

One of his former band members, Maruyama, got him a gig playing guitar with a split-off from Gaido now called Kusare Gaido (Rotten Gaido). By this time, Gaido had split up and reformed so many times that it had become several bands, each claiming the Gaido title.

Gaido had never been a stable band, and the infighting among members was as legendary as the group itself in Japanese rock history. The band had made a trip to Hawaii in 1975 and played at the Sunshine Head Rock Festival on January 1, making them the first Japanese rock band to play on U.S. soil. That year, the band released a flood of singles and live albums. By 1976, Gaido was one of the hottest bands in Japan, but in September they suddenly announced they would be disbanding at the Machida Festival.

On October 16, 1976, they played their last concert in Hibiya. The individual members went on their solo careers, but Maruyama created Kusare Gaido. And Kusare Gaido looked like it might be able to claim the title of the "Gaido of all Gaidos."

For Saigo, Kusare Gaido filled the space left by the speed tribe. The BGLB had played a major part in the growth of the band, forming the bulk of the Gaido groupies. He felt he belonged, and had already started writing his own songs. He thought that, while society was criticizing them, they were going to rise up and be famous.

Maruyama told him he was trying to reform the band under the original name, and put together a new album, which would be their fifth, by the following year. They had Nippon Columbia Records aboard, which operated the Columbia Records label in Japan. This was the big time.

Saigo was working odd jobs to get by. He was still living with his parents, but he assured them that he was on the path to rock stardom, and spent long hours practicing the guitar. At least, as far as his parent were concerned, he wasn't running around with the *bosozuku* anymore and had some sort of life goal.

But Saigo couldn't quite give up his love of driving at full speed. Months had gone by since the anti-speed tribe laws had gone on the books. The motorcycle gangs had decided to lay low to gauge how hard the cops would crack down on them. Yet nobody had been arrested. The law hadn't been broken. The police didn't even seem to be enforcing it. Saigo and his pals decided that the cops were all talk and no walk. They were not about talking or walking; they were all about riding.

One quiet Saturday afternoon in Machida in August 1979, Saigo and his former crew gathered together. They wanted to ride again. Saigo thought it was a very bad idea, but he didn't want people to think he was a coward, so he went ahead and decided to do it anyway. One hundred and twenty vehicles assembled at the Daikyo Gas Station. The run was a disaster. In fact, it made the papers the next day.

### *Bosozoku* leader arrested as "Accomplice;" First Use of Revised Law to Arrest Co-Criminal

The second-in-command of a *bosozoku* motorcycle gang was arrested on the 20th as an accomplice in reckless driving, authorities from the Tokyo Metropolitan Police Transportation Investigators and the Shibuya Ward Police revealed.

In the early morning hours of the 12th, police apprehended four members of a *bosozoku* gang under suspicion of violating the "Cooperative Dangerous Driving" clause of the Road Traffic Act. Included in the group was the gang's second-in-command, an 18-year-old unemployed Machida resident, who was riding on the back of one of the bikes. The suspect maintained he was innocent as he was not in control of the vehicle while the driver was breaking the law. Police arrested him as an accomplice, however, saying that the youth had premeditated intentions to violate the Road Traffic Act.

Saigo was charged with dangerous driving, obstruction of public duty, and other violations. The court fined him 50,000 yen and sentenced him to two months in a juvenile detention center.

In 1980, Maruyama told him the band was getting back together. However, asking Saigo to join was out of the question. Even though Saigo was an original band member, and Maruyama thought his *bosozoku* run was funny, the manager said that a delinquent like Saigo would just drag the band down. Anyway, he couldn't show up to band practice while he was in juvenile detention — so he got cut. The manager told Saigo, "Listen kid, you can gather your delinquent friends and come cheer on the band. Someday, maybe you'll be a band member yourself. Right now, bow out and support the band."

Saigo regrets that final run. "I was at the turning point of my life, and not only did I miss the turn, I ran a red light at full-speed and wound up in jail. I drove off the road into a swamp, and I'm the only one I can blame."

The future looked dark for Saigo. He wasn't going to be a rock star. He wasn't going to be a *bosozoku* gang leader. He was going to to have to get a job. He found work fixing cars. He knew a lot about cars, but it wasn't glamorous. The whole job was frustrating because he had temporarily lost his license and couldn't drive the cars he was working on.

He had steady work and a straight job, but Saigo staying on the tried-and-true path was about as likely as him driving under the speed limit.

## CHAPTER THREE

# Gimme Shelter

In 1981, Saigo met the woman of his dreams. Her name was Rimi, and she was gorgeous, moody, loved fast cars, and liked him. He didn't know what love was when he met her, but he thought she was the most gorgeous woman in Machida. "I wanted her like the way you would want the coolest car on the lot."

He didn't want to lose her, so he got her pregnant as soon as possible. Their daughter was born the following year. They lived together out of wedlock, but that wasn't scandalous in Japan. While Rimi was pregnant, they stopped having sex in her second trimester, and Saigo, not wanting to be unfaithful, pretty much limited himself to going to brothels. He didn't consider going to brothels as cheating; there was no love involved it. To him, it was like getting the oil changed in your car.

Nevertheless, Saigo wasn't irresponsible, and he wanted to make sure his daughter could go to a good school. He began to think about the future. In 1982, a mid-level boss from the second-largest crime organization, the Sumiyoshi-kai, approached Saigo. He asked him if he and his old crew from BGLB would join his registered right-wing organization, Jiritsusha, which had their offices in Kabukicho, the red-light district in Shinjuku, Tokyo. The group was in need of young blood and manpower. In exchange for bringing his men to the group, Saigo would get a title, a business card, and a name to trade upon. In essence, while espousing nationalist values, the group was a front for the Sumiyoshi-kai.

Saigo already spent a lot of time in Kabukicho, a notorious red-light district where all the sex shops were. His extent of political knowledge, however, was limited to knowing that communism was bad and that China was a menace to Japan. As for the divinity of the emperor, he never really thought much about it, but if believing in that was part of being a right-wing leader, then fine, the emperor was a god. He could believe it.

Most yakuza factions have their own right-wing outlet. They allow the yakuza to engage in semi-legitimate extortion behind the guise of collecting "donations." Many of these outlets go back decades. The group that recruited him, Jiritsusha, had its origins in the era before the war.

Not every single solitary right-wing group is affiliated with the yakuza; however, the majority certainly are. Yakuza and right-wing groups function very similarly and mainly just stand for whatever makes them money. By joining this group, Saigo and his crew became yakuza associates. Saigo's group all got uniforms as well. In many ways, they had simply switched in their BGLB hot-rodder uniforms for new threads. The history of Jiritsusha, however, was certainly more illustrious than that of their motorcycle gang.

Jiritsusha was founded by one of the most notorious right-wingers in Japanese history: Taku Mikami, a naval officer who participated in one of Japan's most infamous attempted military coups.

Japan's golden age of civil government was from 1912 to 1926, and was known as the Taishō democracy. The tax qualifications for voters were reduced, giving more people the opportunity to vote. Then, in 1925, they were eliminated. Party politics flourished, and legislation favorable to the working class was passed. Jazz was all the rage, and the arts blossomed.

Beneath all of this, militarism in the country was growing, powered by shadowy right-wing groups, secret societies, and conservative forces within the government. The passage of the Peace Preservation Law granted the police extraordinary powers and censored the press, helping the agenda of the ultra-right.

Tsuyoshi Inukai was a former journalist who was elected to the Lower House of the Imperial Diet in 1890. He was reelected seventeen times, and held the same seat for forty-two years. He became the prime minister of Japan in December 1931, when the tides were already shifting towards a fascist state. He made moves to limit the power of the navy and military. This led to his assassination on May 15, 1932. Eleven young naval officers, including Taku Mikami, stormed the prime minister's residence and shot him to death. They were aided by army cadets and right-wing civilians who were part of a secret yakuza-like society. Inukai's last words were legendary: "If we talked it over, you would understand." Mikami replied, "Dialogue is useless," and made the fatal shot.

The coup d'état became known as the May 15 Incident. The nationalist insurgents attempted to overthrow the government and replace it with military rule. Their original strategy included killing the prime minister at a reception he planned for the silent-era actor Charlie Chaplin, who had arrived in Japan a day earlier. They planned to kill Chaplin as well, hoping the act might incite a war with the West. During the prime minister's assassination, Charlie Chaplin and the prime minister's son, Takeru Inukai, were watching a sumo match. This was probably one of the few times a spectator sport saved lives.

The rebels attacked other government leaders, and tossed hand grenades into the Mitsubishi Bank headquarters in Tokyo and several electrical transformer substations. Aside from the murder of the prime minister, the attempted coup d'état came to nothing, and the rebellion washed out.

Those responsible took a taxi to the police headquarters, confessed their crimes, and surrendered themselves to the authorities. This was not uncommon among the lawless factions of Japan: do the crime and willingly do the time. It was a way of building street cred.

Although the rebels lost, many historians believe that the prime minister's assassination marked the death of democracy in pre-war Japan and the solidification of a military rule. By the time the prime minister's eleven murderers were court-martialed, they were being hailed as national heroes.

During their trial, sympathizers from around the country submitted a petition to the court asking for a lenient sentence. The petition had 350,000 signatures signed in blood. The accused gained sympathy by using the trial as a staged performance to proclaim their loyalty to the emperor, and by appealing for government and economic reforms.

The court also received eleven severed fingers from youth in Niigata, who asked that they be executed in place of the accused. The severed fingers were a gesture of sincerity. It was a ritual that would become commonplace in the postwar yakuza world.

The court handed out a relatively light punishment. Many felt that Inukai's killers would be released in a couple of years, if not sooner. The failure to severely punish the conspirators of the May 15 Incident epitomized the democratic government's inability to confront the military, and thus further eroded the rule of law and order.

When Mikami was released from jail several years early on parole, he became a right-wing activist. He then created the predecessor to Jiritsusha in 1941. After the war, it was taken over by a Sumiyoshi-kai boss and served as a recruitment center for the yakuza organization.

It was during his Jiritsusha days that Saigo met Takahiko Inoue, a boss in the Inagawa-kai, as well as a member of the prestigious Yokosuka family (Yokosuka-ikka). They hit it off. Inoue was in his mid-thirties, and Saigo was just twenty-one. While Saigo was just starting his career, Inoue was already established.

Inoue was from Kyushu, the southernmost part of Japan, where the men were manly and the women were dark. He liked Saigo's American-like straightforwardness and sense of humor. Saigo admired Inoue's tranquil composure and honesty.

By the time Inoue was thirty, in 1977, he was selected to be a managing director of the Inagawa-kai, a distinct honor in a group that had now reached its peak of over 10,000 members. He was the youngest managing director of the group in decades. He also helped run a right-wing group, Daikosha, which was the Inagawa-kai's own vehicle for expressing nationalist sentiments.

Inoue managed to open the first Inagawa-kai office in the sleazy streets of Kabukicho, and despite the heavy influx of gangs already claiming territory there, he managed to survive without bloodshed. He had 100 men directly under him. In his younger days, Inoue had been infamous for getting into fistfights with other yakuza at the slightest provocation, but by the time Saigo met him, he had achieved a certain mellowness and was well liked in the area.

People called him "The Buddha." (He would go on to become an actual Buddhist priest.) He was a bit chubby, and his prematurely gray hair gave him a certain air of authority, as did his tendency to wear dark suits. He had a square pug-like face that was usually adorned with a half-smile. He was quite popular among the local hostesses in the red-light district.

He would occasionally lecture Saigo about what it meant to be a true yakuza. Perhaps he was being a bit romantic. While serving time in prison, Inoue's mother wrote to him and asked him to live the ideals of the yakuza he espoused. And Inoue did his best. He truly believed that without beneficence and goodwill, yakuza ceased to be yakuza, and instead became common thugs and mafiosi. Yakuza needed to help out the locals, or else the locals wouldn't pay them for protection. That meant they should never cause problems for civilians; never bother ordinary people. When there was a chance to do some good, they should rush to do it.

Perhaps knowing that Saigo was on his way to entering a true life of crime, Inoue advised Saigo to get a real job. There would come a time when Saigo wouldn't be able to make money as a right-winger anymore. Inoue himself was a smart investor who ran several businesses, owned over ten buildings, and brought in legitimate revenue to keep his organization together. He was one of the first generations of yakuza to make the transition from being an outlaw to being within the law. He even owned an Italian restaurant.

Inoue collected debts when he first started out as a yakuza, but stopped doing so early on. He still accepted "donations" and protection money, and many business owners in Kabukicho and Shinjuku were happy to pay him. He was the much lesser of the evils in the area. The local merchants and yakuza created a forum for discussing problems in the Kabukicho area, and Inoue was the manager of the association. It was called The Tokyo Central Get-Together Association, and Inoue acted as the peacekeeper in the area and between the various yakuza factions. In the lawless seedy world of Kabukicho, he was the sheriff.

Inoue would often invite Saigo out drinking, although Inoue usually drank for the both of them. He'd start speaking in his thick

Japanese southern accent, making him nearly unintelligible. Saigo would remind Inoue, "Hey, I'm not from the Kumamoto prefecture — I don't understand what you're saying."

"Of course you understand, you idiot," Inoue would sometimes reply, in his Kumamoto dialect. "In a past life, you were from Kumamoto. I know it!"

In Inoue, Saigo felt like he'd found the older brother he'd never had. He asked Inoue to make him his younger brother and seal the deal with the ritual exchange of sake cups, *sakazuki*. Inoue refused, on principle. Saigo was a member of the Sumiyoshi-kai-backed Jiritsusha, and while it was possible to have allegiances that crossed yakuza organization lines, Inoue felt this particular match was wrong.

Nevertheless, Saigo began to refer to him as *aniki* (older brother) in private, and Inoue didn't object.

About a year into his time in the Jiritsusha, Saigo decided to cut out the middleman and form his own independent right-wing group. However, it wasn't going to be easy. Jiritsusha was located in Kabukicho. He lived in Machida. The Tokyo wards were roughly an hour apart by car.

To accomplish this, he decided to set up a branch in his hometown. He had the tacit permission of his boss at Jiritsusha, though not necessarily his explicit permission. In Japan, these things are never clearly discussed, but left vague until they need clarification.

In 1984, Saigo rented an office in Machida's Tsukushino area and gathered sixty young men for his own political organization: Shinnoujuku. The name meant "The Shelter" and/or study hall of the gods and the emperor.

Like other right-wing groups, The Shelter wasn't officially a yakuza group, but it functioned like one. It had all the earmarks, including a *daimon*. The *daimon* is the yakuza equivalent of a family emblem or corporate symbol. Broken into two parts, *dai* translates to "big," and *mon* translates to "family crest" or "coat of arms."

Saigo's group also had a code of ethics that was vaguely defined and written on a scroll; they were still associated with the Sumiyoshi-kai, and functioned in a pyramid-like hierarchy in which the guys at the bottom paid the guys at the top.

The Shelter did a brisk business. Saigo found that the system he had set up for BGLB worked just as well for the The Shelter. Young punks with semi-steady jobs would donate their money and time to be a member of the group. They wanted to use The Shelter's name to impress people, and Saigo and his crew were happy to accept the cash.

They started collecting protection money in the form of "donations" from the bars, hostess clubs, sexual massage shops, and blowjob coffee parlors (pink salons, brothels, and other dens of ill-repute in the area). They offered different types of protection, such as bodyguard services and enforcement services. Like most yakuza and right-wing groups, The Shelter was flexible, and offered different payment plans. Some shops only paid at the end of the year; some paid twice a year. Most places were on a monthly plan. In return, The Shelter would occasionally drag out and discipline unruly customers who refused to use condoms or got too fresh with the hostesses. Sometimes, they'd collect bar tabs from delinquent customers that could sometimes amount to several thousand dollars. The Shelter took the reasonable collection fee of 50 percent. That was still cheaper for the bars than suing someone. That could take years, and amount to more than the bar tab itself.

Saigo was also making money though *kanpa* (fundraising campaigns). They would hold *kanpa* for worthy causes, such as protesting at the Russian embassy to force the return of the northern territories. Granted, Saigo would pocket much of the money, but his organization had an image to maintain. He and his crew would hop into their black vans aka "sound-trucks," which were decked out with the Japanese flag, slogans in Japanese, the group's emblem, and outfitted with loudspeakers that would blast out music or their rantings at ear-numbing volume.

They gained *danbe* (sponsors), ordinary citizens who admired certain groups or individuals, and provided them with funds, support, land, office space, and sometimes just dinner. There was something glamorous about hanging out with men of action that the ordinary white-collar salaryman found exciting. Of course, a right-wing group wasn't as cool as the yakuza, but they still had fans. Old men who felt that Japan had been forced into a war by America that they couldn't win, and had then suffered the indignity of the U.S.-imposed democratic constitution, liked the rhetoric of Saigo's group. Plus, Saigo was a local boy, and some businessmen in the town were rooting for him.

The Shelter created a newsletter, *Shinnojuku Ippo*, and began offering subscriptions to businesses around the neighborhood. The newsletter was a great money-maker. The cost of an ad was anywhere from 30,000 yen to 300,000 yen, depending on the size of the company. Companies and individuals would buy the ads out of patriotic zeal, to pay for services, or out of simple fear. It was implicit in the offer that businesses who subscribed to or advertised in The Shelter's newsletter would get protection from hoodlums, youth gangs, yakuza, and, of course, The Shelter itself. The Inagawa-kai had offices in Machida under Hideo Hishiyama, who was the head of the Hishiyama-gumi. In theory, they could have offered to protect those businesses, but they had very few people on the ground and thus no real presence or influence there. They collected money from only a few businesses, and were hardly a force to be reckoned with.

Some people paid because they agreed with Saigo's half-baked right-wing ideology, but most paid because they were afraid of what might happen if they didn't. Saigo never retaliated against any person or company that didn't want to pay. Just the implied threat of violence was effective. He didn't believe in making good on that threat. It would only piss people off, and give the cops an excuse to do something.

Although the Inagawa-kai was hardly a force in Machida, there was another group everyone had to take into consideration: and that was the Kinbara-gumi, headed by Norimasa Kinbara. The Kinbara-gumi was an organization under Japan's fifth- or sixth-largest organized crime group at the time: the Kyokuto-kai. Kinbara was Korean, and bad-tempered. Kinbara had 120 men in the area, double the number Saigo had.

Many businesses actually subscribed to *Shinnojuku Ippo* because they they preferred Saigo and his crew to the Kinbara-gumi. Their methods were notoriously brutal and uncouth, so they were not well liked. This helped Saigo out immensely. For example, a forty-one-year-old woman opened a small hostess bar near Machida station. Several members of the Kinbara-gumi repeatedly visited the business and demanded payment for her operating on their turf. They'd find fault with her service as well, calling her girls "ugly bitches" and complaining about the whiskey. They would sometimes come in groups, scaring away other customers. They threw shochu, cheap Japanese booze, in her face. They pelted her with ice, and urinated on the carpet. She called the police, but they never came when the yakuza members were still there. Eventually, she paid. The payments the Kinbara-gumi demanded kept escalating over time. That didn't make for satisfied customers.

The Shelter seemed like the better option. Just a month after opening shop, Saigo's bank account was growing significantly. However, Kinbara didn't take the invasion of his turf lightly. He soon called Saigo at his office and ordered him to come visit him, by himself. Kinbara had heard things about Saigo and The Shelter, and he wanted some clarification.

Saigo immediately went to visit Kinbara at the Kinbara-gumi office. Two scary-looking thugs guarded the front door. They guided Saigo to the back office, where Kinbara was waiting for him. True to his word, Kinbara was alone. He had the young Saigo take a seat at his desk and began interrogating him. Saigo was operating on the Kinbara-gumi turf. What was he really up to, and, most importantly, was he taking away Kinbara's business?

Saigo told Kinbara that he was not running a yakuza group. The Shelter, Saigo said, was just a right-wing organization. For some reason, Kinbara decided that Saigo was truly just a clueless punk unaffiliated with the yakuza, but still trying to make money using a bullshit right-wing group. He didn't like what that implied — that Saigo was probably racist; specifically, anti-Korean. After all, saying you're a right-winger is pretty much declaring you hate Koreans and that the Japanese are the best.

So Kinbara made it clear that he was Korean and that Saigo was on his turf. Then he told Saigo to behave himself and to get the fuck out of his office.

On his way out, since Kinbara didn't see Saigo as a threat or a competitor, he made an offer that would benefit himself. "As you get your business going," Kinbara said, "if you run into some expenses or need some cash, let me know. We provide financial services for the locals."

In other words, Kinbara was a loan shark. Saigo said he would remember that, and he did — but Saigo would find that borrowing money from Kinbara was like walking down a slippery slope.

Japan's semi-legal sex industry exists on a mind-boggling scale, yet there are very few books or articles that give even a rudimentary idea of how big a role it plays in the national economy. It's not that the sex industry exists in a gray zone in Japan. If anything, it exists in a pink zone — it's overwhelmingly legal, except for when the authorities decide to make a token crackdown. Even though selling pornography that depicts uncensored sexual intercourse is a crime, paying for sexual services isn't. Services such as oral, anal, bondage, and S&M are legal. The only form of prostitution that the law forbids is vaginal penetration with the penis, and it sets no punishment for the prostitute or the customer if caught. There are exceptions to that, as well. So-called soaplands are one such industry.

The best sex Saigo ever had took place in a soapland. "The women know how to make you reach ecstasy like no ordinary woman could." Inside a soapland, a man enters a large private bathroom, often with a bedroom or sauna attached. His chosen "attendant" helps him bathe, a process that might include an actual bath, though it most famously involves the girl lathering up every nook and cranny with her own naked body. The customer pays for the "bath" up front. Afterwards, the man and his attendant may decide, as two consenting adults, to go to the room next door and to take the encounter further at a mutually decided fee. This post-bath encounter remains completely independent of the soapland's business.

Not only is a soapland a unique experience within Japan's adult-entertainment industry, but they are also among the top tier. The women who work there are well known to be the most beautiful in the industry. They use their entire bodies to wash customers, and provide services in a bed. Because there's a bedroom and bathroom, the working area is large. Customers go there looking for high-class service, so technique is important. The women are thorough and professional. They must be able to give a really high-quality massage, stay in excellent physical shape, wash the customer thoroughly, and provide him with at least one orgasm during the service.

The fees for soaplands are top tier as well. In magazines aimed at women who want to work in the sex industry, this is how the job is introduced:

**Soap**

Intelligence required: \*\*\*

Nudity required: \*\*\*\*

Work when you want: \*\*\*\*

Easy stand-by: \*\*\*\*\*

Calorie burner: \*\*\*\*\*

Payment: \*\*\*\*\* (At a shop)

The payment is the highest because sexual intercourse is understood to be a part of the package. The calorie-burner rating is a reflection of the fact that many women working in the sex industry are very conscious of their weight, and that sexual activity is a form of exercise. Flexible hours are also good for married women or single mothers. Some establishments provide daycare as well.

Almost every time Saigo went to a soapland, he borrowed money from Kinbara. It would soon become a problem. Going to a soapland was an expensive habit that sometimes cost him $1,000 a night. It was not like his friends had much money and, because he was under eighteen, he couldn't borrow money from a bank. Plus, to most people, the amount he was asking for seemed like a lot of money to spend on soaplands.

The more Saigo went to soaplands, the more money he borrowed. He ended up owing the Kinbara-gumi 60 million yen ($60,000). At one point, Saigo's tab was so high that Kinbara goons grabbed him off the street and took him to their office. Kinbara demanded to know what the hell Saigo was spending all the money on and how he planned on paying them back.

Saigo told him, "I go to soapland. A lot. I can't get enough." Kinbara was so dumbstruck that he laughed.

Kinbara wanted his money. But, of course, Saigo couldn't pay Kinbara back immediately. He did, however, promise to pay him back eventually, but asked Kinbara to wait until his lust was satisfied. Saigo told him it would take years to pay it all back, but that would be better than not being reimbursed at all. Kinbara believed that Saigo was a man of his word. He patted Saigo on the shoulder, agreed to his terms, and wished him luck.

Saigo thought to himself, "Hey, the yakuza are sometimes pretty reasonable."

A short time later, Kinbara finally figured out the extent of Saigo's money-making activities. Saigo had long crossed the line between right-wing group and yakuza.

On a bright summer's day in 1984, Kinbara called Saigo's office and said, "I'm going to come by and say hello. Let's have some tea."

Saigo said sure.

Kinbara showed up with two soldiers and his right-hand man, Takeda, who was rumored to be a rather short-tempered and violent individual. Kinbara was dressed in a navy-blue suit, double-breasted, exquisitely tailored. Yet he still managed to look like a menacing thug. However, his tone was cordial.

As they talked, Kinbara mumbled to himself. Takeda had a small notepad, and was taking memos. "A signboard on the wall. A paper lantern on the wall with the group name on it."

Saigo felt something was wrong, but Kinbara assured Saigo that everything was fine. He was just admiring his office. Patriotism must pay well. Kinbara had heard about their local support and wanted to gauge what they were up to. He asked Saigo if he could take a company newsletter from the pile stacked in the corner. He looked over the newsletter, which, in addition to local business ads, had advertisements featuring the names of Inagawa-kai, Yamaguchi-gumi, and Sumiyoshi-kai members.

Kinbara looked at the picture of a Sumiyoshi-kai boss posted on the wall of the office and tipped his head towards it, making eye contact with Takeda. Takeda made another scribble in his notebook.

Kinbara didn't stay long. As he was leaving, he gently tapped the *daimon* on Saigo's *kanban* (signboard). It was the same as the *daimon* on Saigo's men's jumpsuits.

Kinbara thanked Saigo for showing him the office, got up from the leather sofa, and left.


A day later, ten soldiers from the Kinbara-gumi burst through the door of Saigo's office, when they knew he was not there. They went straight up to his second-in-command, Yusuke Yamada.

"You're supposed to be a fucking right-wing group, but you're just a gang."

One by one, they listed everything the group had that made them look like a yakuza group, pounding the desk, rattling off each "tell."

"When you next hear from Saigo, tell him to come to our office. We're going to talk. And we're taking this hostage in lieu of him." And, with little or no resistance, they pried the *kanban* off the wall and carried it out.

They had a point. In almost every way, Saigo's group was indistinguishable from a low-ranking yakuza group, and Kinbara wouldn't stand for it. The loss of the *kanban* was devastating. The *kanban* was a symbol of the group's power, their unity, their face. Just like a yakuza, without a *kanban*, Saigo's right-wing group was nothing but a bunch of punks. Come hell or high water, Saigo was going to take that signboard back.

Saigo summoned all of his soldiers to the office, telling them to bring baseball bats, metal pipes, knives, whatever weapon they could find. The office phones were ringing off the hook, and Saigo sent men to the train station to use the public telephone to call in the stragglers. He had almost 100 men assembled that night, many of them in uniform. They were excited. Nobody really knew what was going on, but they were going to rumble. This was no ordinary excursion. A rusty scent of sweat, anticipation, and fear filled the air.

There was barely room to stand, so Saigo climbed up on his desk and explained the situation. It didn't take long. "Without our *kanban*, we're nothing. We're not going to stand for this. That's why we're going to storm their offices and take back our *kanban!*"

Saigo had thought it was a pretty inspirational speech; he'd expected a flood of raised hands. All he saw was a sea of heads, many of them looking at the floor. There was a long silence.

"Senpai," said one of the crew, "they're yakuza. We aren't yakuza. They'll kill us." There were some murmurs of agreement.

Saigo was outraged. "Listen, our reputation is on the line here. We have to go. We're tough. There's 100 of us. We're young. We're right. We'll win."

There was another long silence. Exasperated, Saigo changed his sales pitch. "We've come a long way together. We are The Shelter. If there is any man here who isn't man enough to go on this mission, if there's anyone here too scared to come with me, then raise your hand now and get the fuck out of my sight. Because if you raise your hand, you're saying you quit."

A single hand went up in the back of the room. Saigo couldn't see who it was because the guy raising his hand was so short that his face was hidden. Other hands followed.

Saigo had his ocean of raised hands, but they weren't the ones he'd been hoping for. Many of the crew shuffled backwards out of the office. Some bowed in his direction, apologizing, and ran out. Saigo was flabbergasted. This wasn't how he'd envisioned it. He'd thought the members of the group that had rumbled with him during their speed tribes days would be up for the good fight. No such luck. Within ten minutes, there were only five of his crew left, including himself. Five out of 100. Maybe that was actually a good number.

Yamada shrugged his shoulders and said to Saigo, "You know, we've been acting like big-shot yakuza. Kinbara and his guys really are yakuza. So you know."

Saigo knew.

He asked them what they wanted to do.

"Let's go get it back," said one of the crew. "If we bring it back, that's our victory."

Saigo couldn't guarantee they'd even walk out alive.

But his small crew was loyal. They thought, if it happened, it happened. So they left their office and headed towards Kinbara. They were unarmed and scared out of their minds. When they arrived, there were several gang members hanging out in front smoking cigarettes. One of them ran into the office, and suddenly Saigo heard the sound of beepers going off. The Kinbara-gumi had sounded an alarm.

They walked into the office. It was Saigo's second visit there. The men inside sprang up from their chairs and grabbed him and his crew. They were frisked, and held in the reception room. Kinbara came out of his office and looked at them, dumbfounded.

"What the fuck do you want?"

"We came for our *kanban*," said Saigo.

Kinbara burst out laughing. "Are you crazy? You think you're getting that back?"

"Please give it back."

Kinbara punched him several times, Saigo stood his ground. He asked Kinbara to please stop hitting him and to give him back his *kanban*.

Kinbara launched into a tirade about what a dirty double-crosser Saigo was and that he had no right to violate the Kinbara-gumi turf. Saigo should just tuck his tail between his legs, get the hell out of Machida, and flee to Tokyo.

Flanked by his men on two sides, Saigo apologized for upsetting

Kinbara and impugning the honor of the Kinbara-gumi. Meanwhile, the word spread among Kinbara-gumi members that Saigo and his crew had been kidnapped by the gang and were being held at their office.

Additional gang members began swarming into the office to jeer at Saigo and to offer suggestions to Kinbara. Some suggested they bury him. Others suggested that, for his insubordination, Saigo should cut off one of his fingers and offer it to the boss.

Saigo didn't budge. Kinbara was impressed. He offered to induct Saigo into his own gang.

Saigo declined his offer.

Kinbara told him that he'd let Saigo live if he turned all his men over to the Kinbara-gumi. Saigo didn't have the nerve to say that these five were all that was left of his crew. He refused to cough up even one man to the Kinbara-gumi.

The gallery of yakuza were still suggesting that they kill Saigo and his men, and bury the bodies.

After what seemed like hours of threats, Kinbara surprised everyone by letting Saigo take his *kanban* back. In return, Saigo promised to dismantle his group, set them all on the straight and narrow path, and get the hell out of Machida.

He was lucky to leave the office alive, but there was no way he was going to leave Machida.

Saigo figured it this way: he owed money to Kinbara. Kinbara told him to join his group or get out of town, but there was another option, in which he could maintain his independence, not pay back Kinbara, and regain his *kanban* and his dignity. As the old saying goes, if you can't beat them, join someone else.

He wasn't going to flee to Tokyo; he was going to talk to Inoue. He was going to join the Inagawa-kai.

## CHAPTER FOUR

# Giri

The first thing Saigo did after restoring his *kanban* to his office wall was see Inoue. Their bond was still tight, and Saigo trusted him. It was a bit of a tricky place because The Shelter was still under the Sumiyoshi-kai umbrella, so while Saigo could have gone to the Sumiyoshi-kai for help, he had never got explicit permission to open his gang office in Machida. He wasn't sure if the Sumiyoshi-kai would back him up if he had to fight Kinbara's group. Inoue was a good person to ask for advice, and he hoped Inoue might take him under his wing. He needed to either be a yakuza or have another yakuza group back him if he was going to survive in Machida now.

Saigo sat in Inoue's office on the seventh floor of a building in Kabukicho. Inoue listened sympathetically to Saigo's tale of woe, from start to finish. Saigo asked to join the Inagawa-kai; to be under Inoue. Inoue shook his head. Although Inoue was a gang boss in the Inagawa-kai, it was still Hideo Hishiyama who ran the Inagawa-kai office in Machida. If Saigo was going to run his gang in Machida, Hishiyama was the one he needed to speak to. This was a good thing, because Hishiyama needed soldiers.

Inoue asked how many men Saigo had left under his command. After he'd brought back the signboard, some of his men sheepishly returned. He had ten to fifteen soldiers he could count on. That was good, Inoue told him. That meant he had some leverage.

If Saigo could bring fifteen men on board, he might be able to set himself up as a fourth-tier yakuza boss (entry level) and have his own outfit. It was likely that Hishiyama would go for it. In addition, things would have to be smoothed over with the Sumiyoshi-kai in order for Saigo to properly go over to the Inagawa-kai. Inoue promised to take care of it in addition to setting up a meeting with Hishiyama.

Hishiyama's office was in his home, which was not that uncommon for yakuza, a two-storey house in the middle of Machida. Saigo and five of his men went and knocked on his door.

Hishiyama's men led them to the foyer to meet Hishiyama. They exchanged ritual bows and introductions, and were led to the main room. Saigo stood while Hishiyama sat back on his sofa, observing the situation.

Hishiyama was a surly-looking fellow. He was prematurely bald, with a long, oval face and eyebrows that looked like they were half the length of what they should be. Perhaps it was his narrow eyes, long flat nose, and lack of eyebrows that made his face seem almost expressionless; as though it had been carved in porcelain.

Saigo asked Hishiyama to be his *oyabun*.

Hishiyama immediately conducted the equivalent of a job interview. He wanted to know how many men Saigo had to call on. He checked Saigo's history, criminal records, past associations, and friends in the yakuza. He then asked for a reference within the Inagawa-kai who could vouch for him. When Saigo referred him to Takahiko Inoue of the Inoue-gumi, Hishiyama's eyes lit up. Although Inoue had referred Saigo, Hishiyama hadn't fully understood the extent of their relationship. The fact that Saigo was close enough to Inoue to have him act as a reference was impressive. After all, Inoue used to be the bodyguard of Chairman Ishii, the head of their family, the Yokosuka-ikka.

At the time, Saigo hadn't been aware of that part of Inoue's life. Susumu Ishii, also called the gentleman yakuza, was an internationally known crime boss. He was the second-generation leader of the Inagawa-kai, and one of Japan's most well-respected godfathers.

Hishiyama made the call, and Inoue gave Saigo a glowing recommendation. Hishiyama nodded and laughed while he spoke with Inoue. After hanging up, Hishiyama laid down the law for Saigo: If he took on Saigo as his *kobun*, then Saigo had to call him *oyabun*. He had to pledge his loyalty to Hishiyama and the Inagawa-kai. It was an oath of absolute loyalty; he would do whatever was asked of him with no questions asked. The yakuza had a saying: if the *oyabun* says the passing crow is white, it's white.

If there was a gang war, he would be called to fight, and might even die. If there was a shooting, he might be asked to take responsibility for the crime, even if he hadn't done it — all for the greater good of the organization.

He told Saigo to think it over and come back the next day. Saigo didn't have to think it over. He and his crew joined the Hishiyama-kogyo on the spot.

By no means was this casual and informal appointment the norm in the yakuza world. Becoming a yakuza and a *kumicho* all at once was unheard of. The standard practice was to either be recruited or volunteer "to become a real man" at a young age and to spend up to two years living in the office of the *oyabun*, working as a virtual serf. *Sumikomi* — the live-in yakuza — were at the bottom of the ladder. If they survived the rigorous hazing and training that came with becoming a full-fledged yakuza member, there was an elaborate sake exchange ritual in which the newbie would become the adopted child of the boss, and the boss would become his father.

The nature of the ritual varied between groups, but the ceremony was often elaborate and required the presence of a Shinto priest, versed in the mystic rites that sealed the bonds between yakuza bosses and their "children."

There was no need for standing on ceremony in the current situation that the two of them faced. For Hishiyama, it was a matter of expediency. He needed soldiers, back-up, and a base to expand in Machida. Saigo provided all that. Saigo's history as a motorcycle gangster, a right-wing group leader, and his reputation as an uncontrollable violent force of nature made him like the Instant Ramen version of a yakuza boss: just add a *daimon* and a *kanban*. Saigo was ready to go.

For Saigo, who did not have much fondness for Hishiyama, nor any real respect yet for yakuza tradition or history, he now had a chance to continue do what he wanted to do: make some money, and tell Kinbara to go fuck himself.

It was a good deal for everyone. Except Kinbara.


Saigo wanted to know exactly what to put on his business card, so he went to Inoue for advice. They met at a reasonably well-lit jazz bar that served good whiskey. Inoue told him not only what to put down, but what it all meant. Although Inoue never went to college, because Ishii encouraged him to read and write more, he understood the yakuza structure and history better than most members. He was able to explain it to Saigo like an anthropologist discussing the social hierarchy of a primitive tribe. He even drew it all out for him on a paper napkin.

The yakuza's power structure was built like a pyramid. The top organization was either called a *kai*, which meant association, or a *kumi* or *gumi*, which meant group or (mafia) family. The big five groups were the Yamaguchi-gumi, the Sumiyoshi-kai, the Matsuba-kai, the Kyokuto-kai, and the Inagawa-kai. Chairman Ishii was the head of the Inagawa-kai. The higher you were on the pyramid, the more people you had below you. Since Ishii was at the top, everyone followed him; although only those who had done the ritual sake exchange with him were considered Ishii's true *kobun*.

Underneath the top tier were usually *ikka* (families). There were several families in the Inagawa-kai, but because the Inagawa-kai chairman heralded from the Yokosuka-ikka, it was the best place to be. Ishii's *kobun*, Hiroshi Miyamoto, took over the Yokosuka-ikka when Ishii became the leader of the Inagawa-kai. Below the *ikka* were other organizations.

The breakdown of Saigo's title went as follows:

- Inagawa-kai (Parent group. *Kai* means "association")
- Yokosuka-ikka (Second tier. *Ikka* means "family")
- Hishiyama-kogyo (Third tier. *Kogyo* means "industrial enterprise")
- Saigo-gumi (Fourth tier. *Gumi* means "team" or "company" [especially in construction])*

Saigo was now the gang boss of the Inagawa-kai Yokosuka-ikka Hishiyama-kogyo Saigo-gumi. He was an *oyabun*, a father to his men, and they were his *kobun* (child figures). For this privilege, Saigo would have to make payments to Hishiyama, to the Yokosuka-ikka, and to the Inagawa-kai ruling elite. The fees could add up. Also, one of his main responsibilities would be going to yakuza-related events — weddings,

---

*   There is a great variation in the names of organizations within the yakuza. There only appears to be one rule — any group called *ikka*, literally "a family", must have other groups below it to remain an *ikka*.

funerals, and memorial services for major bosses — and providing *giri-gake*. Saigo wasn't quite sure what *giri-gake* meant, and had been too embarrassed to ask Hishiyama. Inoue explained: The first part of the word, "*giri*," was the be-all and end-all of the yakuza life. Normally, *giri* means obligation, duty, honor, and, most of all, reciprocity. However, in the yakuza world, *giri* also referred to the cash donations that young yakuza were required to bring with them to each ritual-and-ceremony part of the yakuza life.

It was one of the ways the yakuza at the top could collect money from the people below them without breaking the law or laundering money. *Giri* for the Inagawa-kai was not cheap, but, on the plus side, the Inagawa-kai would have his back. He could put the Inagawa-kai symbol on his business card, and use the power of the name to further his own interests.

As the *kumicho*, Saigo would be busy acting as a figurehead. This required keeping up appearances. He would drive a Mercedes-Benz, wear an expensive watch, live in a huge estate, use a gold-plated lighter, and constantly show his face. So a lot of the real power would lie with his second-in-command, the *waka-gashira* (sub-boss).

Saigo chose Yamada to be his *waka-gashira*. Yamada was intelligent and reserved, and was appointed to the position despite the fact that he was Korean. When Saigo gave orders, it was Yamada's job to make sure they were fulfilled.

Below Yamada would be the executives and, at the bottom, the ordinary soldiers. The Saigo-gumi was now a family of men with fathers, brothers, and sons — but no sisters.* They were not related by blood, but by their pledges of allegiance to those above and below them. Those ties were considered thicker than blood.

---

\* No major yakuza organization has had a woman as an executive member. It's the ultimate men-only members' club.

Unfortunately for Saigo, Hishiyama seemed like a kind of an asshole to him. It didn't feel like Hishiyama was his father. He had more respect for Inoue. When he told Inoue this, Inoue glared at him. For the first time, Saigo felt the presence of the man once known as the Demon Inoue. Saigo braced himself for a blow, but it didn't come. Inoue burst out laughing. He agreed, but wouldn't have ever said it if Saigo hadn't brought it up. But Hishiyama was Saigo's *oyabun*, and he had pledged his loyalty to him. Until Saigo moved up the yakuza ladder, he had to treat Hishiyama with deference and respect, or he wouldn't be a yakuza for long.

Thanks to Inoue, and the fact that he already had his own crew, Saigo went from being just a right-wing party leader to a fully fledged yakuza on top of it. He had no plans to close The Shelter. He'd seen firsthand how a right-wing group could work with a yakuza group. Now he could simply run both.

Saigo rented himself and his group a brand-new office in the center of Machida. His office was on the first floor of a small building. He immediately hung his *kanban* so the world would know exactly where he stood. The signboard had Saigo's group's name embossed in gold over a black background. It was a huge placard, almost as tall as Saigo himself. The object was almost too heavy for one person to move. Saigo was pleased with his new digs, and he loved his new *kanban*. He kept looking at it like a bodybuilder ogling his own biceps. He'd spent nearly $2,000 on that alone. And it was nearly impossible for someone to steal.

In the reception area, a huge blue Japanese porcelain ashtray sat on the long table between the two black leather couches that faced each other. Eight paper lanterns with the Inagawa-kai name written on them, and sixteen with Hishiyama-gumi written on them, were all lined along the ceiling. There was also a glass-framed painting with a black background and the characters for Inagawa-kai written on it in gold.

A painting of the word *ninkyodo* was hung up on the wall. *Ninkyodo* meant the humanitarian way — the honorable way to function as a yakuza. Saigo didn't know what it meant at all. The two *kanji* were written in Japanese calligraphy style, using black ink on a white background. The ink itself was so thick that the characters almost seemed embossed. He just thought it looked cool.

On the wall farthest from the door was a whiteboard calendar with important events scribbled in. Above the calendar were three pictures: the first-generation leader of the Inagawa-kai, Seijo Inagawa; the head of the Yokosuka-ikka, Susumu Ishii; and Saigo's *oyabun* (gang father), Hishiyama.

It had taken Saigo a long time to get to where he was, and it hadn't been a straightforward path. He'd been threatened and beaten up; he'd switched alliances and was once nearly chased out of town. But, when all was said and done, he'd won out. He was ambitious and he was lucky. Why not aspire to be as respected as Seijo Inagawa — the president of the Inagawa-kai?

Even though Inagawa was a yakuza boss, many people considered him a sage. He was born as Kakuji Inagawa in Yokohama on November 13, 1914. He grew up poor, and never completed elementary school. Although his father gambled away the family's money and was a failure in business, he was, in some respects, a remarkable individual.

In 1923, after the Great Kanto earthquake, rumors spread that the Korean workers were looting the local areas. Lynch mobs grabbed them right and left, killing thousands, the innocent and the guilty. Inagawa's father hid one family in their home for days. He told his son, "They're human beings, just like us. We're all the same."

It made a deep impression on the young Inagawa. It did not benefit his father to protect the Korean family, and it endangered them all, but his father had courage, and it was the right thing to do.

Inagawa grew up to be extremely physically powerful and ruggedly handsome. He trained as a judo student and was extremely adept. His nose was slightly flattened, probably because it had been broken on the tatami mats several times.

Unfortunately, there was no way to make a living as a judoka. In 1933, his judo teacher introduced him to the head of a gambling ring — Kentaro Kato. At the time, Kato was the foremost criminal leader in the Kanto region. Inagawa had been considering becoming a police officer, but the yakuza were introduced to him first. Although he correspondingly had a grudging respect for law enforcement, Inagawa decided the yakuza world was the one for him. When asked why he chose the yakuza over the police, Inagawa would joke, "I'm not so good at reading and writing."

His judo experience helped him in the early days of his yakuza life. He once famously threw a disgruntled competing gang boss from the second floor of a house, and singlehandedly ejected the rest of his crew.

He didn't have a lot of time to learn about being a yakuza before he joined the Imperial Japanese Army as a foot soldier in 1935. He took part in the suppression of one of the several military revolts that happened in 1930s. After he served his two years, Inagawa was discharged and returned home in 1937.

At a time when entertainment options were extremely limited, gambling was very popular in Japan. Loose federations of gamblers known as *bakuto* had existed in Japan for over 100 years. These gamblers were the predecessors of the modern yakuza. Shortly after returning home, Inagawa became a formal member of the Tsuruoka-ikka, one of the most powerful gangs in the Kanagawa prefecture. They were a federation of *bakuto*, and running underground gambling dens was their main source of revenue.

Inagawa quickly distinguished himself as a leader, an excellent gambler, and a hot-headed enforcer. Many yakuza have two names — and the second name is meant to capture the essence of who they want to be. So he took on the name Seijo Inagawa. Seijo means "holy fortress."

Inagawa made enemies, just as anyone in the yakuza world does if they're good at their job. He also had a habit of saying exactly what he thought, even if it raised the hackles of those around him. He told one rival yakuza boss to his face that he looked like an orangutan. When any gambler complained that the winner of the evening was "a goddamn Korean," Inagawa would chew them out, even in front of the other bosses.

"There are no Koreans or Japanese here. There are human beings. Anyone gets to play. Anyone gets to win. Shut the fuck up."

The outbreak of World War II put an end to the gambling for a few years. But when the war ended, Inagawa took up where he had left off.

Ethnic Koreans and Chinese, who had been imported to serve as slave laborers for the war effort, were banding together to become powerful criminal forces, particularly in Yokohama. Inagawa formed his own small gang to help Tsuruoka's remaining group in their efforts to dismantle these non-Japanese gangs. Inagawa could understand the resentment and hatred they felt towards the Japanese, but that didn't mean allowing these gangs to run amok. The police were short-staffed, and Inagawa picked up the slack. The "foreigners" were chased from the area by Inagawa's rapidly growing gang in just a few years.

In 1948, Inagawa was sent to the Atami region in the neighboring Shizuoka prefecture to support the Yamazakiya-ikka gambling group. He established the Inagawa-Kogyo (Inagawa Enterprises), the precursor to the modern-day Inagawa-kai, in the cities of Atami and Yugawara.

Inagawa's gang became a big player in the yakuza landscape in the 1950s. By the early 1960s, the gang had established a presence as far north as Hokkaido.

In 1964, the Tokyo Metropolitan Police Department took serious measures to crack down on organized crime by creating a division devoted solely to those efforts. In an attempt to keep a step ahead of the authorities, Inagawa registered his gang as a political party.

It didn't fool anyone. Up until then, the laws had been weak: in order to be arrested for gambling, one had to be caught in the act. The laws were revised, and eventually Inagawa was arrested and sentenced to three years in prison for running an illegal gambling casino.

Inagawa was released from prison in 1969 to find that his gang had dissolved into chaos, clashing both internally and with police. In March 1972, he renamed his organization the "Inagawa-kai," established a Tokyo office in Roppongi, and appointed Susumu Ishii to the position of board chairman. In the same year, the group formed a partnership with the powerful Yamaguchi-gumi — a relationship that continues to this day. When Saigo joined the group, Seijo Inagawa was still running the show.

Many considered him to be the most powerful yakuza boss in Japan. Saigo wanted to be like him. However, Saigo would have served himself better had he heeded the famous words of the founder about the right and wrong way to climb the yakuza ladder.

The words were immortalized in the Inagawa-kai theme song. Yes, the Inagawa-kai have a theme song. If you're going to have a *daimon*, you might as well have a theme song — maybe even two theme songs. The Inagawa-kai, like many corporations, has a fascination with merchandising. Not only are there Inagawa-kai badges, but also Inagawa-kai sake, Inagawa-kai sportswear, Inagawa-kai watches, and, of course, Inagawa-kai *daimon*-emblazoned business card holders. The only thing they lack in comparison to a typical Japanese corporation is a cute mascot character.

The opening bars of the song, "Otoko No Hanamichi" ("The Flowery Final Path of the Man"), written by Tsuruto Hara, describe the motivations of the old-school yakuza and the life esteemed so well:

> I stake my life for this coat of arms (*kanban*)
> When I make a bet, my chivalrous blood dances.
> The flower of Eastern Japan, the Inagawa-kai
> It's better to blossom and then fall apart
> Then come apart and then blossom.
> I want to be a famous man
> I want my name to be known
> The cold wind that soaks our skin
> Is hard and stings
> In our world of *giri* and human feelings.

But the most important yakuza life lessons may be in another song, which Inagawa selected as the theme song for *Shura No Mure*, the 1985 movie about the history of the Inagawa-kai. The movie was one of the last feature films glorifying the history of a still-existent yakuza group.

The song, "Kanagawa Suikyoden," references a famous Chinese novel concerning a nationwide struggle for power on a grand scale, thus metaphorically elevating the lives and struggles of the yakuza in the Kanagawa prefecture to an epic scale. Yet it gives a good idea of the stoic romance and perils of the yakuza life.

Loosely translated, the lyrics, written by Saburo Kitajima, go like this:

> Behind every shining famous face
> Is a dumb ass in the shadows
> Holding them up
> And that's all right.

That's how it is in this world.
Don't let the drizzling rains of the Tazawa mountains stop me
This is what I wanted to do and how I live.

Let's leave no regrets and nothing behind
And live our lives like we were on fire
My childhood friend.
Promises to pick up our bones

If you kick down others,
To climb up the mountain,
Next it will be your turn to fall.

Saigo wasn't cautious as he quickly scaled that mountain. He might not have kicked anyone down, but he clearly pushed some people out of the way. His carelessness would come back to haunt him.

# CHAPTER FIVE

# Shinogi

Saigo quickly began to reestablish his group as a branch of the Inagawa-kai Yokosuka-Ikka. The Kinbara-gumi did not welcome their "official" entry into the area. When Kinbara found out that Saigo was now an actual yakuza, he was livid, and threatened to take action. However, even though Saigo had far fewer soldiers, he had one in particular who aggressively wanted to fight for their territory and rule the town. And that didn't sound bad to Saigo.

This soldier, Daisaku Hanzawa, had a propensity for violence, and a vicious meth addiction, which was not uncommon for yakuza at the time. Meth gave him courage and an element of unpredictability that made him a formidable opponent. He had the fearless kamikaze spirit, Saigo would say.

One day, Hanzawa borrowed a small truck from the office. He just took it. Saigo wondered what the hell Hanzawa wanted with a truck, and didn't know where he was. As he sat in his office, the black phone on his desk rang. It was a member of the Kinbara-gumi. Hanzawa was at their office. He had rammed into some of Kinbara's soldiers with the borrowed truck. They had tried to run as they heard him coming, but many of them were left with injuries, albeit minor. They had been badly bruised.

Saigo thought they were exaggerating. That was totally insane, but it was true. And the only reason they hadn't killed Hanzawa was because he had a loaded gun, which was even more insane because guns were practically unheard of in Japan, even for gangsters.

They wanted Saigo pick him up, promising they'd let them both go without hurting them. So Saigo went to their office, finding the truck parked in front of it. He opened the door. Hanzawa was sitting on Kinbara's desk, holding a gun and playing with it. He was pointing it around the room — clicking the safety on and off. The gun was half-cocked. Half of the guys in the room looked like they were ready to throw up.

When he saw Saigo, Hanzawa put the gun on the table, but kept it in his hand. He was smiling. Kinbara's men were hugely embarrassed and kind of pissed off, but showed visible signs of relief that Saigo was there. He was still trying to figure out what to do when Kinbara himself walked in. He looked around the room. He looked at Hanzawa, who was clearly on meth. So Kinbara let him go this time. Saigo found himself at a loss for words. He cleared his throat. He was terribly sorry about the situation. He decided to take Hanzawa home, and assured Kinbara he would come back later to apologize properly. In Japan, even mobsters had to be polite at times.

Of course, even as Saigo was dragging him out, he didn't make Hanzawa put away the gun. Because you never could be sure. When they got in the truck and were a few blocks away, Saigo took the gun away and slapped him silly. But Hanzawa just laughed. Saigo went back and apologized the next day.

There were repercussions, but no acts of retaliation. In those days, meth-heads got one free pass. Saigo gave him a free pass as well. Hanzawa had almost started a gang war, but he had also instilled the fear of God, so to speak, in the Kinbara-gumi, and that wasn't a bad thing. Besides, Saigo had other things to worry about at this time, like paying his dues.

*Shinogi* is the alpha and omega of the yakuza life. Like many words in the yakuza world, it has multiple meanings that depend on the situation and context. Sometimes, *shinogi* refers to the income a yakuza makes from his various profit-making ventures. Historically, it refered to the edge of a blade. Outside of the yakuza, it can be defined as the means and methods of enduring or overcoming a problem. Sometimes, the noun is attached to the end of a word to indicate it is a stopgap measure to deal with a problem or a means of killing time. Ironically, it can also mean the food served to attendees at a funeral.

The definition given by the National Police Agency describes it best: *shinogi* are the "fundraising activities of the yakuza."

A yakuza going through a tough time doesn't complain about his business. He complains about his *shinogi*. If the *shinogi* isn't good, the yakuza can't pay his *jounoukin* (association dues). If he can't pay his *jounoukin*, that's the end of his yakuza career. When broken up, *jounoukin* translates to "the money you deposit above." Everyone, except the man at the very top, has to pay.

Saigo's *shinogi* was rock-solid. He had close to fifty full-time members working for him, and fifty part-time associates. Money was coming in through multiple revenue streams, such as forcing corporations to buy or sell stocks, collecting debts from others, and making high-return loans. The Shelter had *danbe*, ran *kanpa*, and printed the newsletter, but they were always exploring additional types of *shinogi* as well, from subcontracting work on construction jobs, to forcing people to vacate premises or property. (This was known as *jiage* or "land-sharking".)

Saigo also collected money from all his members. Many made a living running illegal gambling businesses. Saigo didn't touch those businesses himself, nor did he want to know the details. Using Saigo's name was helpful to their business, and he was content with his indirect cut of the profits.

Anything within the Saigo territory was subject to a "tax." So if you were operating a shady business on the Saigo-gumi's turf, you had to pay a form of protection money called *bashodai*, also known as *shobadai*. One of Japan's most well-known red-light districts, Tanbo, was near the south exit of the Machida station. The district had sprung up at the end of the war, and featured a number of restaurants and bars that were also fronts for prostitution. In 1998, there were over eighty shady shops in the area. From these shops alone, Saigo brought in 12 million yen a month. His group also collected an additional 5,000 to 9,000 yen a day from streetwalkers.

Even the public telephones in the area were taxed. A few weeks after setting up his office in Machida, Saigo summoned the local NTT (Nippon Telegraph and Telephone Corporation) representative to his office. He complained about the poor maintenance of the pay phones in his area. The coin-release levers were rusted. There were still telephones that didn't accept pre-paid cards (telephone cards) and only took change; he was unable to make international calls, and this was also unfair to his Korean members, who had to call home now and then. As the local yakuza boss, he felt a civilian duty to make sure that these essential public services were maintained — or so he claimed.

The NTT representative nodded and took notes. A few days later, he came back to the office with an envelope full of telephone cards, worth almost 40,000 yen when combined. Sometimes, Saigo would cash the cards in. Other times, he'd just give them to his men. In the days before cell phones, public telephones and beepers were indispensable parts of the yakuza life.

Saigo also worked hand in hand with local real estate agents, finding them good properties, introducing them to clients, and sometimes forcefully evicting tenants. For this, the agents paid him a good fee, sometimes up to 5 percent of the profits on a transaction.

The Saigo-gumi also made a decent amount of money for keeping silent about shameful activities. In other words, they demanded hush money. Saigo had a network of hostesses, hosts, and other people working in the adult-entertainment industry who would feed him intel on bank presidents, company CEOs, wealthy doctors, and crooked politicians in the area. Sometimes, shady journalists would also drop him a tip. Extortion was a staple of his business, though never a consistent source of income. Blackmail was a complicated business. If you milked the victim for too long, they, or someone close to them, would eventually go to the police.

Scandals always made money. The most common scandals involved bankers or company presidents abusing their authority and making bad business decisions that they wanted to conceal. Adultery and indiscreet affairs were good material for blackmail, too. Get the dirt, name a price, take the payment, and walk away. That was his strategy. He didn't push his luck by trying to get paid over and over again. That's how people got caught. He didn't feel bad about shaking down the wealthy or the stupid. They were victims of their own greed. He was just the hammer of karma.

One summer, Saigo took a local company president on a trip with him and his crew to an inn near Atami. The lovely geishas who worked at the inn served the party and got drunk with them. Saigo left to go to an Inagawa-kai executive meeting the next morning, so he headed back to Machida earlier. That night, the company president and one of the geishas slept together.

The next day, the woman's husband, a local yakuza, showed up at the hotel and barged into their room. He threatened to kill the businessman. The distressed president called Saigo, who returned to the inn and agreed to mediate the situation.

After an hour of discussion, Saigo explained the terms. The company president had to apologize, vow to never sleep with the man's wife again, and pay 100 million yen in compensation. It was almost $1 million, and he had to take it or leave it. Saigo promised to keep the whole thing out of the media and to make sure there would be no further damages demanded. The panicked company boss agreed to pay on the spot, and Saigo made him bring the cash within hours. The money was paid, and the problem was solved.

Of course, it was all a set-up. Saigo and the local yakuza had it worked out from the start. The "husband" got one-tenth of the money. Usually, the woman would be an employee at a hostess bar or other yakuza-run establishment, or sometimes she would actually be the girlfriend or mistress of one of the players in the con. She would get a generous cut as well. Saigo and his crew would keep the rest. The yakuza have been doing this kind of fraud for decades. In the U.S., it's called "the badger game." In Japan, it's called *tsutsumotase*, which is written using the characters for "beautiful", "person", and "situation". In actual usage, *bijin* (beautiful person) is almost always limited to women, beautiful women. Beautiful woman situation.

Negotiating settlements was also a good source of income. For instance, before even going to a court, a person could instead go to the Saigo-gumi and ask them to negotiate settlements in civil disputes or reimbursement claims for damages. Civil cases in Japan can drag on for years and cost thousands of dollars. Even if the court ordered the loser to pay compensation, the court costs and legal fees are almost never included in the compensation. The yakuza could settle a civil dispute in days or weeks. Even though they kept half the money, it was still more efficient and profitable than hiring a lawyer — unless the yakuza later came back and blackmailed you for using their services.

Politics also played a role in *shinogi*. During election seasons, local politicians would ask Saigo's crew to gather up votes. Sometimes, in order to make vote-tampering easier, they'd check to see whether people on the politician's supporters list were still alive. That involved sending a few guys down to city hall to check records. When conducting voter fraud, it's always good to remember that dead men don't vote.

Having political connections helped keep the police off their back. In general, their relationship with the local cops was exceptional. Saigo understood that as long as his gang suppressed street crime and didn't engage in it, all was good. Pissing off the cops was bad for *shinogi*.

The regular monthly income for Saigo-gumi was roughly 10 million yen ($100,000). Saigo paid himself a salary of one-third of the group's monthly revenue. Unfortunately, expenses were high. The association dues, even on the fourth tier, were sometimes over $10,000 a month. That didn't even include the *giri-gake* he'd have to provide when he attended funerals, weddings, succession ceremonies, and other yakuza events — and these events were frequent. He would be invited to a funeral whether it was the death of someone from the Inagawa-kai or another gang, like the Yamaguchi-gumi. He had to show his face, and each month he'd end up kicking close to 20 million yen ($20,000) back to the organization at least.

Some months, he felt that the association dues were unreasonably high, but he didn't mind paying. Rather, he wasn't going to complain. The Inagawa-kai brand made him money.

*Shinogi*, he would often remind himself, also means endurance.

## CHAPTER SIX

# Pig box

Oddly, it wasn't Hanzawa who introduced Saigo to meth, but a woman he met at a hostess club. He'd never done it before, but he found that he liked the feeling quite a lot. It wasn't surprising that he, too, became addicted to it by 1988.

The history of meth in Japanese society is almost as old as the modern yakuza. It ranks as one of the three worst contributions Japanese science has given the world. The second worst is high-fructose corn syrup, and the third worst is the karaoke machine.

Yes, America can ultimately trace its obesity and meth problems to Japan. The process of making high-fructose corn syrup was commercialized by a Japanese scientist employed by the Japanese government. It makes you wonder if this was how the Japanese planned their revenge on the U.S.: fatten them up with a sugar substitute, and then fight them when they are all too fat to even roll out of bed onto the battlefield.

As for karaoke, if you've ever had to spend an evening singing "You are my sunshine" with a band of drunken salarymen, while a Japanese woman with too much make-up and a voice unnaturally high pours you low-grade whiskey and mixes it with water, you'd understand why karaoke makes the top three.

Meth takes first place because the damage it has done to the world has been immense. Japanese organic chemist Nagahiroshi Nagai synthesized methamphetamine from ephedrine in 1893. Nagai had been researching traditional Japanese and Chinese medicine, which use the natural form of ephedrine, *ma huang*. The Chinese have long used *ma huang* to treat asthma and bronchitis because it opens up the windpipes.

The new drug had some other side effects that were welcome. It woke people up, removed their feelings of fatigue, and made them work harder. However, it also made people unnaturally cheerful, chatty, and hyperactive. It could only create this superhuman state for a short time, but the user still needed sleep and rest. If they didn't get it, they'd run themselves into the ground. The Japanese doctors only used it to treat asthma, depression, and narcolepsy.

It was Nazi Germany that realized the value of the drug as a "super-serum." They started to sell methamphetamines as an over-the-counter drug in 1938. The Germany army, realizing it enabled soldiers to work longer and more energetically, began to supply it to soldiers.

Japan quickly followed, introducing it into troop rations. The government made major pharmaceutical companies ramp up meth production. It was primarily for troop usage, at first. But, just as in the United States, often what is developed for military use becomes commercial. By 1940, it was being sold over the counter to the Japanese general public under various names. Hiropon was the bestselling brand. The name allegedly came from the catchy slogan that it would make your fatigue (*hiro*) jump away (*pon pon*) like a rabbit. Even today, addicts are called *ponchu*, which is a combination of the word *pon*, from *hiropon*, and *chudoku*, a verb meaning to be addicted. No one really understood all the side effects, the addictive qualities, or the mental damage it caused after being used for an extended period of time.

The scientific name for methamphetamines in Japanese is *kakuseizai*. *Kakusha* means "Buddha," which originally meant "one who is awake." *Sei* means to "wake up from one's sleep; to become sober." *Zai* indicates a prepared substance. So *kakuseizai* is literally "the drug that wakes you up and keeps you awake (like the Buddha)."

The Japanese slang term for meth is *shabu*, coming from the verb *shaburu*, which means to suck on something. There are a few reasons that the word came to refer to the drug. There is the metaphorical idea that meth sucks the life out of you; that it eventually drains everything from you if you keep using it. The second reason *shabu* is an apt name for the drug is that many users experience an incredible thirst after they get high. Often, according to urban legend, addicts get a craving for sugary soft drinks such as ginger ale or cola. One veteran detective from the Tokyo police insists that the easiest way to tell if you're interrogating a meth-user is to offer them a Coca-Cola — if they take it and gulp it down, you're dealing with someone high on speed or a heavy user.

Nothing had ever made him feel as good as *shabu*. He remembered sitting naked in his apartment one day, feeling like every nerve in his body was pulsing.

There was sex, and there was sex on *shabu*. Many women in the water-trade (hostesses, prostitutes, massage girls) were addicted. It made the sex better, and it was easier to endure unpleasant customers in a meth-induced fugue. Some women dissolved the powder into liquid and used it with a lubricant before sex — it gave them and the customer an unbelievable high.

Saigo never had much self-control, and he didn't see doing meth as a problem because everyone was doing it. Plus he liked the courage and power it gave him. When he was on meth, he became the man without fear. But it didn't take long for him to go overboard, and the side effects didn't take long to manifest themselves.

In February 1988, he began to feel as if he was being watched all the time; that someone was out to get him. He didn't know who or why, but he needed to hide. The Saigo-gumi was temporarily taken over by Yamada because he wouldn't come out.

Saigo accused his wife of cheating on him with another man. When she denied it, he kicked over the table in their room and accused of her lying. "I want to leave you," he told her. "Let's call it off."

She tried to calm him down, "When you get off the drugs, you won't feel that way."

"You lying bitch. I know what you're up to. Get out."

She did, and she took their daughter with her. Now he was all alone. In his frustration and irrational state, he shot himself up with a nearly lethal dose. He didn't sleep for seventy-two hours. He began hallucinating, and became convinced that he was surrounded by policemen and yakuza from rival organizations. He thought even his own soldiers were going to kill him.

He gathered all the newspaper in the house and a roll of packing tape, and tried to cover every window. When he could still see light coming through the windows, he taped towels, pieces of cardboard, and anything else he could find over the newspapers until no one could look in and he couldn't look out. He made one small peephole that he could open and close at will. When he looked through the hole, he saw the chrysanthemum symbol of the police on a hat, and a man wearing that hat.

The Machida police were alerted by a neighbor, and came knocking on his door. He opened it, and there stood Detective Lucky.

People called him Lucky because he only smoked Lucky Strike cigarettes. Lucky was from Okinawa. He was dark skinned and had a bright smile full of teeth. His relatively short haircut had a very slight pompadour that made him look like a Japanese Elvis, but anytime someone told him that, he'd say, "I hate Elvis and I hate karaoke — in that order."

Saigo half-opened his front door and glared at him. Lucky was the last person he wanted to see.

Lucky asked him point blank if he was doing meth. He knew the answer. He ordered Saigo to give him the drugs and to go with him to the police station, where Lucky could arrest him.

Saigo thought about it. He was going crazy on the stuff, and he needed to get off it. He didn't think he could do it on his own. So he admitted he was on it.

And Lucky took him in.

He was held for the full twenty-three days allowed under the law. He went into withdrawal. It was a long, painful incarceration.

His juvenile record had been expunged when he became an adult, so he had no criminal record. It was his first time to be charged with violations of the stimulants law. He vowed to never use meth again, and the judge gave him a suspended sentence.

It didn't take long for him to violate the terms of his release. In early May, Saigo once again boarded up his windows with cardboard and started screaming loudly in the night, waking up his neighbors. When he did venture out of the house and drove down the highway, he would imagine there were angry yakuza hiding in his trunk. He would sometimes stomp on the brakes after speeding up, just to ensure the collision would kill the gangsters hidden in the trunk of his car.

On the evening of May 19, he heard a window being pried open. Lucky was peeling back the cardboard, peering through the darkness, using a flashlight. He put the light on Saigo. He was clearly high again, and while Lucky could get a warrant and arrest him, doing so would be a pain in the ass. So he ordered Saigo to turn himself in within twenty-four hours. He needed to just grab his stuff, go to the police station, take a drug test, and do his time before he did something more stupid.

"Even your boss Hishiyama is worried about you," Lucky said.

Saigo wasn't surprised that Lucky had been talking to Hishiyama. That's what organized crime cops did — especially the ones in the intelligence-gathering division. He'd seen Lucky visit Hishiyama a few times. Hishiyama would usually try to give Lucky gifts of cigarettes and expensive booze. Lucky would take the carton of cigarettes, but not the booze.

Saigo closed the window and thought about Lucky's proposal. He was in big trouble. He decided to hide in the garbage room of the apartment complex. No one would look for him there. He went downstairs, made a fort out of garbage bags, and barricaded the door. No one could find him now.

This worked for a day, but eventually the smell of the garbage was too much, and he returned to his apartment.

A few hours later, Lucky pounded on the metal door of his apartment. Saigo let him in. He had come alone. Lucky knew he was high. He ordered Saigo to give him the drugs. Saigo meekly handed over the syringes and a few small bags of powder. Lucky took the drug kits, the dope, and everything else. He weighed the bag of meth in his hand like he was holding a handful of diamonds. He sighed. The amount Saigo had in his possession made for extra jail time.

Lucky told Saigo that if he flushed the meth down the toilet and took a urine test, Lucky would pretend he'd never seen the meth. Saigo took the deal.

He was arrested the next day on several charges of the Stimulants Control Act. He was tried and found guilty in the lower Tokyo court;

his prior suspended sentence was revoked, and he was now sentenced to a total of two years and eight months in prison.

He'd never been in prison before, although it was considered a rite of passage in the underworld. In yakuza slang, he was going to *butabako*, which meant "pig box," even though no one really used the word 'pig' to denote yakuza or cops in Japan. Animal terms are used all over the world to designate entities within each country's underworlds. In Japan, cops aren't pigs; they're dogs. Squealers and rats are also dogs. As for pigs, they're just stupid and/or unclean dishonorable people.

Saigo should have been sent to a prison for first-time offenders, where the conditions are slightly more humane, but he was already a known member of a yakuza group. He was sent to Fuchu prison, the largest prison in Japan, which held roughly 3,000 prisoners. He'd heard that life there would be tough. He had no idea of how awful it would really be.

Upon entry to the prison, he was stripped naked, and every cavity in his body was searched. The guards made it to clear to him that he was a nobody on their turf. "It seems like you were a boss out there. You had a name and your colors, and you swaggered around like you were hot shit. But in here, you're just a pig."

Other guards repeated to him variations of this refrain as they processed him.

"You lost your human rights the second you walked in here."

"You were sent here because you committed a crime. Outside, your *oyabun* may be your god, but while you're here, we're your *oyabun*."

The prisons were still governed by laws created in the Meiji period. Prison society was and is a world unto itself. Many of the prison guards were the sons, and sometimes daughters, of prison guards. It became a family occupation.

Prison life was a series of petty punishments. If you spoke out of turn, you might be forced to sit in *seiza*, an uncomfortable kneeling pose,* for minutes or hours, until your legs fell asleep and you fell over on your face. Guards always found this amusing. If you made a sound when you fell, that was another punishment. If your shoulder was sore and you rubbed it: penalty. If you looked out the window, or allowed your gaze to wander, you'd get a warning. If you did it again, more punishment.

The guards had a philosophy about their work. They believed it was their job to be ruthless and to earn enough money to support their family. They were convinced that the tougher they were, the lower the rate of recidivism would be. They had no idea of "reforming" the prisoner — that wasn't the goal. Their job was to make life so unpleasant that no criminal would ever want to come back.

Saigo shared a room with five other men. He had his futon, and was allowed a few books. On his second day in prison, he had taken a written examination so his intelligence could be assessed. He'd done very well, and was assigned a job producing electric motor parts for Toyota automobiles at a metal-working factory on the premises. The job was perfect, because he liked cars, and it required some skills and intelligence. The working day started at 6.00 am. Breakfast was at 6.20 am, and he had to eat without speaking and do his own dishes. Only fifteen minutes was allowed for lunch. No talking was allowed.

Even during work, speech was forbidden. If Saigo wanted to speak to someone, and sometimes this was necessary to finish the work, he had to raise his hand first. The guard would say, "*yoshi*," and then he could communicate verbally.

Dinner was served at 6.00 pm in absolute silence. Speaking during dinner could result in severe punishment, including solitary

---

* In 2022, the Kanagawa lawyers' association strongly advised Yokohama Prison to cease and desist using forced *seiza* as a punishment, arguing that it was illegal and an extremely painful form of corporal punishment.

confinement. The food was plentiful, but awful. They were served huge bowls of *kokumai* from a rice crop that had been harvested three or four years prior. It smelled awful. Saigo suspected that prison was called the pig box because of the smell of the rice. There was always more food than he could eat.

After cleaning up, he would go to his room and have some time to read before lights went out. Then the day would start over again.

The prisoners were allowed to take a bath twice a week. They would have to shower before soaking in the tub, and keep their hands visible at all times. On his first day, while he was showering in front of the guards, one of them noticed that Saigo's Mongolian spot was still pronounced and bluish. They made fun of him for it.

The Mongolian spot (*mokohan*), often found on Asian children, is a blue spot found near the base of the spine. It looks similar to a large bruise, and usually goes away as a person gets older. Because it's associated with youth, the Japanese slang for "wet behind the ears" is *mada ketsu ga aoi* (your butt is still blue). Blue-assed Saigo suddenly felt very much like a helpless child. In the outside world, he would have punched someone in the face for such smart-ass remarks, but in prison, he had to shut up and endure them.

Everyone got bullied by the guards. If you reacted, you were punished. If you disobeyed orders, you were punished. The stress drove some of the prisoners crazy.

The different yakuza gangs were friendly to each other, unless they were in a war on the outside. It was a good time for them to get to know each other and to create cross-organizational friendships.

Even with close monitoring, fights would still break out — sometimes very violent and bloody fights. That wasn't surprising when you had a bunch of convicts, many of them yakuza, working in a factory carrying hammers, steel objects, and tools. However, even if you saw a fight breaking out, trying to break it up would only get you in trouble as well. It was an unwritten rule: don't interfere.

Six months into his time, he would break that rule. One of the men working next to Saigo attacked another man with a hammer, smashing the man's face, and splashing blood all over the walls. One of the blows glanced off Saigo's shoulder. Without thinking about it much, he blocked the assailant from killing the other prisoner. He didn't know either of them, but he couldn't stand by and let a fellow human being be bludgeoned to death. As the guards rushed in to break up the fight, Saigo rubbed his shoulder where he'd been hit; it was painful.

The guard saw him do it and concluded that Saigo had been part of the fight. Starting a fight was a serious infraction. That got him put in "the leather cuffs."

The cuffs consisted of a wide leather belt that was put around his waist; his left hand was fastened to his back via a shackle on the belt, with his right hand over his belly. He was warned that if he complained, they'd put the muzzle on him as well, the *boseigu*.

The guard told him, "Get ready for the worst two days of your life."

He was taken to the "protection room" (*hogobo*) — a step above solitary confinement, made to sit down, and do nothing. The room was three meters in length and two meters wide. The walls were covered with twenty-centimeter-thick sponge so the prisoner couldn't smash his head into the wall or hurt himself. The door had two slot-sized holes: one in the top where the guards could peer into the room, and a hole in the floor where they would put his food.

In the farthest corner of the room was a drain over which the prisoner was expected to defecate and urinate. It was hard to do this with both hands strapped to your torso. The trouser had a hole under the anus so that the prisoner could relieve himself, but it was small, so there was no way to go to the bathroom without pissing or shitting on yourself. In theory, you could move around so that your penis dropped down when you pissed, but it didn't always work. There was no toilet paper in the room, because of course, you couldn't use your hands to wipe your ass. A television camera was in the upper-right-hand corner of the room, so this exercise in humiliation could be seen by the guards at all times.

The guards would come in to check on him every three hours. Sometimes, they would reverse the binding of the hands. Under no circumstances would they completely remove the cuffs, although they would loosen them slightly. Food was served in the equivalent of a dog bowl.

Saigo realized that the only way he could eat was if he crawled over to the bowl and ate the bowl of rice with his face stuffed inside. Fittingly, the term for eating in the cell was *inugui* (eating like a dog). He decided that he'd rather starve. They could treat him like a dog, but they couldn't make him act like one.

Because he wouldn't eat, they threatened to leave him in the cell a third day, but Saigo just stared at the guard silently, and they let him back into the prison population.

He vowed to himself that if there was another fight in front of his eyes, he'd rather let somebody die than be sent back to the cell again. And then, when he thought about it some more, he decided that probably wouldn't be any easier. The only thing to do was avoid being around when a fight broke out.

These days, the guards are less brutal. In a prison in Nagoya on December 14, 2001, three guards decided to discipline an unruly prisoner with a high-powered hose. They pulled down the inmate's pants and sprayed the water into his rectum. The inmate died the next morning from severe rectal injuries and bacterial shock.

The incident brought worldwide attention to the deplorable state of life in Japanese prisons. The Japanese courts found all three men guilty of criminal assault resulting in death. They were all given suspended sentences, so none of them ever went to jail. It's hard to imagine what would have happened if they had.

The incident resulted in some reform, but that was long after Saigo got out.

The guards wouldn't always physically punish the prisoners. Sometimes they'd take away privileges; you'd lose your right to take a shower, or to go to the prison yard and exercise.

At night, the prisoners were allowed to speak to each other, as long as it was done quietly and calmly. There were no hidden cameras in the room (at the time), so their conversations couldn't be overheard. There were also no air conditioners or heaters in the room. Saigo was always freezing or sweating. It was never comfortable. They'd talk about their life before prison, their crimes, and, if they were yakuza, their *oyabun*.

There were Koreans, Romanians, Taiwanese, and American prisoners, and they were expected to speak and understand Japanese, but most of them couldn't speak Japanese well when they entered. The longer they stayed, the better they got at communicating. Saigo thought that prison must be even more hellish if you had no idea what you were supposed to do and kept breaking rules that you didn't know or couldn't possibly know because you were informed of them in words you couldn't understand.

One of his temporary roommates was a black man from Rochester, England. He had been a gangster back home, and was serving time for manslaughter. He'd been in prison before in England. He explained to Saigo just how bleak things were in Japanese prison compared to home.

He told him, "I will never ever come back to Japan. Fuck this country."

He told him that in English prisons you got your own room. You could read the books that you wanted, and there was no "protection room" and no leather handcuffs. You could speak when you wanted to, and you could see your family members often. The other prisoners thought he must by lying. In Japan, Saigo was only allowed to see his wife and daughter once or twice a month. The idea of conjugal visits seemed otherworldly.

Even the number of letters he could get were limited, and always screened before he got them. Sometimes sections would be blacked out. There was no television. The book selection was limited and, of course, reading material about yakuza was forbidden. When Saigo was able to get a weekly magazine, articles about the yakuza would be cut out before he could read them.

One thing that he did learn to appreciate about Japanese prisons was that no one got raped. He learned from foreign prisoners that that happened often; newbies would be picked out by the tougher cons, held down, and sodomized.

The only freedom they had was exercise twice a week. The exercise yard was vast, and they could spread out. There were only three guards looking after hundreds of them, so they could have serious discussions, plan for life after prison, and work out their differences.

Saigo made friends with a member of the Yamaguchi-gumi. He was oddly humble and polite. In addition to being a yakuza, he was a carpenter who could really make things. It was good to make friends with a barbarian from the West, which is how eastern yakuza thought of western yakuza.

Good times were few and far between. Punishments were constant.

It was almost an education. Perhaps that was why the yakuza also referred to prison as *daigaku* (college). It was the place where you learned to suffer in silence, obey, swallow your pride, and be tough. It was, in its own way, excellent mental training. You had the opportunity to learn how to behave like a proper yakuza by watching how the senior yakuza conducted themselves. You listened to their stories. You networked, and made friends that might last a lifetime. You might also make some enemies, but learning not to immediately retaliate was important, too.

Rimi didn't visit often. A few months into his term, she brought divorce papers along. "Sign them," she asked. "Promise me, for our daughter's sake, that you won't remarry. Please don't bother us. We're starting a new life." Saigo protested. He promised he'd change. She didn't budge. She just pushed the divorce papers at him. He signed them. And that was that.

The months went by, and then it was time to leave.

It was 1990. Saigo was given a few days' notice. He was able to tell his old gang that he was coming home, and he knew they'd be there to greet him.

The paperwork and process for leaving the prison were laborious. One of the final steps was taking his fingerprints in the holding room. They used transparent ink, which was almost like glue on his hands, and had him spread his hands out on the records sheet. They didn't appear to match his entry records. The guards insisted that he wasn't Saigo, and accused him of being someone else. Part of the problem was that his hands were so huge that they didn't quite fit on the paper.

The certification and re-entry process smoothed up when a long-time guard heard the commotion and came in to insist that the Saigo trying to leave the prison was the same Saigo who'd come into the prison.

At the exit, he was given back his clothes, and was allowed to change into them. The only thing the guard said to him as he was checking out was, "Don't come back too soon." Saigo had a thousand things he wanted to say, but he held his tongue.

As soon as he walked outside, he saw his crew. There were five black Mercedes waiting for him, to bring him back home to Machida. There was Yamada and a number of soldiers. Saigo felt like no time had passed at all. He soon learned otherwise.

## CHAPTER SEVEN

# Back in The Shaba again

Japanese Buddhism posits six realms of existence: there's heaven and hell, and then there's the realms of hungry ghosts, fighting spirits, animals, and humans. Colloquially, the world of ordinary humans is considered *shaba*. In the yakuza world, it's also used to contrast between life in prison and life outside prison. *Shaba* was the world outside prison.

When a yakuza gets out of prison, he is traditionally thrown a celebration called a *shushoiwa*, or a "getting-out-of-prison celebration." A dinner is held, and everyone brings envelopes full of cash to show their respect for the returnee and to aid them in getting back to business.

Following the celebration, it is customary for the returnee to visit the people who rank above him in the organization and to properly greet them and let them know that he is back and still exists. So, shortly after Saigo got out of prison, Hishiyama took him to see Coach at his home in the Ikebukuro area of Tokyo. Coach was a former professional baseball player and one of the highest-ranking members of the Yokusuka-ikka, way above Hishiyama. In fact, he was even Inoue's boss.

In the Inagawa-kai, when greeting superiors, it was customary to get on your knees, place both hands on the ground, and bow so low that your head touches the floor.

When Hishiyama took Saigo and two others to pay respects to Coach, Saigo noticed that the house had Western flooring, not tatami. In the living room, when Hishiyama and company put their hands on the ground and bowed to Coach, only Saigo kept his hands on his knees and did a consequently slightly shallow bow.

Coach was offended by this. He did not address Saigo directly, but instead yelled at Hishiyama. Hishiyama apologized profusely.

Saigo, who was still slightly befuddled due to his long time in prison, and nervous about meeting a senior yakuza, interrupted without thinking. There wasn't a tatami mat there, and he had been told to put his hands on the tatami and then bow. "This isn't tatami; it's just a floor."

Coach slapped him with full force on the side of his head, knocking him sideways like a broken Japanese *daruma* doll. He ordered Hishiyama to educate "this kid" better. Saigo had spoken out of turn and had been rude.

Saigo righted himself, and bowed deeply and correctly to Coach. Hishiyama apologized again, prostrating himself in front of Coach along with Saigo, again and again until they hastily left.

Saigo thought to himself that Coach was an asshole and that Hishiyama had no spine.

Things had changed since he'd been gone. That was only natural. He had a couple of new soldiers under him now. One who particularly interested him was Akira Mizoguchi. Mizoguchi had been kicked out of Japan's most respected college, Tokyo University, in his third year, and was easily the most erudite guy in the group. His other nickname, Ikijibiki, meant "the living dictionary," but Saigo never used that nickname when addressing him.

Mizoguchi's father was a very high-ranking boss in the Inagawa-kai — ranked much higher than Saigo. After deciding he wanted to follow in his father's footsteps, Mizoguchi was placed under Saigo's command in order to avoid favoritism.

Saigo felt he owed his own parents a visit for all the support they had given him while he had been in jail. He went to their house on a Sunday night, had drinks with his father — something neither of them really did much — and blissfully passed out in the guest room.

He woke up Monday morning, surprised to see his father still home at 10.00 am. As he was eating his breakfast of toast, eggs, and bacon while his dad picked at his warm rice and cold fish, Saigo looked at the time. It was now 11.00 am. His father should have been at work by now.

As it turned out, Saigo's arrest had triggered a series of events that resulted in his father being forced to retire from his job at the Bank of Japan. Saigo was stunned.

The Bank of Japan used to do an annual investigation of its workers to make sure that no one was subject to conflicts of interest that could result in financial malfeasance. The initial hiring process weeded out most of the bad apples, but times changed, and so did people. The standard checks included making sure that none of the employees had borrowed excessive amounts of money from loan sharks, or even from the semi-legal consumer loan companies — which could legally charge as much as 29 percent interest.

Marital problems, scandals, arrests — any of these things could get someone fired. Saigo's father worked in the division that handled the printing of money, so the checks there were the tightest. The bank conducted its own investigations, even sending people to the employee's neighborhood.

Mr Saigo's neighbors had shocking news for the investigators: Saigo's son was a hot-rodder, and had been arrested for drug use. The internal-controls department called him in for a hearing, and asked him if the rumors were true. Mr Saigo, being a very honest man, answered in the affirmative. He told them his son used methamphetamines and was a member of the yakuza. He believed that when his son got out of jail, he would turn over a new leaf and be a better man.

His supervisors hadn't known at all about his son's organized crime connections. They'd just wanted to know if it was true that his son was in prison. Mr Saigo's explanatory answer only made matters worse.

He was called into the office and told politely that he would normally be fired, because having a criminal in the family was grounds for dismissal. However, since he was so close to retirement, they would let him leave the company instead, if he did so immediately. In return, they promised him his full pension. He took the offer.

Saigo felt terrible. It was one thing to take responsibility for his crimes and go to jail, but he hadn't foreseen how this would affect his family.

He felt guilty, so Saigo started looking for ways to employ his father.

He called up one of his *danbe*, and asked him for a loan and to sell some of his land to Saigo. With an investment equivalent to $200,000, he set up a car-repair and painting service. They specialized in foreign cars. He gave the company to his father to run, along with his cousin Taro. His dad now had a job.

Saigo had been a mechanic and car repairman for someone else before — but now it was him running the business (although the day-to-day management was entrusted to his father). It was a niche business. Saigo immediately let every yakuza know that he was running a new company that would take care of any damages to their much-prized automobiles at reasonable (for yakuza) prices.

At the time, the yakuza were so flush with money, and so many of them had foreign cars that needed special care, that business boomed. During Japan's economic bubble, money flowed. The bubble lasted from 1986 to 1991. Everyone had too much money, and the yakuza were making sure to get a piece of it. In many ways, they not only profited from the bubble, but helped create it. They would pay exorbitant amounts for repairing small defects in a car — a scratch on the body, scuffs on the hubcaps, a stain in the upholstery, a fleck of peeled paint. They wanted their cars looking brand new at all times.

His dad had a job, and Saigo felt much better.

Mr Saigo paid great attention to detail, and his politeness, demeanor, and sincerity made him well liked by customers. Dealers in foreign cars who didn't want to work with angry yakuza started sending their clients to Saigo's shop.

Two or three months after being released from jail, Saigo met Hiroko. They were introduced to each other through a non-yakuza friend they had in common. She was three years older than him, and, unfortunately, due to the norms of Japanese society, her age would have most likely kept her from finding a husband. Saigo had promised his first wife he wouldn't remarry, even though there wasn't really any logic to the promise. Still, he had given his word, so he wouldn't remarry. At the same time, he felt lonely. She understood his circumstances, and they decided to date anyway.

She was good-natured, always smiling, motherly, and patient. She was able to put up with Saigo's bad temper and yakuza life. They soon moved in together.

Unfortunately, Saigo didn't have much time for her or his family. He was busy getting back to work. A few months after turning over the car-painting business to his father, Saigo went to visit him. When his father answered the door, he was wearing a worn-out suit, looking haggard and unhappy. His mother was silent as well.

Saigo sat himself down in front of the low-set table called a *kotatsu* they had in the front room, and caught up with his father. Saigo smoked a cigarette and asked his father why he hadn't bought a new suit yet.

His father responded that he didn't have the money. Saigo was puzzled. His father was supposedly making 400,000 yen a month. That was a lot of money.

"Your cousin hasn't been paying me," Mr Saigo said. "So I don't have any money."

Saigo was furious. His cousin Taro had joined the Saigo-gumi right before Saigo went to prison, and had taken to the gangster life like a fish to water. The problem was that he wanted to look the part in every way, and was willing to dip into the company's coffers to fund the transformation. He bought a Lincoln Continental, fancy suits, and a gold-plated Rolex. He did all this with the money that he was supposed to be putting into the business.

His father knew that Saigo would probably be angry about this, and thus had refrained from saying anything earlier. Saigo once joked that if his father was ever shot, the first thing he would do, if he even went to the hospital, would be to apologize to the nurses for getting blood on the floor.

Saigo immediately fired his cousin from the gang and from the company. His father continued to run the auto-repair and painting business, and he began doing Saigo's books as well. The organization grew to such a size that Saigo couldn't remember everyone's names anymore. He thought about making flashcards, but never got around to it; so, when his father did the books, Saigo began to assign numbers to the individual soldiers by the order in which they joined: Soldier 1, Soldier 2, and so on. This helped Saigo immensely. Numbers were easier for him to remember than names. If you're going to run an organized crime group, it helps to have someone who is a good organizer, and he was lucky his father was exactly that.

Business did so well that Saigo got an unexpected visit at his office from Kinbara. Kinbara came with only his driver and his bodyguard. It was a surprisingly cordial visit. Kinbara had come to remind Saigo that he still owed him about $60,000 — money that Saigo had borrowed to spend time in Japan's seedy sex parlors — and now that Saigo's business was doing well, wasn't it about time to pay him back?

Saigo asked for a little more time. The company was just starting, and $60,000 was a lot of money. Kinbara agreed to wait.


Since Saigo grew up in Machida and knew many of the residents, he asked for local support, and the local merchants welcomed him back. He was able to get his yakuza business back on track pretty quickly as a result. It also helped that, while Saigo was in prison, Yamada had done an excellent job of managing the business and maintaining good relations with the local people. He had really kept the revenue flowing. His network of old friends helped, too. His *shatei* (younger brothers) from the local motorcycle gang became his emissaries — sort of like salespeople.

The town still had a problem with youth gangs and street crime. Saigo wouldn't work for free, but he could guarantee that people wouldn't be mugged, and that customers visiting the seedier parts of the city wouldn't be accosted or harassed by blackmailers, conniving journalists, private detectives, or streetwalkers.

If there was graffiti on the walls, he'd find who did it and have his men teach them a lesson. If there was a bout of purse-snatching in an area, the purse-snatcher would be himself snatched off the street and have his legs broken. If there was a problem, he'd fix it, and his proactive handling of problems made the area safer for everyone.

Saigo also did smaller jobs, such as keeping the peace in the areas full of love hotels. Love hotels are for couples, illicit or legitimate, to get some privacy and have sex; that's why the rent is usually charged in two-hour slots. Some have all-night services available. The love hotel owners were having problems with the street gangs. They had problems with unruly customers who'd leave without paying. They had problems with vagrants who would accost customers leaving and beg for money, or make vague threats if they weren't paid off. The love hotel owners asked another local yakuza boss to put Saigo in charge of security, and then said they would pay him 20 million yen for the service.

Part of the reason that cops couldn't crack down on yakuza was that the cops had a policy of "no intervention in civilian affairs." So if the yakuza were shaking down debtors, loan-sharking, or receiving "voluntary donations" — well, that wasn't a problem. After all, the yakuza were still passing themselves off as humanitarian organizations. The major yakuza organizations had solid political connections, and there was enough money to go around for everybody.

During this time, the National Police Agency estimated that the income of all the yakuza in Japan from illegal and semi-legal activity was about 1.3 trillion yen.* However, many yakuza experts at the time felt they were grossly misrepresenting how much money the organizations were bringing in and their revenue streams. For one, the amount of revenue credited as coming from the sale of methamphetamines (34.8 percent) was exaggerated. The rest of the money came from gambling (17 percent), protection money (9 percent), debt collection and civil affairs (7 percent), and extortion from companies (3 percent). Legitimate operations accounted for 20 percent of the income, although 10 percent of those operations came

---

* They made this estimate once in the National Police Agency white paper in 1989. At the time, 1.3 trillion yen was equal to just over $10 billion. In today's money (2022), adjusting for inflation, it would be around $23.6 billion.

from yakuza-run companies. And on top of that, the official numbers were seriously underestimating the financial power the yakuza held. A former National Police Agency bureaucrat suggested that the real income of the yakuza at the time was seven times the estimate put forth by the NPA, and that the amount of money coming from corporate coffers, willingly and unwillingly, was astronomical.

Saigo's group was bringing cash to his office in bags.

Things were going well for Saigo, and he finally had enough money to go to Kinbara's office and pay him back.

When Saigo and his crew arrived at Kinbara's office, it created quite a commotion. Everyone assumed that Saigo had come to "*o-rei mairi*" (pay his respects) — which is yakuza slang for taking revenge. In the normal world, it means to formally come by and say thank you.

Saigo walked up to Takeda, who was blocking the door, with his hand in his coat as though he was ready to reach for a gun, and nodded to him. Saigo held up both hands, and had one of his soldiers bring a small bag forward and show it to Takeda. It was full of 10,000-yen bills.

"That's what I owe your boss. I'd like to pay it back myself."

He walked into Kinbara's office, where Kinbara was standing up behind his desk, glaring in Saigo's direction. Saigo gently plopped the bag full of cash on the desk.

"Go ahead, count it. There's 6 million yen in there. I owed you money. I paid my dues, with some interest, and now we're even."

Kinbara took the bag, took out the money, and counted it. He nodded. "Tell me something, Saigo-kun. Did you really blow all this money on getting blown?" Kinbara never knew what to make of that story. In his entire life, he had never met any yakuza who spent tens of millions of yen at soaplands. "Was it really so good?"

"Well, yes, it was,' Saigo told him.

"You are so stupid."

# CHAPTER EIGHT

# Tattoos hide fear

There were a number of things that Saigo wanted to do now that he was a free man and back on his feet, and the first on his list was get a proper tattoo, like a real yakuza. Of course, he wanted to cover up his blue ass as well. It turned out that his time in prison was like going to a three-year exhibition of tattoo art. Everyone showered together, and he had a chance to see the best and worst of traditional tattoos — thousands. He was particularly enamored of the tattoos of two yakuza he met there, one from the Yamaguchi-gumi and one from his own clan. They had gotten their tattoos done in Numazu City in the Shizuoka prefecture. He decided he would follow in their footsteps, and asked one of them for an introduction to that tattoo master. Many famous tattoo artists only accepted new clients after proper introductions.

Tattoos are as Japanese as sushi and samurai. The yakuza have their own word for tattoos: *gaman* — endurance. When done the traditional way, the tattoos are expensive, time-consuming, and painful.

The Japanese take great pride in endurance. *Gaman* was the favorite word of Seijo Inagawa, the founder of the Inagawa-kai, and he didn't mean tattoos. Bearing the unbearable, that was the mark of a man. Japanese men take great pride in their ability to endure suffering. It's the culture in which *seppuku,* suicide by ritual disembowelment, was considered a noble way to die, provided that you did it right and showed no expression of discomfort or pain as you slowly and methodically cut open your stomach.

There is even a word for the activities in which males compete to show who is tougher: *gaman kurabe,* literally "comparing endurance." This is why drinking contests in Japan among university students can turn deadly, and sometimes do — no one wants to give up and show he or she is the weaker. Jokingly, some yakuza refer to comparing their tattoos to those of other yakuza as *gaman kurabe,* but they are well aware that it is a pun of sorts.

The tattoos also illustrate what are considered the other great virtues in the Japanese underworld: loyalty, patience, commitment, and persistence. A full-body tattoo can take up to 500 hours to be completed, and the yakuza receiving the tattoo is expected to stay with the same tattoo artisan until the end of the process. Of course, the process never really ends. There is always some coloring to be added, some shading to be done, outlines to be defined — and as the tattoos fade slightly with time, some retouching. The level of commitment the tattoos show to the organization can be easily gauged; if you have the name and crest of your gang tattooed into your skin, it makes switching allegiances next to impossible.

There is one other meaning attached to the tattoos that some yakuza don't even consciously recognize: they are symbols of wealth. A full-body tattoo, or even one that simply covers the upper body, can cost thousands of dollars — it's the equivalent of turning your skin into an ostentatious solid-gold Rolex. The yakuza brandishing the elaborate tapestry on his upper body is also telling those around him that he has money to burn.

Japan has a long history of tattooing; it has over the course of the centuries been for decoration, for punishment, for ritual, and also to show membership of tight-knit social groups. Tattoos have never been and will never be solely the province of the yakuza — although for many Japanese, and Westerners as well, Japanese traditional tattoos and the yakuza are inextricably linked.

The Chinese historical record *San-Kuo Chih* (*Account of Three Kingdoms*), compiled sometime before 300 AD, notes that the denizens of the Kingdom of Wa (Japan) were sometimes tattooed to show their social rank. The *Kojiki* (*Record of Ancient Manners*), put together circa 700 AD, and one of Japan's oldest written works, hints that tattoos in Japan served ritualistic or magical purposes. The *Kojiki* also contains the first recorded account of a striptease in the land of the rising sun. There is no mention of whether the goddess performing the striptease was tattooed.

Historians are not all in agreement, but over the centuries, Japan continued to use tattoos to indicate social rank and to create a visual record of criminal behavior that would follow a lawbreaker more persistently than a Google search ever could. The tattoo as a mark of hereditary status certainly had its place.

Japan never had slavery or a complex caste system like India, though it did have a class system, which was regimented by occupation and closeness to the Imperial line. There were always the *hinin*, "non-people" — this would include jailers, executioners, and gravediggers — who did distasteful tasks and also dealt with criminals. As Buddhism flourished in Japan, it created a new underclass known as the *burakumin* ("people of the village"). They engaged in tasks considered sinful under Buddhism, such as the slaughtering of animals and making leather products. They also did filthy and dangerous work that the Japanese upper class would not do. They were called "people of the village" because they lived in separate communities from the rest of the Japanese (and, in some isolated parts of Japan, still do). These two groups were often marked with crosses or lines on their upper arms to keep track of them, and to keep them away from the greater community.

The *Nihon Shoki*, another of Japan's earliest written historical (and sometimes mythical) records, has a note about a man named Azumi No Muraji who had been tattooed across his face as punishment for treason. Ichiro Morita, in the book *Irezumi: Japanese Tattooing* writes that in 460 AD, *geimen* (tattooing the area around the eyes) was one form of punishment. The punishment was later replaced with branding the flesh of a criminal. These "flesh punishments" included cutting off fingers, ears, and noses. The eye tattoo was revived in 1672, and, in a great humanitarian leap forward, in 1720 most of the "flesh punishments" were replaced with tattoos being inked on the body. Being punished with a tattoo was considered getting off easy. There were good and bad things about this system. It definitely made it clear to the public that the tattooed individual had a criminal record. However, it made it hard for such individuals to reintegrate into society.

After 1720, malefactors were marked with symbols indicating they had been found guilty of past crimes, and the area where they came from. In the Tama region, a man might have the kanji character for dog tattooed on his forehead. In other areas, the markings would be different — two stripes on the arm, or something else. However, the enterprising marked men found a way to game the system. According to Morita, "The (tattooed) men began to hide their markings in elaborate artistic tattoos." It's quite possible this influenced the early yakuza and their associates to get tattooed. Eventually, some of them used these tattoos to intimidate others for acts of extortion and other crimes. The tattoos that were carved on the criminal for punishment were used in "reverse for profit." In other words, the tattoos became the futile equivalent of a yakuza *daimon* — something to strike terror into the hearts of peasants and townsmen, and make them cough up money. On September 25, 1870, the Meiji government abolished tattooing as a form of criminal punishment.

However, despite the government use of tattoos to classify people, punish felons, and maintain "living" criminal records, the popularity of tattoos among Japanese commoners grew steadily in the Edo period. After 1750, perhaps due to the popularity of a Chinese novel translated into Japanese as *Suikoden*, which depicted the tragic, honorable, and heroic lives of 108 outlaws, tattoos became the rage among the lower classes.

The novel was tremendously successful, going through many translations and editions — it was almost counter-revolutionary. Several of the heroes in the book were tattooed Robin Hoods fighting against corrupt government officials, and the books were lavishly illustrated. They depicted these heroes in all their dragon-tattooed glory, and they became inspirational figures for Japan's emerging middle class known as *chonin* (townsmen). Among the *chonin* emerged small groups of vigilante law-keepers known as *otokodate* (street knights) and participants in a new occupation — firefighters. In Japanese, they were called *hikeshi*, literally "extinguishers of fire." Both the firefighters and the street fighters embodied modified warrior codes and worked on behalf of the commoner, not the feudal lord. If you wanted to discuss Edo-period Japan in *Star Wars* terms, the samurai were the Storm Troopers, fearlessly flying into battle at the will of their lord and master, Lord Vader, and dying anytime — while the street knights and the firemen were the champion of the little guy, the Rebellion. The samurai were the arm of oppression; they wore armor and were clean-skinned, with no tattoos. The street knights and firemen were heavily inked and unruly, but sworn to protect the weak and to fight injustice. It's not surprising that they were the most celebrated figures of popular culture.

The firemen of the era didn't quite possess the skill sets you might imagine. The only way they knew to put out fires was by knocking down adjoining buildings, to create a gap so that fire couldn't spread. Their heroic and highly visible exploits earned them a great number of local fans, and they flaunted their status and solidarity within their group with colorful tattoos. The firemen were often separated into *kumi* (groups), just like the modern yakuza, and it was not uncommon for members of one *kumi* to share similar markings. However, these Japanese firemen were so rough and aggressive in doing their duty that writers of the day question which did more damage: the fire or the firemen.

These burly firefighters, who favored tattoos with water symbols such as the carp, and who had a fearless proclivity for dangerous work, are considered by some to be the antecedents of the modern yakuza — or, at least, many yakuza would like to believe as much. In a short time, perhaps emulating the fictional heroes they read about, it was not just firemen and street knights, but gamblers, construction workers, and artisans who were getting adorned with elaborate pictorial tattoos. The tattoo artists decorating the bodies of their newfound clients often made the inkings with one eye on the woodblock prints illustrating the Suikoden.

Some of the techniques being used to make wood-block prints, *ukiyo-e,* and other artworks of the time were simply applied to the human body. The tools were often the same, although everyone knew that the human body is much softer than wood.[*]

Of course, the government, sensing that fun and rebellion was always dangerous, banned the practice in 1812, but it continued quietly among the lower classes. Tattoos were an assertion of individuality and liberty that the government found disturbing. The anti-authoritarian tone of the Suikoden did not charm them either. Tattoos were an inkblot on the face of Japanese morality.

---

[*]  Ian Buruma, in the book *The Japanese Tattoo.*

Evidence of the popularity of tattoos despite the ban can be found in the Tempo era (1830–1844), during which public tattoo contests were banned. Japan underwent a rapid modernization phase in the Meiji era (September 1868–July 1912), but the ban on tattoos was still formally in place — for Japanese citizens. However, visiting Westerners found the traditional Japanese tattoo to be a thing of remarkable artistic beauty. Foreign sailors had them done — even the Duke of York, who would later become King George the Fifth, and his older brother, got tattoos. The Duke of York had a full dragon carved on his forearm by the famous tattoo master Horicho, who hailed from Kobe — where the Yamaguchi-gumi would later start up. Future tsars, European royalty (including Queen Olga of Greece), and many more happily bought the services of Japan's tattoo masters to put some color and oriental mystery into their lives.

However, in the build-up to the World War II, tattoos were discouraged — they were frivolous and rebellious. Among the yakuza, certain artisans, and some laborers, the practice continued, but it was only after the war ended and the yakuza numbers swelled in the postwar chaos that the tattoo made a huge comeback.

Saigo was ready to get an *irezumi*: the Japanese form of tattoo that means "the ink that is put in." It was to the yakuza what a white shirt and necktie were to the Japanese salaryman — an indispensable part of the uniform.


When Saigo arrived at the tattoo studio, he already knew what he wanted: a carp, cherry blossoms, and a dragon. He'd seen those on other yakuza, and liked the way they looked. He had little to no idea of what the symbolism meant; he just knew they looked cool.

Some tattoo artists would look at the man they were going to ink and decide on their own what was the best tattoo for the individual.

Saigo's tattoo master let the individuals choose. Although the ink used in traditional Japanese tattoos is black, it appears blue when it goes under the skin. The tattoo master told Saigo that it would be much more impressive to have a carp shaded in hints of blue with a splash of color, rather than a gaudy burning-red rendition. Saigo agreed.

The carp is one of the most loved symbols and tattoos of the yakuza. It's a manly fish. It swims upstream against the current, even bravely climbing up waterfalls, and when it gets caught, it sits quietly on the cutting board without flapping and flailing, bravely awaiting its death. It is the most stoic of fish. The Japanese word for carp is *koi*, a homonym for "love," and in that sense, it is also auspicious.

The cherry blossoms are a symbol of transience and, in some respects, freedom from the fear of death. The cherry blossoms only bloom for a short time each year before withering and falling, or being blown off the branches by the wind as they weaken. In this way, too, the cherry blossom is shorthand for the yakuza ideal of living fast and dying young — and acknowledgment that life as a yakuza can be very short and that death can come any time.

Saigo had opted for the traditional tattoos done not with electric needles, but with a combination of blunt instruments, *sumi* (Chinese ink), and awls that dug into the flesh — a style known as *wabori*. It is probably the most painful method of getting inked up you can choose. A small series of triangular edged awls and gouges are used to push the pigment under the skin. His tattoo master would use a complicated technique to add subtle shading to the whole of the tattoo, and brute force to give the scales of the carp on Saigo's back a three-dimensional aspect — which was exactly what Saigo wanted.

He wanted the cool-looking tattoos, but was not quite prepared for the immense pain and the blood. While he was waiting, he watched others being tattooed, and it looked a little painful. The master was working primarily on the outer epidermis of the man before him, going over an outline that he had drawn on the body with a felt pen. Some of the best tattoo masters don't even have to draw an outline. (Horiyoshi the Third once said that he could see the outline on the body as though it was projected there — as clear as a children's coloring book.)

With one hand, he stabbed into the flesh, holding the skin with the other hand, constantly wiping away the blood. It didn't look much more painful than getting a shot — but, admittedly, a series of flu-shots one right after another didn't seem pleasant.

The tattoo parlor was fairly spacious but poorly lit, slightly grimy, and held a strange scent in the air. It was the smell of blood, sweat, fear, rust, steel, stale cigarettes, and something musky, almost erotic as well. The master would sometimes light a stick of incense before carving up a customer; the scent of sandalwood didn't drown out the numerous odors in the room, but simply complemented them. It smelled as if someone had opened a brothel in a locker room next to a coffee shop. It wasn't a place where you felt like staying for longer than you had to.

When Saigo lay down on the floor, the master asked him two questions: How much pain can you take? How badly do you want the three-dimensional component on the carp scales?

Saigo answered that he was a man, he was ready for pain, and he wanted a tattoo that told the world that. The master grunted. Normally, the process of creating a tattoo was divided into four parts. First, there was the drawing of the outline: *sujibori*. This was done using a sharp-edged tool and pigment to press the lines into the skin. This carving of the outline involved sticking the needle deeply into the skin, again and again. Then came *bokashi*, the shading and coloring of the areas already outlined with the needle. Finally, there was *gakubori* — digging a frame, which decorated the surrounding area outside the component parts of the tattoo with a pattern.

The master wanted Saigo to understand what the full process would entail, so he began with the scales of the carp, doing a few to the point of completion. The initial carving of the outline stung and was painful, and Saigo didn't flinch, but when the master began the *bokashi*, Saigo felt pain like nothing he had ever experienced. The master drove the needle in so deeply that it hit the bone; Saigo had to gnaw on his cheek not to scream. The master poked and dug; Saigo could feel his skin stretch. He grunted; he sweated, he clenched his fists. He lasted ninety minutes, and only blacked out once. But just for a second.

Five hundred dollars for a ninety-minute session — the first of many sessions he would undergo over the next four to five years. It seemed like a fair price — unless you broke it down into a per-centimeter scale. He didn't care. Fuck it, it was worth it.

He drove himself home that night and went to bed. The scales tattooed on his skin were bumpy and inflamed. The pain was immense. Yet he was happy. He'd started down the path of being a real man and dealing with real pain. As time went by, he would gradually notice that the deep penetration that was part of the traditional tattoo methods was destroying his pores. His flesh was cold where the tattoos had been carved. By the time he was done with the full-body tattoo, his normal body temperature had been permanently lowered — it was as if his entire body was covered with a permanent first-degree burn. He had trouble sweating and adjusting to slight temperature changes. He found it hard to deal with the cold and the heat; his body always seemed to be out of sync.

At the time, he wasn't thinking more than a few weeks into the future. He had no idea of the damage he was doing to himself. Tattoos, he'd later tell his son, are pretty damn impressive, but in the end they amount to self-inflicted punishment.

There has not been a great deal of scientific study done on the extent of physical damage caused by traditional Japanese tattoos. Here's what we do know: the traditional tattoo needle penetrates the dermal-epidermal junction and goes deep into the dermis. This totally and terribly disrupts the function of epidermis as a barrier, causing a wound and lodging the ink openly into the dermis. The way the wound heals affects not only the quality of the tattoo, but also the quality of the skin function after the wound has healed.

The ink stays in place for years by tricking the body's complex immune response. The immune system is structured to defend the body against a wound, and the ink is taken as an infection about to occur. The immune system responds to the invading ink by generating certain types of cells, which serve functions such as healing wounds, and detecting and destroying foreign substances, cellular debris, and pathogens.

The healing may leave scar tissue that affects the sweat glands. The needle or awl may also damage sweat glands as it stabs through them. There are about 100 sweat glands in every square centimeter of skin, so it's not surprising that some damage is done.

The master gave Saigo a choice of which ink to use in dyeing parts of the tattoo red. He could use tattoo pigment imported from America, which was cheap and safe, but faded quickly, or he could use tattoo pigment from Germany, Cadmium Red, which could only be applied in small doses because it was poisonous. Although a highly toxic compound, Cadmium Red was brighter and lasted longer. Saigo chose the dangerous dye. He wanted the scales on his carp tattoo to have a red luster.

Even if he had understood the risks he was taking, the damage he was doing to his body, and that it would eventually cost him an amount equivalent to the purchase of a top-of-the-line Mercedes-Benz, he would have still done it. Why?

Because the tattoos on his body would become Saigo's way of charting his rise up the yakuza ladder — a permanent and unchanging record of his successes, his income, his failures, and his loyalties.

## CHAPTER NINE

# How to make 50 million yen with a fistful of yen and some pussy

His debts paid off, his body tattooed, Saigo was now making good, steady money, but he wanted to pull a big score.

It was a cold day in February 1991. Saigo was sitting on his sofa, practicing the guitar, when Mizoguchi burst into his office, very excited. There were a bunch of *burakumin* outside the Daiwa Bank making a scene. Mizoguchi had seen three or four of them arguing with the manager.

Saigo had an idea. He ordered Mizoguchi to gather some guys, drive the van up to the bank, grab the guy in charge of the *burakumin*, throw him in the back, and bring him to Saigo. He wanted to talk to him.

Saigo didn't have anything against the *burakumin*, but he wasn't fond of dealing with them. Saigo suspected that many of his fellow yakuza, and even one of his soldiers, were *burakumin*. The yakuza were a meritocracy.

Mizoguchi dropped off Akihito Morita at Saigo's office thirty minutes later.

In addition to being the leader of the Burakumin Liberation League, Morita was a fastidious undertaker who worked in a poorly run crematorium. He arrived dressed in a black suit, white shirt, and black tie. He carried a brown leather briefcase. His short-cropped hair was dark black with specks of gray, and he was wearing his trademark tortoiseshell glasses.

From behind his cheap metal desk, Saigo motioned Morita to come into the main office and sit down. They exchanged business cards. Both were rejects from society, so Saigo thought they should get along.

Morita wanted to know why Saigo's soldiers had dragged him to the Suguwara-gumi office. After all, the bank wasn't under their protection.

Morita explained that he and his people were just trying to gain an audience with the branch manager. The bank was refusing to extend a loan to a local business run by a *dowa*, as Morita called him. *Dowa* is the polite term for *burakumin*. Morita claimed the bank had refused to extend the loan because their management was racist.

Saigo wasn't completely convinced by this. He sat back, smoking his cigarette.

"Well, it's a little more complicated than that," Morita admitted. One of the loan officers at the bank was lending a lot of money to a friend of Morita's, without asking for any collateral. This friend, who managed a love hotel, had a deal with the loan officer. Many banks require their finance department to make a quota of loans per month. So the loan officer and Morita's friend had an arrangement whereby the officer lent the hotel manager money, thus making his monthly quota. The officer also got a kickback on the loans. Unfortunately for them both, the Daiwa Bank had fired the loan officer. When the love hotel manager was late paying back his loan, the bank seized his property.

According to Morita, this wasn't fair. The Burakumin Liberation League wanted to discuss the problem with the bank's branch manager, Mr Motomura. Morita wanted to speak to Motomura to request an extension on the loan.

Saigo could tell that Morita was actually trying to blackmail the bank, but was having trouble getting close enough to the branch manager to do so. Once Saigo made it clear to Morita that he understood his real intentions, and Morita finally acknowledged the truth, Saigo advised Morita against pursuing his strategy. If Morita kept trying to blackmail the bank using his present plan, he would go to jail. He was making too much of a ruckus, and his group could easily be arrested for forcible obstruction of business. The arrest would discredit them.

So Saigo and Morita both attempted to come up with another solution. Saigo suggested writing a letter, but Morita pointed out that mailing Motomura a letter would leave a chain of evidence that could be used to accuse Morita's group of extortion or attempted extortion. An off-the-record conversation would be the best way to handle the problem.

Morita came up with an alternative plan that would require Saigo's manpower. In return, Saigo would get half of the total profit. Saigo listened to the plan, and liked what he heard.

That evening, Saigo, Mizoguchi, and Yamada got on the phone to gather 100 men. Most of them came from the Saigo-gumi, although Yamada recruited a good number of people from the South Korean Organization of Japan who would work for pay.

As instructed, each person showed up with a one-yen coin and their cheap personal seal (*inkan*), which is used in Japan as a signature to sign documents. At 9.00 am, Saigo, dressed in his trademark black suit and navy-blue tie, showed up at the window of the Daiwa Bank. He told the teller that he wished to open an account, and placed one yen on the counter. The aluminum coin looked very small when placed under his huge index finger.

The woman at the counter looked puzzled. Why would anyone want to go through the process of opening a bank account just to deposit one yen? She politely questioned him to make sure she understood.

She had, in fact, understood correctly. Technically, anyone could open a bank account, as long as they had at least one yen. The woman nodded, and began to do the paperwork. As she asked him questions and for ID, two more men with one-yen coins came up to the tellers on both sides of her. Behind them, a line was forming.

A few minutes later, her supervisor came over. He interrupted the conversation and asked her to hurry up a bit. There were 100 other guys outside, each with one yen, who wanted to open accounts. She looked outside, and there were indeed about 100 men dressed in black suits. Some of them had tattoos visible on their arms; many of them had facial scars.

The supervisor looked at Saigo for a second, and asked him directly if they were his friends. Saigo looked over his shoulder and feigned surprise. "Oh, yes. Most of them are my men!"

The supervisor apologized to Saigo, and explained to him that they were too understaffed to handle the 100 men waiting with one-yen coins to open accounts. Saigo told the supervisor that he hadn't told his men to follow him, and he didn't have the right to tell them not to. The supervisor should just be happy to have so many new customers.

When the supervisor still seemed upset over the new customers, Saigo accused him of discriminating against yakuza and *burakumin*.

The supervisor told Saigo that, of course, their background was not an issue. He just wished they could come at a different time so that the bank's other customers could get into the bank. Saigo said he might consider asking them to leave *if* the branch manager asked him directly.

The supervisor apologized again, and told Saigo that the branch manager was a little busy at the moment, and did not usually come out to meet new customers. Saigo continued to accuse the bank of discriminating against him and *burakumin*. The supervisor did his best to be polite.

By the end of the day, half of Saigo's men had managed to open accounts. The branch manager, however, still refused to meet with Saigo.

When he got back to the office that evening, he told Morita that things hadn't gone as planned. Morita suggested they move to plan B.

That night, Saigo gave instructions to his remaining fifty men. The next morning, before eight-thirty, they were to bring to the office a one-yen coin; their personal seal; a friend with one yen (with their personal seal), and a cat. If they didn't have a cat, they were told to go borrow one or catch a stray.

The next morning, Saigo was again the first to the teller's window. This time, he brought a small paper bag with about 300 one-yen coins, and asked to make a deposit. He spread the coins across the counter. The teller asked how much Saigo was depositing, but Saigo wasn't sure.

With a polite sigh, the teller began to count. For the first few minutes, the only sound to be heard was the coins plinking into a bucket as she counted them one by one, but then the caterwauls began. There were 100 guys, each with a one-yen coin and a cat, waiting outside the bank to open an account. Some were tossing the cats back and forth to each other.

The cats were not happy.

There were other customers in the bank now. They looked out the window to see where the noise was coming from. Once they saw the mob of guys in black suits throwing cats, they left in droves.

The supervisor ran up to Saigo, his face flushed. He asked Saigo what the hell he was doing, and accused him of animal abuse. Saigo calmly responded that cruelty to animals would be killing the cats and eating them — but that's what the supervisor thought *burakumin* did anyway, right?

The supervisor shook his head back and forth violently. He wasn't saying anything bad about *burakumin*. He was saying that Saigo's crew was torturing the cats. Saigo defended his crew. They were just bored, waiting for the supervisor to open their bank accounts. They were just playing with their cats to kill time.

Strictly speaking, Saigo knew it was animal abuse. The cats hadn't done anything wrong. When they had discussed the plan, Morita hadn't seemed particularly concerned about the welfare of their feline accomplices, but Saigo thought differently. He gave explicit instructions to treat the cats as nicely as possible while still making a scene. Members who dropped a cat while tossing it back and forth were told they'd forfeit their salary for the day. Under no circumstances were the animals to be harmed. Saigo wasn't a pet lover, but even he had a limit.

He specifically told Hanzawa, the group's most feared enforcer, "If you kill the cat, I'll kill you." Maybe that was why Hanzawa was the only one to show up with a German Shepherd. The dog kept barking at the felines, which added to the caterwauls and confusion. Fortunately, Hanzawa stopped it from eating the cats by judiciously pulling on the leash. The dog and Hanzawa seemed to get along. The cats didn't like Hanzawa or the dog.

Regardless, the fact stood that they were disturbing the other bank customers.

So the supervisor called the police, and three officers were soon on the scene; but once they saw 100 yakuza lined up with cats, they weren't sure how to handle it. The cops questioned the men about their intentions and the ownership of their animals. The men all had coins and seals, and they all stuck to their cover story: they were going to open an account, and they were taking their cats out for some fresh air.

One cop came inside and spoke to the supervisor. Saigo could hear the conversation from where he stood. If Saigo's group had threatened one of the tellers, or had done something violent, maybe the cops could have done something about it. But as it stood, the men weren't violating any laws. The supervisor was livid. They were abusing the cats and disturbing the customers — but playing catch with cats wasn't a crime. Doing something like twirling the cats by their ears or killing them would be a crime. If they were doing this to a cat that belonged to someone else, maybe that could be considered a crime, too. Some of them were just holding their cats. Others were even hugging them.

They weren't directly threatening the bank's customers. Granted, the customers were disturbed by Saigo's crew's actions. If they kept it up, the bank could file charges of obstruction of business, but the crew would have to do it several times. Ultimately, there was nothing the police could do.

The cop left, and the supervisor went upstairs to the second floor of the bank. A few minutes later, down came the branch manager, Motomura. He looked like he was in his mid-fifties, was slightly paunchy, and wore a gray pinstripe suit. His gray hair was slicked back, revealing a large forehead. He finished off his look with gold-rimmed glasses, which made him look very much like a typical Japanese banker.

Motomura spoke to Saigo in a very calm, almost friendly tone. He invited Saigo to go upstairs to speak with him.

That's what should have happened from the start, Saigo said. He wanted their talk to be brief so his friends wouldn't have to stand outside in the cold with their poor little cats.

When they got up to the second-floor office, Motomura sat behind his desk, and Saigo sat across from him, his back straight. Motomura offered him a cigarette, and Saigo took it. They both lit up, tapping out the ashes in the crystal ashtray on Motomura's leather-bound desk.

Motomura was straightforward. He wasn't going to give Saigo cash. That was fine. Saigo didn't want cash. He was there for a loan.

The Daiwa Bank required collateral. A loan without collateral would never be approved by their head office. But Saigo knew that hadn't stopped one of the bank's former loan officers from lending a lot of money to the love hotel manager. That individual had been fired, but the bank had never pressed criminal charges, saying it didn't seem necessary.

So why did Saigo need to provide collateral? He asked whether the bank was getting a kickback. Motomura denied it, and asked Saigo if he was trying to blackmail him.

Saigo said he wasn't, because the bank hadn't done anything wrong. He was just pointing out that the bank had made loans without collateral, and he wanted to take out a loan, also without collateral.

Motomura had been working for the Daiwa Bank for most of his career. He had been the manager of the Machida branch for seven years. The bank's reputation mattered to him, as did the jobs of the people working for him. A scandal would get people fired — his branch might even be closed down. He didn't want that.

He asked Saigo if he cared about the welfare of his workers. Saigo did, so he understood where Motomura was coming from. Still, he requested 50 million yen.

Motomura didn't balk or blink. He just nodded and stroked his chin. He decided to give Saigo the funds from the "neighborhood countermeasure funds." Many banks and business used to keep emergency funds for dealing with problems in the neighborhood, including noise pollution, parking, and general disturbances. These so-called neighborhood countermeasure funds were also often used to pay off the local yakuza.

Motomura knew Saigo had no intention of repaying the loan, so he would only authorize the transaction under two conditions: One, Saigo would never make the incident public.* Two, he would never try to extort money from Daiwa Bank again, regardless of the branch.

Saigo gave Motomura his word, and promised to shut down anyone else who put the bank in the same situation.

"Good. Please understand that if you ever show up again at our office again, I will call the police and demand they defend us from you. If you can promise this will never happen, that you will never come back, we have a deal, and we are on good terms."

Saigo understood, and since he was a young yakuza, Motomura offered him important advice about dealing with the situation. He suggested that Saigo make two or three token payments on the loan. If he never paid any of it back, it would be easy to demonstrate that he had committed fraud — that he had never intended to pay back the loan.** If he paid back some of it, he could always argue that he had meant to pay back all of it, but that his business had gone bad.

Returning to the first floor, Saigo motioned Motomura to follow him, and they walked outside to where Saigo's men were lined up. In a loud voice, Saigo told his men that, apparently, it was not a good idea to wield cats next to the Daiwa Bank. So, although he hated to ask, he hoped they and their cats could go to another bank and deposit their money elsewhere.

The men responded in unison. "Hai!" Several came up to Motomura and said, with a bow, that they were sorry for the inconvenience. Some of them released their cats on the spot, and the

---

\* Daiwa Bank is no longer in existence, so talking about what happened won't affect anyone now.

\*\* In legal terms, it's called *sai* — the will to deceive. Police have to prove it exists to make a fraud case stick.

animals ran away as fast as they could. The other men, still quietly holding their cats in their arms, bowed once and walked away.

Saigo went back inside the bank. He sat down with the supervisor, and began filling out the necessary paperwork. The loan was deposited into Saigo's Daiwa Bank account one week later. He had already deposited 301 yen in one-yen coins, and was pleased to see his balance suddenly balloon to 50,000,301 yen.

Saigo gave 20 million yen to Morita. He paid 20,000 yen to each man who had lined up outside the bank for those two days. He kept the rest of the money for himself, and eventually made exactly two payments of 100,000 yen each on the loan.

Saigo was not completely convinced the bank wouldn't take back the money, so he liquidated the account and put it in the Saigo-gumi safe, which was located at the back of his office. It was always good to have cash on hand.

Part of the handsome profit went into the down payment for his new compound that he bought in Machida. The compound included both his home and the Saigo-gumi office, connected to each other on a large plot of land, surrounded by an iron fence. Security cameras were placed in strategic locations along the walls, at the door, and near the garage. The locals sometimes called it Fort Saigo.

He decided that there was more than enough space to have his parents move in with him. He promised his mother and father that their living quarters would be separate from the yakuza offices and the dormitory for the new young yakuza under his supervision. They took the offer, and moved in with him.

At the beginning of March, he was in his office, counting money, when Mizoguchi told him that he had a guest, Motomura. Saigo was surprised and perplexed. The bank had never called to ask for the loan to be repaid. He wasn't sure why Motomura was there, but he couldn't very well turn the man away.

Motomura was in slacks and a sports coat. He wore black-rimmed glasses now, and his gray hair was cut short. After exchanging formalities, Motomura told Saigo that he had come by to tell him that he would no longer be working at the bank. The successor was aware of their arrangement, and he just thought he should let Saigo know.

Saigo assured Motomura that he would not call on Daiwa Bank again, and asked him whether he was being transferred.

"I was essentially fired," Motomura said. He had spoken to the head office about what had happened at his branch, and while they understood, they were not forgiving. Motomura was allowed to retire and to keep the majority of his pension. He supposed he'd seek work at another bank.

Saigo felt something akin to regret, maybe even guilt. He hadn't reckoned on Motomura getting fired. Saigo opened the safe and took out 5 million yen. He stuffed it in an envelope and handed it to Mr Motomura with both hands, bowing so deeply that his head touched his desk.

"I can't take this," said Mr Motomura.

Saigo walked around his desk and put his giant hand on Motomura's shoulder. He then stuffed the envelope in the inner pocket of the man's sports coat.

"Motomura, it's never a good idea to refuse a gift from a yakuza. For what it's worth, I'm sorry. But please understand that if you ever show up at our office again, I will call the police, and demand that they defend us from you. If you can promise this will never happen, that you will never come back, we have a deal and we are on good terms."

Motomura was silent for a second and then laughed. Saigo patted him on the shoulder and then bowed to him once more. He asked Motomura to take the money and to use it to start a new life — and, for God's sake, to never tell anyone how he got the money. That would ruin Saigo's ruthless image.

Motomura took the money and left. Saigo never saw him again, and both of them kept their promises.

Saigo learned a valuable lesson from his alliance with Morita: it was possible to take a million times more out of a bank than you ever deposited there. For a smart yakuza, the right financial institution was just a large ATM. You didn't need an account number or a passcode to take out the money — you just needed the right information. After all, the underworld was really just another variant of the information industry.

# CHAPTER TEN

# The professor: Susumu Ishii

To understand the importance of the faction Saigo belonged to, you have to know the history of the Professor. Susumu Ishii's reign over the Yokosuka-ikka and Inagawa-kai would not be long, but he changed the way yakuza did business, and unintentionally showed the world just how much influence the underworld really exerted in the overworld.

Susumu Ishii was born on January 3, 1924, in Minami-Senju, Tokyo. Even as a young boy, Ishii was known for his soft-spoken ways, calm demeanor, and roughly six-foot height. He attended the prestigious Kamakura Middle School, but was kicked out in his fourth year after defending a girl in his class from thugs on a school trip. He beat the bullies so badly that he was expelled for violent behavior. He was one of the brightest students in his class, but, having steered off the right path, he found himself doing odd jobs for a living.

When the world war began, he found work in the Yokosuka Naval Yard. Even though Ishii had never graduated from high school, he worked in the ship architectonics division, because his superior officers realized that he was incredibly intelligent. There, he met his lifelong friend Hiroshi Miyamoto.

Miyamoto was working in shipbuilding yards, doing the final outfitting and maintenance of ships that were preparing for launch. He was the leader of a small adolescent-filled *gurentai* gang in the area. The *gurentai* functioned similarly to the yakuza, with a complicated system of older and younger brothers, but often with no official *oyabun*. Ishii and Tajima-kun, one of Miyamoto's disciples, were friends. When Tajima was called up for service, he introduced Miyamoto to Ishii.*

Towards the end of the war, Ishii, still in his teens, enrolled in the Yokosuka Naval Academy's correspondence course. He graduated at the top of his class, and was accepted into the navy. The navy sent him to the Hakejima base, where he was a signal officer for the Kaiten squad.

The Kaiten-tai were the navy's version of the kamikaze, often referred to as human torpedoes. In the days before computerized tracking and radar, the Japanese navy created torpedoes called *kaiten*, which they hoped would be more accurate. They managed to put humans inside the torpedoes to steer them into targets.

The Kaiten troop and its unique torpedoes got their name from the battleship *Kaitenmaru*, a legendary naval vessel in Japanese history. The name meant also meant "turn around." There was hope the Kaiten would turn the war around in favor of the Japanese, who were clearly already losing.

The prototypes were created in the summer of 1944. They were in use by November that year. By the end of the war, the squad had created 420 units. Contrary to urban legend that getting in the ships meant you could never get out, the human torpedo could be opened from the inside, but there was no escape mechanism, no ejection seat. Once it was launched into battle, whether the soldier succeeded or failed, one thing was certain — he would die.

---

\* Tajima would die in a suicide attack in Saipan a year later.

While the torpedoes were also equipped with oxygen, the air inside was often contaminated with excessive carbon dioxide and gas fumes. Some soldiers may have suffocated before even reaching their targets.

Every mission in these human torpedoes was a suicide mission. In fact, the odds of survival in a Kaiten were worse than being a kamikaze pilot. You could either collide with a target, get blown up, and die, or miss, sink, drown, and die. Either way, you were going to die. Although all the pilots were "volunteers," no one could legitimately refuse a request to volunteer in the Japanese army.

It was nearly impossible to steer the vessels. Some joked that it required "six hands and six eyes." Out of the fifty attacks in total that they undertook, the Kaiten are believed to have only sunk three major ships, greatly damaged one, and inflicted a small amount of damage on another.

Ishiii spent almost a year in the signal communications department for the troop. He witnessed brave men and frightened men set off to their "glorious" deaths, only to die futilely due to engine failures and other technical glitches. The Kaiten were supposed to be infallible weapons of destruction, capable of taking out aircraft carriers. In actuality, they were, for the most part, a colossal failure.

If the war continued, Ishii knew he would have to pilot one sooner or later. Fortunately, the war ended before he had to volunteer.

Ishii was discharged from the navy in December 1945. He drifted back to Yokosuka, and got a job working at a delivery company. There he ran into his old friend Miyamoto. Ishii told him many times, "Many of my friends died, yet I made it back to Yokosuka without ever fighting in the war. I guess I'm lucky."

The city was in chaos. Supplies were short. Because Ishii was the smartest of the disaffected youth in the area, Miyamoto asked to become Ishii's younger brother. Ishii accepted. In a bar in Yokosuka, they performed a poor man's version of the *sakazuki*.

The ritual exchange of sake forms the bonds between groups and between individuals. It cements the structure of yakuza life.

Ishii was not drinker at all, but for the ceremony he managed to down the one small glass of sake that Miyamoto's lackeys poured into his cup from a giant bottle. Miyamoto and Ishii shared the sake from the same bottle, and they pledged their loyalty to each other. It wasn't an elaborate yakuza ceremony, but it sealed the deal between them, and Ishii took over the loosely formed gang that Miyamoto ran.

Miyamoto and Ishii's gang traded in black-market items, ran gambling parlors, shook down business owners, sold stolen merchandise, and did anything else they could do to survive. Ishii made sure they minimized the amount of friction they had with the locals.

Ishii worked during the day and hung out at to the local dance hall, running the gang at night. Somewhere along the way, he managed to round up a few nice suits, and always wore them. His dapper dress and great height made him easy to remember.

Ishii's strength and character helped him win a loyal band of followers. One of his right-hand men was Joe Hirozaki. Before the war ended, Joe was on the kamikaze short list. He had resolved to die once, so he wasn't afraid of anything.

In early 1946, Joe got drunk and started a fight with two U.S. military officers. They promptly kicked the crap out of him. Ishii and Miyamoto were alerted to the fight and, not knowing the full circumstances, Ishii plunged in. After landing a few ineffective punches, Ishii kicked one of the soldiers in the balls. That had an effect. With the rallying cry of "Kick them in the balls!" he led his men to victory. Ishii tried to help Joe stand up, but quickly discovered the man stunk of cheap sake, and he couldn't get him to stand up on his own. Not wanting to go to jail, Ishii and his crew fled the scene before the military police arrived.

A few weeks later, Miyamoto, Ishii, and Joe were at the Moon River Dance Hall, where they ran into their rival youth gang, Tadahiro Suenaga and his crew. The dance hall was where the gangs gathered in their off time.* It was two versus ten, but, before the fight began, Joe got behind Suenaga. He still owed Ishii for his intervention, so he pressed a gun against Suenaga's back and threatened to shoot him dead on the spot.

Suenaga backed down, took his crew, and left. Funnily enough, Joe's gun turned out to be an empty juice bottle. Ishii had a way of accumulating favors that seemed to cash themselves in right when he needed them.

He was naturally lucky, and tried his luck by gambling whenever he had enough money to. By all accounts, he was an infamously exceptional gambler — especially in games where luck seemed to be the one and only determining factor in victory.

There were many kinds of gambling, including card games such as *hanafuda*. But the big game of the day was *chō-han*.

Even now, skill has nothing to do with the game. It's all a matter of luck. There are two six-sided dice. If the dice aren't fixed, the odds of winning are 1:1. The dealer shakes up the dice in a bamboo cup or bowl. He turns the cup over onto the tatami mat or table, keeping the dice hidden. Players place wagers on whether the sum of the numbers are *cho* (even) or *han* (odd). The dealer finally lifts up the cup, displaying the dice. The winners collect their money.

The house doesn't always win when the yakuza are running the gambling game, but they always get a share of the winnings. Most of the time, the *bakuto* made their money running the games, not necessarily by winning them.

---

* At the time, dance halls were also home to prostitution, but not overtly.

The dealer sometimes acts as the house, collecting all losing bets. In many cases, the players bet against each other. This requires an equal number of players betting on odd and even results, and the house still collects a set percentage of the winnings.

In those days, the players sat on a tatami floor. The dealer sat in the formal *seiza* posture, and oversaw the game. The dealer was sometimes shirtless to prevent accusations of cheating. When shirtless, if the dealer had any elaborate tattoos, they were prominently displayed.

Many yakuza movies, including the film *Shura no Mure*, feature *chō-han* scenes.

Ishii's flamboyant betting style and stoic attitude towards both winning and losing caught the attention of a local *bakuto* leader named Gihachiro Ishizuka. Ishizuka was a powerful boss in the area who controlled the Yokosuka docks.

Ishizuka's name meant "pile of stones." It suited him well. He was a short, squat guy with a simian face and a broad smile. Nothing got in or out of those docks without him having a say in it.

Ishii met Ishizuka while gambling. They exchanged greetings, but had no contact after that.


For months, Suenaga and Ishii's gang skirmished over turf, women, and perceived slights. Ishii stayed out of it, although he would get reports from Miyamoto. The gang wars escalated, as gang wars tend to do. Post-world war chaos only exacerbated the problem.

The police were disorganized, understaffed, and poorly armed. Rounding up a bunch of hoodlums was low on their list of priorities, especially if the hoodlums were attacking each other.

One night, in 1946, Suenaga's crew jumped Miyamoto's gang while they were sleeping off a night of drinking at Miyamoto's home. Several men were hospitalized. Fortunately, nobody died.

Miyamoto was absent that night. When he found out what had happened, he was outraged. To attack someone while they were sleeping was against the vague rules that governed the *gurentai* (thugs).

The payback was vicious. Miyamoto's gang caught two of Suenaga's crew leaving a dance hall, and beat them unconscious. They debated taking them hostage. They could use the guys as bait to lure Suenaga into a trap — that would really teach him a lesson. But would Suenaga risk his own neck to save two of his men? They decided he wouldn't. Knowing this, and the fact that Ishii wouldn't approve of such tactics, Miyamoto let the guys go.

After a few weeks of Miyamoto's guerrilla warfare, Suenaga and his crew sought out Ishii at his home, hoping to broker a deal. In Japan, when people come from the same background and are trying to figure out where they are on the social ladder in the vertical society, age is a major factor. Suenaga and Ishii had known each other since before the war, and were on an equal footing in terms of seniority. Suenaga wasn't Ishii's *senpai* (senior) or *kohai* (junior).

Ishii laid down the terms. Suenaga had to apologize for his midnight attack on Miyamoto's crew, pay their hospital bills, and pay additional compensation. Suenaga agreed, but when Ishii presented the compromise to Miyamoto, he wouldn't take the deal. "It's not a problem that can be solved with money," Miyamoto said.

Suenaga changed his strategy. He sought out Ishizuka and became his *kobun* (child role). Suenaga and his gang were now under the Ishizuka family umbrella, and felt emboldened. With a yakuza group backing him up, Suenaga proceeded to attempt to wipe out his competition.

Ishii's "secret weapon," Joe, didn't help matters. Joe stormed into Suenaga's office with a dull sword, and carved up several of Suenaga's men before being caught and beaten to a pulp.

Suenaga chose a plan that Ishii would have called unethical and vulgar. He offered to return Joe alive to Ishii's gang if Miyamoto would show up at a deserted temple in the area and make apologies for the gang's troubles. Suenaga told Miyamoto to come alone. If he showed up with his gang, they would kill Joe.

But, as the boss of the group, Ishii insisted on going there alone in Miyamoto's place. Miyamoto had intended to go himself, but Ishii had gotten wind of the problem.

"I'd lose you and I'd lose face. Losing both would be hard to deal with," he told Miyamoto.

The underworld abounds with terms referring to the importance of "face." Face is everything.

Japan itself has been called a "culture of shame" (*hajii no bunka*). The importance placed on the opinions of others and how one is viewed by society creates an invisible cage around each person, which keeps them in place and well behaved. In the small, tight-knit, and densely packed communities of Japan, "face" and the importance of preserving it plays an important role in regulating behavior. The language itself requires every person to pay attention to who is above, below, and equal to them in Japanese society. The conjugation of verbs, the proper pronouns, the terms of address — all these things change depending upon the difference in status of the individuals speaking.

The words to describe "face" vary in the Japanese language and in yakuza slang, but even when the words change, the importance remains. "Face" is the center of the yakuza life. Becoming a big man in the yakuza is referred to as "selling one's face" (*kao wo uru*). To "lose face" (*kao ga tsubureru*) is the worst thing that can happen to a yakuza; it's the ultimate insult. In yakuza society, preserving face and becoming famous is paramount. It directly relates to one's rank and standing in yakuza society. In other words, "face" is an expression of an individual yakuza's prestige. Therefore, there are few things more loathed by a yakuza than someone "smashing your face" or "putting mud on your face." A simple thing such as referring to a yakuza without adding an honorific to their name such as "–san" or "–kumicho" can be deadly.

When a yakuza is insulted or humiliated, they are very likely to physically attack the person who did it, with extreme prejudice. Gang wars have started over trivial insults. This is one of the reasons that part of the initial training of a yakuza is so much about learning to speak correctly, bow correctly, address elders correctly, and learn one's place in the hierarchy — all to avoid giving offense unnecessarily. In general, yakuza have a very poor sense of humor in regard to anything that might jeopardize their prestige.

Ishii left Miyamoto behind and went to the temple alone, but not unarmed. He had a pistol in his belt. When he arrived at the predetermined spot, Ishii's luck was still with him. Joe was alive. With him was the gang boss, Ishizuka.

At the temple, Ishizuka surprised Ishii with an apology and an explanation. "I am truly sorry for this recent series of events."

Ishizuka had heard about the trouble Suenaga had been having with Miyamoto, but he didn't know it involved Ishii. He found out that Ishii's friend Joe had made a suicide attack on Suenaga's boys, and that they had kidnapped him and were using him as bait to lure their rival. That didn't sit well with Ishizuka. He thought it was dishonorable and underhanded, so he banished Suenaga from his group.

It was at that temple with Ishizuka and Joe that Ishii graduated from being a punk to being a yakuza. He asked to join Ishizuka's group and to bring his men with him. From that point on, Ishii began learning the ways of the traditional yakuza.

He learned rituals, decorum, and a more businesslike way of doing things. He also paid taxes on his income, and insisted all his men do the same. He famously said, "Yakuza are given life by the ordinary citizens. We should do as they do and pay our taxes as well."

In 1948, at the age of twenty-four, Ishii became the *waka-gashira* in the Ishizuka-ikka. Saigo was roughly the same age when he became a yakuza forty-four years later. Ishii also supposedly supervised some of the group's lending operations.

The Korean War broke out in 1950. For the Ishizuka-ikka and Ishii, it was a stroke of good fortune. The Yokosuka docks were flooded with work, sailors, and money. The Ishizuka-ikka got a cut of all of it.

Ishii ran the show at the Ishizuka-ikka for many years, catching the eye of senior members of the Inagawa-kai and, finally, Seijo Inagawa himself.

In 1955, Ishii was introduced to Kiichi Inoue (a different Inoue from the one whom Saigo would befriend in the future), a top gang boss in the Inagawa-kai. Inoue was known as one of the four emperors of the Yokohama area, a major port near Tokyo. The Inagawa-kai had taken control of Yokohama, and wanted to incorporate Yokosuka in their turf. Inoue felt the young gambler and former ship designer would be the perfect person to help them move in. He asked Ishii to become his *kyodaibun* (yakuza brother), and Ishii accepted.

Ishizuka retired in 1961, when Saigo was just one year old. Ishizuka gave Ishii his place as the head of the Ishizuka-ikka. At the same time, thanks to Kiichi Inoue's efforts, the Inagawa-kai put the Ishizuka-ikka under their umbrella. Thus, Ishii got a second title: branch manager of the Inagawa-kai Yokosuka-ikka.

In 1962, with the Inagawa-kai backing him up, Ishii gained territory in the Kofu area, further expanding Inagawa-kai territory.

The expansion into Kofu involved bloody gang warfare, but that was part and parcel of the business. Wars over turf or territory, called *nawabari* by the yakuza, were essential to being a successful yakuza. *Nawabari* literally means "roped-in area." The more turf your organization had, the longer your "rope" border — and the more face you had. When someone acted up within your *nawabari*, or set up an office there, it was understood as a hostile invasion. The understanding of every yakuza was that if you gave an inch, you lost a mile. Gain an inch, and it felt like a mile. The tug of war was never-ending.

In May 1963, Inagawa summoned Ishii to his home in Atami to make him an offer. He asked Ishii to take over the formerly independent Yokosuka-ikka crime family. If Ishii accepted, the Yokosuka-ikka would become a part of the Inagawa-kai.

Ishii was delighted at the offer, but his delight was dampened by problems happening within the Inagawa-kai that he couldn't ignore. Inagawa was seriously considering banishing Kiichi Inoue from the group.

Kiichi Inoue had been a huge force in the expansion of the Inagawa-kai, but he had become arrogant. He was holding gambling events in the greater Tokyo area under the Inagawa-kai name, without having the permission of the boss or kicking back any of the *terasen* (handling fees) from the events. Inagawa might have been able to overlook being short-changed, but Inoue was telling anyone who would listen that he had made the Inagawa-kai what it was — that the organization had got big only thanks to his efforts. This infuriated Inagawa.

Ishii felt greatly loyal to Kiichi Inoue. After all, it had been Inoue who introduced him to the Inagawa-kai. He felt that without Inoue, he would never have been selected to take over the

Yokosuka-ikka. Ishii understood that from Inagawa's perspective, Inoue's behavior was unacceptable, but thought Inoue deserved a second chance.

On the other hand, Inagawa's mind was basically made up. There didn't seem to be anything Ishii could do to change it.

In the middle of the night, while his servants and family were sleeping, Ishii used a short knife, a hammer, and a cutting board to sever the tip of his left pinkie. He carefully wrapped it in a brand-new white handkerchief. In this act of severing his finger, *yubizume*, he made a sacrifice to spare Kiichi Inoue from being banished.

He had his driver take him to Inagawa's house in the morning. When he arrived, Inagawa met him in the reception room of his spacious house, surprised to see Ishii come back so soon.

Ishii placed the white handkerchief on the tablet between them, and spoke to Inagawa. "*Oyabun*, may I ask that you accept this in exchange for not banishing Inoue from the organization?"

Inagawa opened the handkerchief to see Ishii's severed finger. He glanced at Ishii's left hand wrapped in a bandage. He took a deep breath, and loudly cursed for a bit.

The severing of fingers as a gesture of apologizing existed long before the postwar yakuza, although it's no longer a welcome act in the modern yakuza. In this day and age, yakuza try to hide in the shadows. A severed finger is a liability, not an asset.

In the old days, even among severed fingers, there was a hierarchy. A finger given up for another person is sometimes called an *ikiyubi*, "a living finger." It denotes self-sacrifice, and is highly respected.

If that *ikiyubi* is rejected, and thus pointlessly chopped off, it is called a *shiniyubi*, meaning "a dead finger." A severed finger is also called a *shiniyubi* if it was cut off to atone for one's own mistakes.

"Inoue is lucky to have a great friend like you," Inagawa said, accepting Ishii's offer and not letting his finger be viewed as "dead."

Inagawa was impressed. Few men had such loyalty to their blood brothers, especially when it was not immediately in their own interests. It was probably at this time that he began to consider Ishii as his successor.

The Coach, a disciple of Ishii and, in the future, Saigo's boss, would later become the eighth-generation leader of the Yokosuka-Ikka. When Coach chose his successor, he would also use the same criteria as Ishii in making the decision. People want to follow a leader who knows what loyalty means. The yakuza, for all their talk of honour and loyalty, are constantly fighting among themselves and stabbing each other in the back, sometimes in more than a metaphorical sense.

A man with loyalty who was willing to sacrifice for his friends — that was a rare man in their world, maybe in any world.

Ishii was the moral compass of the Yokosuka-Ikka, and the ideal.


Near the end of the summer in 1963, Kiichi Inoue and three of his men were in Tokyo drinking at an expensive nightclub. There, Inoue made a breach of decorum that would result in his downfall. He was lucky it didn't get him killed.

As they sat, smoking imported cigarettes, and drinking whiskey and water, Hisayuki Machii walked in. Machii was the legendary leader of the Tosei-kai, one of the most powerful yakuza groups in Tokyo at the time. He had two nicknames: "The Tiger of Ginza" and "The Bull." The Bull described him better, because of his flat nose and perpetual scowl. He had a deserved reputation for violence.

Machii was proudly Korean during a time when Koreans were treated as second-class citizens in Japan. Meanwhile, other important Korean Japanese figures, such as the national idol and pro-wrestling champion Riki Dozan, made great efforts to keep their ancestry quiet. No one outside his Korean fans in Korea and close friends in Japan knew he wasn't 100 percent Japanese.

Machii's group primarily was composed of Korean yakuza. He was on good terms with Japan's ruling powers, and had staunch anti-communist views. He promised the ruling class he would keep the left-wing Japanese Korean residents associated with North Korea under control, and that he would keep an eye on the remaining Koreans. He was also being paid by the CIA to collect information about political activities in Japan and Korea, and to make sure that Japan did not turn into a communist country.

Machii had connections so deep that Kiichi Inoue couldn't have possibly known them all. As of February 1963, Machii had a formal relationship with the third-generation leader of the Yamaguchi-gumi, Kazuo Taoka. Inagawa himself oversaw the *sakazuki*. A well-known yakuza associate and fixer named Yoshio Kodama arranged the meeting. He was also a CIA informant, con-man, and possible war criminal — not to mention the founder of Japan's largest political party, the Liberal Democratic Party (LDP) back in 1955. He knew all the right people and all the wrong people. With his wealth and connections, he was more powerful than the prime minister himself.

When Machii walked by Kiichi Inoue, all that Inoue saw was another familiar yakuza face. They'd met many times at numerous yakuza functions, but had never really talked. Inoue, wanting to be friendly, called out to Machii. His choice of honorific was terribly mistaken.

"Hey, Machii-kun, how are you?"

Machii stopped in his tracks and looked back at Inoue. He recognized who he was, and was not impressed.

Machii turned to Inoue. "You. I don't recall being so friendly with you that you can call me Machii '*kun*.'"

Inoue's reply to this was the Japanese equivalent of, "Fuck you, you arrogant prick." Inoue's crew jumped to their feet as soon as their boss spat out the words. Machii's bodyguards stiffened. Inoue told his men to back down.

Inoue apologized, sort of. "I had no idea you were such an important person, but we can talk that over sometime." He and his men immediately split. Machii, thinking nothing of it, went to the VIP room in the back and got drunk.

Inoue decided that he had been insulted. He had lost face. He reasoned that the Inagawa-kai was going to have to eliminate Machii sooner or later if they were going to expand into Tokyo. On his own, without bothering to consult anyone, he decided to move that plan forward.

Inoue ordered his men to prepare to kill Machii when they had a chance. He reached out to Ishii for help, and Ishii sent his men up to Tokyo. Miyamoto was one of them. They were supposed to stake out Club Muse, one of Machii's haunts. Their orders were to take him out, but to avoid getting entangled with other members of the group. At first, they all thought the leader of the Tosei-kai had provoked the fight, but quickly realized that the whole conflict was a matter of Kiichi Inoue's personal pride.

The Inagawa-kai wasn't going to go to war just because Kiichi Inoue's ego had been bruised.

Within a week of the incident, Machii, Kodama, and Inagawa met at Kodama's house to discuss the problem. They agreed that the Inagawa-kai had no problems with Machii and that Kiichi Inoue would need to be taken care of — not killed, but sentenced to a fate that was almost worse in the yakuza world. He would be banished.

Inagawa summoned Ishii and told him the news. "There is nothing you can for Kiichi Inoue now. Chop off another finger, and it's a *shiniyubi* (dead) for sure. I'm sorry, but he has to go."

Ishii politely argued that for Kiichi Inoue, who had spent his entire life as a yakuza, being formally banished would be like being ordered to commit *seppuku*.

Ishii suggested another solution. He promised that he would convince Kiichi Inoue to retire. Banishment would be a shameful way to end his yakuza life, but to retire on his own would leave Inoue with some dignity.

Inagawa wasn't convinced. What if he refused to retire?

Ishii was prepared for that possibility. "I settle the matter then. I'll forcibly 'retire' him myself."

Inagawa agreed to the terms. If Inoue wouldn't retire and tried to break away from the group, there would be trouble. Banishing him might also cause trouble. Ishii's solution seemed equitable, fair, and reasonable.

Ishii promised that, before Inoue retired, he would bring him to Inagawa and his brothers to apologize for his acts of impropriety and to say goodbye.

Ishii went to see Inoue, and packed a gun in his belt in case he needed to adopt the alternative retirement plan.

Inoue and Ishii met at a hotel in Ginza. Ishii came alone. Inoue sent his bodyguards out of the room, and told them to wait downstairs.

Ishii explained the situation to him and the choices that Kiichi Inoue had left. At first, Inoue was angry and refused to listen. However, in the face of Ishii's calm resolve, he gradually understood the position he was in, and calmed down. He asked Ishii to ensure that his men would be reabsorbed into the Inagawa-kai. He glanced at Ishii's hand, and thanked him for the sacrifice Ishii had made on his behalf.

Finally, he promised to apologize to Inagawa and to formally ask to retire. The last words he said to Ishii that day were reportedly, "I really don't have a choice. If I don't retire, it would mean you'd spend a long time in prison. You don't deserve that."

He was alluding to his suspicion that, if he had refused the offer, Ishii would kill him on the spot. Ishii did not say a word. The silence was his affirmation.

Kiichi Inoue retired without incident, becoming *katagi*, an ordinary person. For the yakuza, it was an awful fate — to be *ordinary*. Whether Kiichi Inoue was happy after retiring, no one knows. It was as though he vanished from the world.

However, Inagawa, keeping to his word, absorbed Kiichi Inoue's soldiers into the Inagawa-kai — the same umbrella organization that Saigo would join twenty-one years later.

Ishii was supposed to be made the fourth-generation leader of the Yokosuka-ikka, a second-tier organization of the Inagawa-kai, but Ishii had a problem with the Japanese word for four: *shi*. *Shi* also means death. Like many gamblers, Ishii was very superstitious, so he refused the position of the fourth-generation leader.

The organization agreed to make him the fifth-generation leader instead. So, in early November 1963, a succession ceremony for Ishii was held at the Yokosuka Kanko Hotel. On the same day as his succession ceremony, a fourth-generation leader was crowned. The seat was immediately turned over to Ishii, who became the fifth-generation leader of the Inagawa-kai Yokosuka-ikka.

Hundreds of people attended the event.

An old photo album shows yakuza outside the hotel, in a single-file line, crowding the streets as a black limousine rolled past. At the entrance, an army of black-suited yakuza stood watch while their seniors strolled in.

At the reception desks, more men in dark suits dutifully noted the name of each man coming in and the amount of cash he brought with him to the ceremony. Cash was stacked in piles on the table. *Giri* was always expensive.

Seijo Inagawa was present at the event. His hair was slicked back, and he looked tan and buff. He wore a black robe and a *hakama* (men's kimono). For the ceremony, the Inagawa-kai posed as a political group to avoid crackdowns by the police, even temporarily changing its name to Kinsei-kai, but everyone knew it was the Inagawa-kai. Ishii was given a position as the organizational committee chairman, and Yoshio Kodama joined the new group as an advisor.

The hotel was top of the line. It even had a color television in the lobby. The banquet hall was full of men. The only visible females were a small group of geisha who were serving food. It was a man's world, after all.

Every major organized crime group in Tokyo had a representative in attendance, except for the Yamaguchi-gumi. Relations with that group were not going well.

In pictures from the ceremony, Ishii towered over everyone, tall and aloof. Inagawa stood close to Ishii, smiling, but still managing to look stern.

The ceremony was simple, and finished quickly. Sake was drunk, cups were exchanged, the crowd clapped, and the new lineage of the Yokosuka-ikka was displayed on the wall in handwritten letters on fine Japanese paper.

Ishii was listed as fifth-generation leader Tadahiro Ishii — not his real first name, but his yakuza first name. His hand-chosen yakuza name was more auspicious. The first character, *yu*, meant "only; simply; merely." The second character, *haku*, meant "wide learning; esteem; fair." The character is used in the word *hakase* (professor) and the word *bakuto* (gambler).

For a man as superstitious as Ishii, it was important to do whatever he could to stay lucky — but luck only goes so far.


The yakuza could see the writing on the wall in 1961 when Tokyo was chosen to host the 1964 Summer Olympics. In a cabinet decision made in February that year, prime minister Hayato Ikeda set forth Japan's first violent crimes prevention prospectus.

Unfortunately, it did little to deter the growing violence among Japan's powerful yakuza groups. The following year marked the beginning of violent and deadly gang conflicts across Japan.

In 1963, Japan saw violent skirmishes in Hiroshima, Yamaguchi-gumi battles in Kobe, and shootings in Tokyo. December 1963 was marked by two pivotal yakuza-related events.

On December 8, a member of the Sumiyoshi-kai stabbed pro-wrestler Riki Dozan in a Ginza nightclub. The assailant ran away, but didn't get very far before being caught and brutally beaten by members of the Tosei-kai, the predominantly Korean Japanese yakuza group. Dozan died in the hospital a few days later. It was bad publicity for the yakuza. It was like the mafia had killed Japan's Babe Ruth.

On December 21, at the Tsuruya Hotel in Atami, members of the Inagawa-kai, Sumiyoshi-kai, Kokusui-kai, Tosei-kai, and every other major yakuza group in Japan gathered to form the Kanto-kai. It was a federation of right-wing nationalist yakuza that spanned almost all of eastern Japan, and it was all assembled by the LDP founder Yoshio Kodama himself. Of course, Kodama and his political allies attended the reception. The federation was seemingly tied together under a shared anti-communist, pro-capitalist, right-wing ideology. The yakuza gained additional goodwill by offering to supply troops to safeguard the arrival of President Eisenhower.

Shortly after, all their efforts were pissed away. The Kanto-kai did something very stupid: they blatantly interfered with Japanese politics, dictating terms to the ruling Liberal Democratic Party. They issued a warning to the LDP, blasting them for wasting their energy on internal politics. "LDP members: Immediately stop your infighting." They also praised Ichiro Kono's faction of the LDP. It was not a coincidence that Kono and Kodama were close friends. The warning was sent to 200 individual Diet members in the lower and upper house combined. It listed seven yakuza groups within the Kanto-kai, so the LDP members knew who they were dealing with.

Former newspaper editor Masunosuke Ikeda was livid. He was a senior member of the House of Representatives, which is the lower house of the National Diet, who hailed from the rural Yamagata prefecture. Masunosuke made sure that the document was taken up in the LDP committee on Measures to Preserve Law and Order. It was the first time the yakuza had banded together to openly give orders to the ruling party. The police and prosecutors were told to force the Kanto-kai to dissolve and to do something about the yakuza.

In January 1964, the National Police Agency drew up the Violent Crimes Countermeasures Plan and began the First Top-Down Yakuza Crackdown. The Tokyo Police set up the Special Organized Crime Crackdown Headquarters, whose ultimate goal was to bring down the top yakuza players by arresting them, cutting off their funds, and diminishing their ranks. In February, they kicked off the war by arresting any yakuza they could, on any case they could make.

In March, the National Police Agency designated ten organizations, including the Inagawa-kai, as national organized crime groups. The agency ordered police across the nation to crack down on them whenever possible. The gambling laws were revised as well, so it was possible to arrest yakuza for gambling without catching them in the act. Within a year, more than 1,000 yakuza were arrested nationwide on gambling charges alone.

The Inagawa-kai, being primarily a group of gamblers, took a lot of that heat. Over 400 members were arrested on gambling charges during their 1964 fiscal year. Ishii was not exempt. He was arrested twice. The second time, he was arrested alongside Inagawa himself, who was sentenced to three years in prison.

The arrest stemmed from a legendary night of gambling at a party in the resort town Hakone on March 29, 1964. The Inagawa-kai threw a party to celebrate the retirement of a Sumiyoshi-kai leader. Top bosses of major yakuza groups gathered together and gambled lavishly. In one night, more than 550 million yen was spent. The hosts collected about 40 million yen in handling fees.* The amount of money changing hands in the one night was mind-boggling. The incident later became the inspiration for the 1968 yakuza film *Socho Tobaku*.

By January 1965, the Kanto-kai had been dissolved.

Ishii called Miyamoto and another trusted lieutenant to his home in Yokosuka. He greeted them dressed in traditional Japanese clothes, and told them what was painfully obvious. "The days when yakuza could make a living by gambling are over. It's time to move on. The police only need a pair of dice and some testimony to put us in jail."

There was talk among the yakuza to consider limiting the games to only wealthy patrons of the yakuza. They thought that customers were ratting them out to the police, so perhaps carefully choosing the clientele would eliminate the problem.

Ishii didn't agree. The problem was that even a wealthy businessman might complain to his wife or girlfriend after a huge loss. She would then call the police. In some cases, the businessman himself might make the call out of spite.

It didn't matter how the gambling customers got caught — they would tell everything to the police: who came, where they sat, how much money they spent. The yakuza kept their mouths shut, but they couldn't expect the same discretion from the rich businessmen, celebrities, and industrial magnates who participated in their gambling events.

Ishii decided it was time for a new course of action. In 1967, with the aid of businessman Kenji Osano and funding from the Heiwa

---

* At the time, 550 million yen was worth $1.5 million. Adjusted for modern-day inflation (2022) 550 million yen is worth $14 million.

Sogo bank, Ishii set up his first real company, Tatsumi Sangyo, a construction firm. The Kanagawa government listed it as a designated firm for public works projects. Ishii was on his way to becoming a new type of yakuza — one that ran legitimate and profitable businesses. This made life much easier for his family, which included a beautiful wife and a young daughter. To the outside world, he now looked like a businessman, not a thug.

The path that Ishii took was unusual, but he set a precedent within the Yokosuka-ikka. He chose a young Kyushu-born yakuza named Takahiko Inoue to be his bodyguard, and to follow Ishii's example. That same Inoue would later mentor Saigo. Ishii had many revolutionary ideas for a yakuza boss, but his teaching was that every yakuza needed two streams of income: legitimate and non-legitimate. Of course, the legitimate job was usually boring — you could hire *katagi* to do that. It was the ill-gotten gains that were the most fun — at least Saigo thought so.

Ishii's time in jail had made him rethink how he wanted to live and survive as a yakuza. At his new company, Ishii made himself the CEO, Miyamoto the vice-president, and a smart businessman the executive director.

The wealthy customers and politicians who had been guests at his gambling events created a solid network for securing public works and general construction projects.

By 1969, the Inagawa-kai's territory expanded to include Yokohama, Kawasaki, and finally parts of Tokyo. They set up offices in the Roppongi neighborhood of Minato-ku, one of the twenty-three wards, under the name of Ingawa Kogyo (Inagawa Enterprises).

Of all Ishii's business ventures, Tatsumi Sangyo was the only venture where he was listed as a director. He ruled the other ventures from the shadows.

In 1986, Inagawa chose not his only son, Yuko, but Ishii, the mentor of his son and the head of the Inagawa-kai Yokosuka-ikka, to be his successor.

Thousands of yakuza, including Saigo, attended the ceremony, held on May 5, 1986, at the Inagawa-kai main family headquarters in Atami, in the sixty-tatami-mat-sized hall. In addition to yakuza, the attendees included politicians, movie stars, celebrities, bankers, and some of the heads of Japan's largest financial firms. Every major yakuza group sent their envoys: the Yamaguchi-gumi, the Sumiyoshi-kai, and even the Korean Japanese yakuza group Tosei-kai.

The long driveway leading up to the house was lined with low-level yakuza standing silently in their black suits. They guarded the streets as the senior-ranking yakuza strode into the main hall, almost all dressed in *hakama* (formal Japanese men's kimonos) with the crest of their yakuza group boldly embroidered on the clothing. It was a royal event, covered by every major newspaper in Japan.

The ceremony was performed with the rare grandeur reserved for a succession ceremony. Each yakuza group has a slightly different variation of the ceremony. On that day, it was done in accordance with the *bakuto* tradition — the way of the gamblers. At the end of the great hall was a Shinto altar devoted to *Amaterasu-ōmikami*, the goddess of the sun. Holy sake, food from the mountains, rice cakes, and other offerings were laid before her. There was a white cloth stretched in front of the altar where the guests of honor sat.

With their backs to the altar, Inagawa sat on the right, and Ishii on the left, as was customary for the successor.

After the elaborate prefatory remarks, which included the greetings and inspection of the sake, Inagawa drank from the succession cup. He gave it to the master of ceremonies, who then handed it to Ishii, while saying, in almost archaic Japanese, "This cup of sake you are about to drink is of great significance. As you drink it dry, you will take upon yourself the heavy responsibilities and great duties of the second-generation leader of the Inagawa-kai. With those feelings in your heart, we beseech you to please drink deeply from the cup."

Ishii, who remained calm and seemed somewhat detached during the event, took the gold sake cup and drank the contents in three sips, as tradition demanded. As soon as he finished, a huge roar of applause rose from the crowd. Inagawa and Ishii both stood up and switched places. Banners were unfurled. The changing of the guard was complete.

Saigo had no idea just how large the Inagawa-kai was until he witnessed the succession ceremony. He didn't fully understand it, but the seriousness of it all impressed him.

The Yokosuka-ikka was now a very good name to have with Ishii in power. The Inagawa-kai had close 9,500 members, including associates. The Yokosuka-ikka had close to 2,000.

Ishii made a big impression on Saigo. He didn't look like a yakuza. He seemed aloof, like someone in the world, but not of it.

Sometime during 1987, Saigo's *oyabun* put Saigo on Ishii's security detail, just for a day. Saigo was an up-and-coming yakuza, and had a reputation for toughness. For Saigo to be chosen to protect the legendary chairman, and to have even spoken to him directly and be acknowledged by him, was a rare honor.

In an organization like the Inagawa-kai, it was a long way to the top.

## CHAPTER ELEVEN

# You've been naughty boys: the first anti-organized crime laws

Even now, it's hard to succinctly explain the power that the yakuza and people like Ishii had in postwar Japan. Japan's award-winning film director Kitano Takeshi perhaps put it most eloquently: "Japan has two governments. One is the public government. The other is the one that issues orders to public institutions: the hidden government."

Kitano knows a great deal about the yakuza, as many in the entertainment industry do. It is one of the few industries left in Japan where the yakuza still have solid power.

In his book, *Kitano Par Kitano*, Kitano discusses "the dark powers" of Japan. He laments that, in recent years, due to internal struggles in the Inagawa-kai, there are many members who no longer uphold the group's code of ethics. Many of his films can be seen as a critique of the changing yakuza and, in particular, the Inagawa-kai. His films *Outrage* and *Beyond Outrage* are loosely based on the moral disintegration of the Inagawa-kai. The catch copy: "They're all bad guys."

—

There is a reason the yakuza managed to be tolerated by Japanese society for so long. There used to be a code. It wasn't much of a code, and it may have been perfunctory. Some yakuza never paid it heed, but many did. Everyone knew what it was. This was what Takahiko Inoue had tried to tell Saigo many years before.

Many Japanese people feel that the only thing worse than organized crime is disorganized crime. Disorganized crime includes purse-snatching, robberies, break-ins, muggings, rape, and petty theft. The yakuza keep disorganized crime at bay. They give people a feeling of safety within the neighborhoods and entertainment districts they control.

Saigo's scroll of the yakuza code of ethics hung up on his office wall in Machida. The code was the standard for any Inagawa-kai Yokosuka-ikka member during his time in the organization. The code, written in Japanese cursive, set the conditions for what would get a member kicked out. The first was: no using or selling drugs. Saigo didn't sell drugs. However, every now and then, he would weaken and go on a meth binge — but that was a rare occurrence.

The other rules included no theft, robbery, indecent acts, or sexual crimes. There were other rules about relationships among yakuza, and there was a fairly recent addition to the code: do not have any unnecessary contact with the authorities.

At every Yokosuka-ikka meeting, these rules were read out loud, and everyone understood. One thing that should be noted was that extortion and blackmail were not expressly forbidden. Their logic was that if you were being blackmailed by the yakuza, you had done something bad to deserve it. They were enforcing "social justice" by fining people for their misbehavior.

However, public tolerance of their activities was wearing thin by the 1990s. The National Police Agency did a survey in 1990, finding that 40 percent of the 2,000 companies surveyed had faced shakedowns from organized crime, and nearly one-third of those said they had paid up. Amounts paid ranged from 100,000 yen to 100 million yen. Of the remaining 60 percent, who said they hadn't been shaken down, many were probably lying.

Yakuza were still considered legitimate. They operated in the open, with their corporate emblems on display. They wore badges, walked the streets in groups, and were afraid of nothing. The police couldn't act against the yakuza unless the victimized companies complained, and it wasn't a crime to pay off the yakuza. They were free to ask for "donations," and the companies were free to give it to them. Many large corporations not only gladly paid the yakuza for their protection, but paid the yakuza to help them make money.

Meanwhile, the wars between the yakuza groups were escalating at a pace that scared the general public. Yakuza activities became increasingly anti-social, and cozy ties between the ruling elite and the yakuza became nationwide scandals (sometimes even international scandals). Japan had reached a point where the yakuza problem was too big to ignore any longer.

Ishii passed away in 1991 at the age of sixty-seven. He died from a massive brain tumor, leaving behind a mountain of bad loans and missing money. He was buried in Ikegami Honmonji, a Buddhist temple in Tokyo whose funeral plots are sometimes called the yakuza graveyards. Later, Machii, who had ruled the Tosei-kai, Japan's Korean mafia, would also be buried there. Riki Dozan, postwar Japan's most beloved pro-wrestler, and secretly Korean, who was killed by a Sumiyoshi-kai gangster, is there as well. And if you look closely, you can find the grave of a *tekiya oyabun* that has the name of Prime Minister Yasuhiro Nakasone engraved upon it. A walk among the tombstones there is like a taking a stroll through yakuza history.

The same year that Ishii died, the National Police Agency introduced the first laws to specifically target the yakuza. The new comprehensive anti-organized crime laws were titled "The Countermeasures Against Violent Groups," and went into effect in 1992. They were heralded as the end of the yakuza, but for Saigo and his crew they were a blessing.

Although created with all the best intentions in mind, the watered-down version that passed had some unexpected results, to say the least. The countermeasures against violent groups, contrary to their intended purposes, made extortion and related criminal activities much easier to carry out.

There is a saying in Japanese, *namabyoho wa kega no moto*, which roughly translates as "a half-baked knowledge of the laws of martial arts is the cause of injury." It proved to be true for the anti-organized crime laws as well. The way the new laws were set up was so lax that it made enforcement difficult and the likelihood of arrest for violations extremely unlikely.

The laws were intended to immediately allow the police to crack down on yakuza activities, encourage members to leave, and force them out of the public eye. But the laws were a complicated mess, full of holes, and carried such light punishments that they seemed pointless. However, they did serve as a warning to Japan's 88,000 yakuza that times were changing. And they gave the police a solid excuse to go in and out of the yakuza offices whenever they wanted, as well as to put a check on the visible presence of the gangs.

The laws forbade many types of *shinogi* — extortion, collecting protection money, blackmail, debt-collecting, and all other such staples were technically banned. Under the new laws, whenever a yakuza committed any of these acts, the victim could go to the police. The police would issue a cease-and-desist order to the yakuza in question. If they continued to do it, the police would issue a "Do not do this again" preventive order, and if the yakuza also ignored that, he faced arrest and/or a fine — up to year in jail, or a fine of up to 50,000 yen, or both.

However, it almost never went that far. Before the new laws came into effect, the police would build a case and make an arrest. But now they'd give the yakuza a warning first to cease and desist. It was like baseball rules for them — two strikes and you're out. For most yakuza, the warning was enough. For some people, simply having the yakuza go away was more than enough. At least the police moved quickly.

There was also a relatively unknown addition to the law: if you were an individual asking the yakuza to do any of the forbidden activities, and they kept doing them, you faced the same penalties.

One thing the laws effectively did was force the yakuza to retreat further from the public eye. The use of their coat of arms was strictly forbidden.

The law also attempted to force the Japanese people to recognize them by another name — not yakuza, *gokudo*, or *ninkyaku*, but as *boryokudan* (violent groups). The yakuza were incensed by the new moniker given to them. The Japanese have traditionally believed that words have a spirit residing in each of them called *kotodama*. If you change what people call something, you change what it is. The yakuza did not like being called *boryokudan*. The word had no dignity; no hint of grace or nobility, but simply described what most of the gangs were.

Organized crime groups changed their names to have a more corporate sound. They took their signboards down from the outside their office buildings and brought them inside. For example, the Inagawa-kai Yagita-ikka Takada-gumi in the Saitama prefecture became Takada Enterprises. The gang boss was still listed on the company registry, but the front company functioned as the new face of the group.

In his seminal 1992 book *Yakuza Company*, investigative journalist Takeshi Arimori argued that the new laws would push yakuza further into the corporate and business world as they took on the trappings of legitimate entities in order to comply with the law. He was correct.

In May 1991, the Yamaguchi-gumi became a corporation registered under the name Sanki. It was officially created on March 28, 1991. March 28 is a highly auspicious day in the underworld — it is the birthday of Kazuo Takaoka, the third-generation leader of the Yamaguchi-gumi. The company was officially involved in renting office space and rooms, managing golf-practice courses, managing parking lots, and buying and selling antique arts and crafts. They were also involved in real estate sales, purchases, management, and rentals. You could argue that it wasn't exactly an accurate picture of the Yamaguchi-gumi, but it listed the headquarters of the group as the office headquarters, and gave the group a new corporate face.

Saigo was amused by the laws. It meant that his men didn't get thrown in jail on extortion charges — they got warned first. This meant they could collect some money before the police shut down their operation, and the risk of his underlings actually having to do jail time was drastically reduced. The two-warning system meant that there was even more time to squeeze cash and protection money out of the usual customers.

The police had essentially installed an early-warning system for the yakuza.

The general public wasn't very impressed with the system either. The police could only issue a cease-and-desist order if there was a complaint from the parties directly involved, the penalties were light, the yakuza themselves weren't banned, and the entire yakuza franchise system, including the payment of association dues from the bottom to the top, had been left intact. The laws ensured that the economic impact on the yakuza was benign at best.

The laws also required the police to officially recognize yakuza groups under certain criteria, such as the ratio of members with criminal convictions as "designated yakuza." Each group was entitled to a public hearing before the police officially designated them as "violent groups."

At the first hearings, the reactions of the yakuza groups facing designation were indignant, for the most part.

In 1992, at the public hearing held at the Tokyo Metropolitan Police headquarters, the chairman of the Sumishiyoshi-kai made a spirited defense of their existence:

> We, the Sumiyoshi-kai, in 1946, shortly after the end of the war, put our hearts and souls into the world of the yakuza. We have never felt like these so-called violent groups. We don't believe we are such a thing. Frankly, we find it an unbearable nuisance to be called as such. However, while we we cannot say these are good laws, we cannot disobey the laws made by those above us.

The Yamaguchi-gumi insisted that they were a humanitarian organization and that to classify them as a violent group was a complete misunderstanding of the group and its goals.

The Inagawa-kai had a surprisingly different reaction to the new laws. On April 10, Izumi Mori, the general affairs director of the Inagawa-kai, spoke on behalf of the group. Mori stated that Inagawa had told his organization that Japan passed this law because they had been bad. They needed to watch their behavior.

"Indeed, we must reflect upon our past actions," Mori said. "It does not matter what the laws are. They are laws laid down by the nation of Japan, and we will humbly and strictly accept them."

There is little doubt that Inagawa truly believed the axioms he spouted, that the yakuza were not supposed to cause harm to ordinary citizens.

In fact, it was at his insistence that Kanto-Hatsuka-kai, a federation of yakuza groups in eastern Japan, added a new rule to the provisions in July 1993. All the rules were supposed to be binding on all members.

The new rule stated: If during a gang war, an ordinary citizen or a police officer, or anyone who has no connection to that conflict, is hurt or damaged, then the person(s) responsible shall be temporarily banished from the yakuza world or permanently expelled.

The anti-organized crime rules resulted in one small change in Saigo's group. The earlier version of the rules was written, "For the sake of my *oyabun*, I will lay down my life and take the lives of his enemies. I will never leave the group." Saigo pointed out to Coach that this was the kind of thing that might touch upon certain aspects of the new laws. Coach thought it over and decided to take that part out, but to leave everything else in.

While the Inagawa-kai placidly accepted the new laws, the Yamaguchi-gumi wasn't going to just let it go. In 1993, the Yamaguchi-gumi took the government to court, claiming that the new anti-crime laws violated the constitution. They filed the case in their hometown, Kobe. Their lawyer, Makoto Endo, was one of the most liberal and greatest criminal defense lawyers in the country. He argued on their behalf that the anti-organized crime law was breaching the constitutional guarantees of equal treatment under the law and of freedom of association.

In one of the earliest March 1993 hearings, Masaru Takumi, the *waka-gashira* in the Yamaguchi-gumi, and their most financially savvy member, declared — with a straight face — that his organization had nothing to do with violent groups.

"The essence of our spirit is to help the weak and fight evil. We sent donations to victims of the volcanic eruptions at Mount Unzen and received letters of thanks from the children. We are a humanitarian organization."

The Yamaguchi-gumi eventually dropped their court case, and there was no more real opposition to the laws. Takumi, however, never changed his official stance that the Yamaguchi-gumi was not a violent group. He was shot to death in a coffee shop on the fourth floor of the Oriental Hotel in Kobe in August 1997. An innocent bystander was killed by a stray bullet in the attack.

Yet the odds are that if Takumi had somehow miraculously survived the attack, he would probably have insisted that the shooters were a breakaway faction of the Yamaguchi-gumi, and thus not representative of the group. Perhaps he would have been half-right.


The 1992 Countermeasures Against Violent Groups laws forced each police department to set up an intelligence division to keep tabs on the local yakuza. They had to know who was rising and who was falling.

In the brief golden age at the start of Saigo's career, the police and the yakuza got along very well. They shared a set of values, in some respects. Most gangsters were vehement right-wingers, extremely patriotic, and anti-communist, and often displayed the Japanese flag prominently in their offices. The police tolerated the yakuza, like Saigo and his crew, because they weren't involved in street crime. In fact, the yakuza would police their own neighborhoods and the entertainment districts with ruthless efficiency. Petty crime, muggings, theft — that scared away customers, and without customers the establishments couldn't make money, and if they couldn't make money, the yakuza couldn't collect protection money.

However, the police had to keep tabs on the yakuza. The cops assigned to the organized crime-control divisions were expected to know who was who in the organization and to be aware of any problems that might end up resulting in a bloody and disruptive gang war. Saigo made their job easier by providing a full list of his men with their dates of birth, addresses, and positions. The list sometimes included guys who weren't listed members. Naturally, the police were thankful.

Detectives from the organized crime control division in the Machida police department would drop by Saigo's office now and then. They'd have a cup of tea, talk about recent events in the underworld, lament the surge of the Yamaguchi-gumi into the Tokyo area, and exchange information.

Once a year, the police would have a special crackdown during organized crime month. The senior detective from the organized crime control division would always call Saigo a week in advance to remind him of it. Saigo would always thank him. The implicit understanding was that Saigo would cough up a few men on whatever charges the police could come up with so that the police department quota was met. In addition to the annual special crackdown, every now and then the police would raid the office, to show the general public that they were policing yakuza, but they'd always call Saigo to make an appointment.

Saigo would make sure to have stacks of newspapers, magazines, and other paperwork lying around the office so that the police could have something to carry out. It looked bad for the police to walk out carrying empty boxes from a raid. The younger officers were bad at pantomime. Try carrying an empty box and making it look like it's full of documents — it's not easy.

In the 1990s, Hishiyama even planted guns in the office to leave for cops to "find" on a scheduled raid. The local police could never identify the gun owners, but still earned points for upping the number of guns seized that year. It was a win-win situation.

This practice of providing weapons to the police more or less stopped after 1995. There was a disastrous incident during annual Autumn Gun Control Month, which exposed the overly cozy ties between the cops and the thugs they were supposed to be policing. The Ehime police, located in southern Japan, needed to increase the number of seizures of illegal guns for the year, so they turned to the local yakuza for help. Senior police investigators asked a local gangster to buy four or five handguns. They even provided the cash for the guns to the gangster's girlfriend. The senior yakuza, who was already raking in the money running traditional *shinogi*, such as gambling and prostitution, was happy to cooperate.

The guns were put in place. The Ehime Police Department staged a "raid" and confiscated the weapons, thus helping to maintain the Ehime prefecture's first-place position nationwide for the number of seizures of illegal weapons. It turned out that the same thing had been taking place in the Gunma prefecture for a number of years. People caught on.

Saigo had a close friend in the Inagawa-kai who was also very pleased with the new laws. His name was Kazuo Kawasaki, but everyone called him Purple. He had apparently gotten the name in his younger years, after scolding one of his soldiers. He'd sent the kid to collect the interest on a loan that had ballooned to several thousand dollars, and the kid had beaten the crap out of the defaulter — leaving marks that got him arrested and charged.

When the soldier got out on bail, Purple dressed him down in front of the other soldiers, and gave them new instructions. He told them it was bad to hit people. It left marks. Bruises.

There was a debate within yakuza circles about whether choking someone was kosher when collecting a debt. Verbal abuse, pinning dead animals to the door, kicking, punching, slapping, threatening, or whacking a deadbeat across the face with a phonebook (which hurts a lot, but leaves no marks) — all these things were considered acceptable.

Purple argued it was much better to choke someone than to hit someone. "But you have to remember this iron-clad rule," Purple said. "Only choke someone until they turn purple; choke them longer, and you might kill them or give them a seizure, or something. And then it'll be really hard to collect the money."

He demonstrated on the soldier he had been scolding. He showed them how to pull up the shirt and squeeze the neck through the shirt so as not to leave telltale finger indentations. The most important thing, he noted, was that you should only choke until they started turning slightly "purple."

He could have used the word "*murasaki*," but he wanted to show off his knowledge of English, so he said, "purple."

And no one understood what he meant. He said it a few more times, yelling, "Purple! Purple!" By this time, the person being choked had almost passed out and looked to be in terrible pain.

One of his soldiers pointed at the now unconscious and possibly dead young yakuza that Purple was choking, and said calmly, "He's purple."

Purple released him immediately. The kid fell to the ground and hit his head on the dirt — and started wheezing and coughing. Fortunately, he wasn't dead. However, unfortunately, everyone remembered Purple's insistence on using the word "purple" in the face of all reason — and so the nickname stuck with him.

Saigo met Purple at an Inagawa-kai funeral early in his career. He was stocky and muscular, but neither tall nor short. He had a penchant for wearing gold necklaces, flashy Italian suits, and ostentatious wristwatches. He had dark skin, and his eyebrows were so thick that they dominated his face and made his protruding forehead even more pronounced.

Purple was primarily a *tekiya*, the type of yakuza who make their money running the food and souvenir stands at major festivals in their area, or selling their wares on the street. Along with the *bakuto* (gamblers) and the *gurentai* (goons), they came to prominence in postwar Japan. They worked at trading centers or fairs, selling products of dubious quality or value; for example, they would sell miniature bonsai trees that didn't have any roots, or lie about the origin of a product. Many of the *burakumin* became *tekiya*, as a way out of otherwise inevitable poverty and disgrace.

Under the new laws, Purple's main source of revenue wasn't affected at all. He made his money primarily when the local temples and shrines in the Meguro ward had their annual festivals — and there were many. He was in charge of making sure the food stands and small shops were all there, serving reasonably sanitary food and drinks, and offering interesting toys, trinkets, and charms. He ran some of the stands directly, and everyone else paid *shobadai* (rental fees) for the rights to sell their wares on his turf.

The temples and shrines would give him a cut of all the proceeds that came in that year. It was a reasonably stable business. Bad weather could result in a bad turnout, so, like a farmer, he was somewhat at the mercy of the elements.

All in all, even if festival attendance wasn't what it had been years before, there were usually good crowds, and he made a good, honest living.

He spent some time as an ordinary yakuza — collecting bad debts, protection money, and repossessing cars in his younger days, but was too much of a softie to really enjoy the work. He took over his father's festival-management business. His father was also technically a yakuza, but was part of a non-designated small *tekiya* organization.

*Tekiya* are not unknown. One of Japan's most popular film series is about such a type of yakuza, and beloved icon of Japanese virtue. There is no Japanese person who doesn't know Tora-san from Shibamata. He's Japan's most famous tramp and the star of the world's longest-running movie series, *Otoko wa Tsurai yo/It's Tough to be a Man*, as certified by *The Guinness Book of Records*. It was supposed to be a single movie, released in 1969, but became the first of forty-eight movies made over a period of twenty-seven years, with almost two releases a year. The series ended with the death of its main actor, Kiyoshi Atsumi, in the summer of 1996.

All the Tora-san movies were directed by Yoji Yamada, who succeeded in creating a Japanese character so popular that his movies are shown in airplane flights to Japan in the "local movies" section.

Tora-san doesn't have a home. He's a *tekiya*, who earns his living by traveling in remote Japanese towns and selling his wares. In the very first movie, he even visits a local yakuza office to pay his respects. This scene is allegedly no longer included in televised versions. In 2011, The *Sunday Mainichi* pointed out that under the new organized crime exclusionary ordinances, even Tora-san films were problematic. Shochiku Studios opened a Tora-san Museum in the middle of Shibamata, in Katsushima Ward, in 1997.

While Tora-san was a sweet, lovable, and gentle soul, not the same could be said for Purple.

He could afford an apartment, a wife, and a Mercedes. He had a full-body tattoo, and was going to learn to do tattoos himself. He had the best life a yakuza could have. His only problem was that he had such a high libido and overbearing manner that eventually his wives would get tired of his constant demands for sex, and would leave him. He married several times over the years.

Purple had income streams from his festival sales and a business making the low-quality products sold at the fairs, and collected some protection money from the locals. He did some loan-sharking on the side, but his rates were reasonable. The 1992 laws affected him in no way at all. People didn't even really think of him as a "yakuza." For Saigo and his fellow yakuza, the laws that were supposed to decimate them only seemed to empower them.

# CHAPTER TWELVE

# Tourist trap

Hideyaki Ogawa, an Inagawa-kai Endo-gumi member, was a thin man with a long horse-like face. He had a gravelly voice and a bad temper. On the morning of August 20, 1993, he came by Saigo's office to borrow his Mercedes. Ogawa had to drive to Yokohama to collect money from a man named Sabura Yamamoto, who was apparently running a small loan-sharking business under the name of Yamamoto Travel.

Saigo offered to go with Ogawa, but Ogawa demurred, saying Hishiyama had said the job was going to be easy. Hishiyama and two other Inagawa-kai yakuza were already accompanying him anyway.

If Hishiyama said the job wouldn't be a problem, then the job wouldn't be a problem. The *oyabun* was always right. But Saigo and Hishiyama weren't getting along. Hishiyama was dealing and using meth. It made him erratic and unreliable. Saigo, having firsthand experience with meth, knew this all too well. Meth-heads make for bad *oyabun*.

Saigo was glad he wasn't going on the mission.

Around 5.50 pm, Saigo got a frantic call from one of his soldiers who had gone with Ogawa. "Hishiyama got shot up. Ogawa-kun, I think he was shot, too."

The group's collection visit to the Yamatmoto Travel business had all gone wrong. It had turned into a shooting match. Yamamoto had a gun, and so did his partner. The soldier was pretty sure that Hishiyama had escaped after he was shot, but he didn't see. He had run out of the office fast. It was all he could've done.

Saigo ordered his soldiers to get out of the area. He decided to take Hanzawa with him to the tourism office. He needed to be sure who had survived, who had died, and what had really happened.

Meanwhile, Purple had been told that shots had been fired at the Yamamoto Travel company where his fellow Inagawa-kai members were. In less than ten minutes, he was at the scene. Saigo's car was parked in front of the building. He knew it was Saigo's car — it was the most expensive Mercedes on the market, and the license plate read "Machida 3000." All Saigo's cars had the number 3000 on the license plate. The trunk had been shot up. The back window had a bullet hole in it as well.

He ran into the office, and found a body lying face down in a pool of blood. The body was still convulsing, and the head had been smashed in, but he was still somehow alive. There was what looked like pieces of brownish jelly on a bloody baseball bat on the floor nearby. There were some skull fragments sticking out of the mass where the head had once been, as though they were placed there as garnishes on a fancy cake.

Purple knew he only had a few minutes before the police arrived. The room smelled of sweat, tobacco, creosote, iron, and rust. There was a bullet hole in the wall near the door. Clearly, there had been a shooting, and the man had been shot in the back while trying to run away.

Purple couldn't tell who it was — he needed to look at the face. It wouldn't be easy because if he touched the body, he'd be covered in blood. The top of the head was emulsified, so he couldn't grab the man by the hair. He lifted up the head of the corpse by the ear and turned the face towards his. Suddenly, a voice screamed at him from behind.

"What the fuck are you doing?" Purple was frozen in place. The voice was coming from behind him. It scared the hell out of him. He turned his head and looked towards the door. There was Saigo, dressed to the nines and looking pissed off. Hanzawa was next to him.

He was so shocked, he let go of the guy's ear, and the head fell back to the floor with a squish. Saigo was pretty sure the man on the floor was Ogawa. Purple lifted the man by the ears again to try to see his face.

Purple's handling of the body irked Saigo. Purple was treating the body as though it was a dead dog or cat.

Purple was not fazed. He stared at the face. "Yep, it's Ogawa." Purple reached into Ogawa's jacket, took out his wallet, and looked at the driver's license, just to be sure. Ogawa gurgled something, shuddered once more, and was absolutely still. They all went silent. Purple felt for a pulse. There was none.

Saigo just stood there for a few seconds. He fumbled in his pockets, and got out a pack of cigarettes. He stuck one in his mouth, and glanced at his watch as he lit it. He looked at the body, and decided they'd better get out of the office before the cops showed up.

They got in Saigo's car and drove as far as they could from the scene. They didn't have much time. If this was the beginning of a gang war, they needed to avenge their comrade before peace was called. They stopped a few blocks from the office to call the police and let them know that there "had been the sound of gunshots."

A few hours later, Saigo and Purple pieced it together. Yamamoto was a corporate blood brother of the Yamaguchi-gumi Kodo-kai, the most violent faction of the Yamaguchi-gumi. He wasn't an ordinary civilian. He'd been operating his loan-sharking business on Inagawa-kai turf. That itself was a problem. The Yamaguchi-gumi and the Inagawa-kai had made a peace treaty years before, but it definitely didn't allow the Yamaguchi-gumi to open offices in Inagawa-kai territory.

On that day, Hishiyama, Ogawa, and two other soldiers entered the office around 5.30 pm. There were only two people working in the office: Yamamoto, who was behind his desk, and another worker. Hishiyama exploded in rage, flipping over the reception table and kicking a chair across the room. He turned to his crew and said, "Let's kidnap these assholes and take them up to the mountains. Beat some sense into them. If they won't pay, we'll make them pay interest with their bones. Grab them."

It turns out that Yamamoto knew he was in trouble with the Yokosuka-ikka before the crew arrived. He already feared for his life, so when he heard those words, he panicked, grabbed a .38 caliber Smith and Wesson revolver from his desk, and fired. His assistant was panicking, too. Only Ogawa had a gun, and he returned fire while the rest of the crew fled. On their way out, Hishiyama got shot in the back, and one of the other soldiers got shot in the gut. Ogawa's gun jammed after two or three shots. He made a break for the door, but Yamamoto shot him. The bullet pierced his heart and stopped him in his tracks. Yamamoto and his crew wanted to make sure that Ogawa was dead, so they grabbed two baseball bats out of the closet and crushed in his head with them. Then they ran.

The whole thing was messy. The Inagawa-kai had a right to take revenge, but it would be only a matter of hours or days before a peace settlement was arranged, and then their hands would be tied.

The first order of business was to see what Hishiyama wanted them to do.

Hishiyama had been taken to the Kitazawa Hospital. They went past the reception and barged into the emergency room, where Hishiyama was lying on the bed, on his side. There was a doctor with him and a policeman nearby. Hishiyama's eyes were closed. Saigo immediately started to ask questions. Was he okay?

When Hishiyama heard Saigo's voice, he half-opened his eyes and said, "Hey, Saigo. Just do them in."

The doctor was checking the machine readings for Hishiyama, and apparently hadn't heard them speaking. That was a relief. Saigo slapped Hishiyama in the face, to the surprise of the attending physician. The doctor didn't know what to do, and shuffled back a bit. Saigo leaned down and whispered to Hishiyama, very quietly, "If you say 'Do it' here in this very place, they'll automatically suspect I'm the one who 'did it' after I do it. So shut up."

Hishiyama started to say something else, but Purple slapped his hand over the boss's mouth and yelled "shut up" in his ear. Purple wasn't trying to be rude to his boss, but he had to be firm to keep them all from getting arrested. Then Saigo gently asked Hishiyama if he could speak to him for a second. Hishiyama nodded, and Purple lifted his hand off Hishiyama's mouth, but hovered it over his lips, ready to clamp down if he started saying the wrong things.

Hishiyama apologized to Saigo for being rash, and then Saigo asked about the gunshot wound in Hishiyama's back.

The doctor was standing there dumbstruck, trying to listen to the conversation. He cleared his throat. They needed to operate on him, and were planning on doing it very soon. The prognosis sounded bad.

The doctors had only treated two gunshot wounds since the hospital had opened years before. They were at a loss as to how to proceed, but at the same time they were really excited to be doing the procedure. "It's so rare to actually get hands-on experience treating gunshot wounds."

The doctor told Saigo that at least one bullet had penetrated Hishiyama's belly and gone straight through his kidney into the area around his spine. They could see about 5 millimeters of the bullet's head sticking out of the flesh, which was helpful.

Saigo found himself feeling a little nauseous as the doctor went on explaining. With regard to possible infectious diseases due to the bullet's entry, there wouldn't be any problem. The bullet had burned all the internal flesh in the course of its trajectory.

The surgeon who was going to be in charge of the operation also came into the waiting room to explain. Hishimaya was lucky: if the bullet had touched any of the nerves around the spinal cord, he could have been paralyzed. If the trajectory had been off by a centimeter, the shot could have been fatal. Still, there was no guarantee that the surgery would be successful, because the surgeon had never done a procedure like this before. "So if he dies, don't come kill me."

Saigo went to see Hishiyama before he went in for surgery. Back in the emergency room, an organized crime control division cop and his partner were trying to talk to Hishiyama. Hishiyama saw Saigo's face, and yelled, "Get those fuckers now before it's too late. You're going to lose your chance to counterattack."

The cops turned and greeted Saigo. The chief detective pulled him aside and said, "You're not going to do anything stupid, right?"

Saigo assured him that that was the case, with Hishiyama shouting all the way into the operating room.

Hishiyama was clearly not in any shape to be giving orders, so Saigo had to go to Coach, Hishiyama's superior, to figure out what to do next. The conversation was brief. Coach told Saigo that Yamamoto was a Kodo-kai member and that they did not want to quarrel with the Yamaguchi-gumi. They would establish a peace agreement. However, until there was an agreement in place, Coach would pretend to not know what was going on. Coach would stall the agreement for a couple of days, which would give Saigo enough time to carry out whatever plan of revenge he came up with, and Coach would look the other way.

Coach then handed Saigo a duffel bag containing about 4 million yen in cash. The money was a substitute for Saigo's monthly organization dues. Coach decided Saigo couldn't waste his time making money. He had to put everything he had into fighting — and fight like hell.

At this point in his career, Saigo never kept a gun anywhere on the premises of his office or in his home — but he always had one hidden with a friend or associate. He had to call his friend in the Gunma prefecture to get his gun, and while he waited for it to arrive, he and Purple searched for the location of a Kodo-kai office in Tokyo. They were going to find an office and shoot it up, and maybe everyone inside. That's how it was supposed to be. They asked a friendly soldier in the Kyokuto-kai, and were given the address of a Kodo-kai branch office in Shinjuku.

They only had two guns. Yusuke Yamada wanted to go, too, but Saigo needed him to stay back. He needed someone he trusted to look after his soldiers in case he got jailed. He'd take Hanzawa instead.

And, of course, Hanzawa was up for it.

It was dark by the time the pair arrived in Shinjuku, and it took them a while to find the address. The building was five stories high, maybe forty years old, and sandwiched between a house and a parking garage. They walked up to the steel door of the office, which was accessible from the outside, took out their guns. They knew that when they fired their shots, the Kodo-kai soldiers would come out shooting within seconds, and maybe Saigo and Hanzawa would die, but that was okay.

Saigo had never fired a gun before. He aimed squarely at the door, pulled the trigger, and the bullet ricocheted back, grazing his left foot and making a hole in his shoe. He jumped back in surprise and pain while Hanzawa fired several shots into the door, only one of which bounced off it. And then nothing happened.

Hanzawa and Saigo looked at each other, and then decided to knock on the door. There was no answer. The whole building was empty. There was no one inside; nobody to witness what they had done. Still, they didn't want to get in trouble for firing shots, so they left immediately.

When they got a few blocks away, Saigo called the Shinjuku Police from a phone booth to report the shooting. They wanted it in the papers.

They soon found out that the Kodo-kai had closed down their office in the building months before, because the entire building had been condemned. The shooting wasn't reported in the newspapers because nobody had noticed it.

The next day, Saigo got a call from Coach, asking him what the hell was going on. Saigo explained what they'd done. Coach was unimpressed. He had never liked guns. There wasn't even a tiny article about it in the newspaper. "You call yourself a man? You can't even shoot up a building?"

Saigo apologized. Coach wondered if he'd even hit the building, but how could he miss an entire building? Coach also wondered how it was possible for him not to have realized there was nobody in the building. "You miss a lot, kid."

The only thing that appeared in the paper was a short article on the shooting at the tourism agency — and it was incorrect. It said

Hishiyama had just been shot in the hand.

The Inagawa-kai Yokosuka-ikka and the Yamaguchi-gumi Kodo-kai achieved a peace treaty several days later. The head of the Kodo-kai, Shinobu Tsukasa himself, came to the Inagawa-kai headquarters to apologize. Monetary damages were assessed, and there was a ritual exchange of sake.

And that was that. There was no revenge. There was no gang war. They had acted foolishly, as yakuza often do. Most of them end their careers without ever firing a shot, yet many of them die over stupid shit. And life went on. Except it wasn't the same for Saigo. For the first time, he realized that the path he'd chosen might result in his own early and bloody death. And the fact was that he didn't want to die — not yet.

He didn't want to die. He had to think that over. He had always envisioned himself as a modern-day kamikaze, ready to put his life on the line for the group, who feared nothing. Yet now he found that he wanted to live. He was doing well in the organization, and was still in a relationship that made him happy every day.

Hiroko acted like the ideal yakuza wife, managing all her relationships with tact. She was motherly, and hung out with Coach's wife a lot. She would call his wife "older sister," and they even went on trips together. Still, they weren't equals. When her "older sister" took out a cigarette, Hiroko would light it for her.

Everyone liked her; even Saigo's soldiers and his parents.

He not only liked her; maybe he even loved her. He had a family, a good life. He didn't want to throw that away in a gang war. He wasn't afraid so much of dying; he was afraid of losing the good life he had finally achieved.

He thought to himself that he was getting soft. He arranged to have another tattoo session. Maybe he'd have a dragon engraved on his leg. Maybe the pain and the tattoos would cover up the fear he felt now.

# PART II

# MERIT BADGES

# 貫目

## CHAPTER THIRTEEN

# Lean on me

In early 1994, Saigo was nearly kicked out of the yakuza. Instead, he got promoted. Although he was doing well, Saigo was not well liked by everyone in the Yokosuka-ikka faction of the Inagawa-kai. Hishiyama knew Saigo's weakness: Saigo was once again addicted to meth — and the more money Saigo made, the more meth he bought.

He soon reached the point where it began altering his behavior and his work performance. He would skip executive board meetings because he was too high to attend. He'd stay up for days on end without sleeping. He'd become violently angry at little or no provocation. He began hallucinating. At one point, he smashed his car into a dividing wall on the highway, convinced that a rival yakuza member was in the trunk of the car shooting at him while another yakuza was on the top of the car trying to break into the vehicle.

Saigo's father and mother didn't know what to do. Saigo's father wasn't concerned just for the welfare of his son; he was concerned for the welfare of the entire Saigo-gumi, which now totaled over fifty people.

Over time, Mr Saigo had come to see his son's crew as members of one large corporate family — his family — and he was practically the human resource chief, branch manager, and accounting department. He was doing the books for the group, keeping account of the income and expenses. Saigo was spending money on meth at an alarming rate. He'd deny it, but his father wasn't a fool. He knew where the money was going, and he knew what his son was doing with it. Saigo was becoming unreliable and unpredictable.

His father knew that talking to Hishiyama and asking for help wouldn't help. Hishiyama was jealous of his son, and would use Saigo's meth addiction to get him kicked out. Plus, Hishiyama also had a meth problem. The notion of Hishiyama looking after his son was worse than a blind man leading another blind man.

So Mr Saigo kept thinking about how to handle the problem, and he thought perhaps he should talk to Coach. Of the yakuza Mr Saigo had met in his life, Coach struck him as one of the few who really followed the principles of *ninkyodo* (the humanitarian way).

Coach and Saigo's father were only two years apart in age. They had first met at a barbecue that Coach held on the outskirts of Tokyo, and they had hit it off immediately. As time went on, they would see each other at extravagant dinner parties sponsored by the Inagawa-kai. The two began exchanging gifts twice a year, as Japanese ritual dictated: *O-seibo* towards the end of the year, and *O-chugen* in the summer.

Sometimes, the Yamaguchi-gumi would send to the Inagawa-kai headquarters a few hundred pounds of fatty, marbled, melt-in-your-mouth-delicious Kobe beef — the finest beef in the world. Coach would pack a few pounds in ice, call up Saigo, and tell him to bring it to his father.

The Inagawa-kai was also heavily invested in the sake-maker Koshinokanbai. As an honorarium, the sake-maker would send crates to the major Inagawa-kai offices. Coach didn't drink; neither did Saigo, but Saigo's father did. So when the sake arrived, Coach would call up Saigo, and Saigo would always protest, "But I don't drink."

"Neither do I, stupid. But your dad drinks. Give it to him."

Saigo's father would always write a formal thank-you letter whenever Coach sent him and his wife something. Coach was impressed by this politeness, and would often ask Saigo how his father had ended up with a no-good son like him.

After consulting with Josephine, Mr Saigo wrote a very formal letter to Coach. He asked him to "take my son as your own son" and to please beat some sense into him. He told Coach that his son was constantly shooting up meth and they could not get him to stop. He had become paranoid, violent, unreliable, and lazy. Saigo was a slave to the drugs, and he could kill himself or someone else if he didn't stop. He needed to be straightened out, and taught honor and respect. Most of all, he needed to never touch drugs again.

Coach was upset. He'd call Saigo every day and ask him if he was shooting up.

Saigo would lie. He kept lying until, one day, he told Coach the truth.

Coach roared at him over the phone, cursing Saigo furiously. He ordered Saigo to come to his office immediately, and hung up. Then he called back two minutes later.

Saigo picked up the phone. Coach was still pissed off, but less so. He told Saigo to stay in his office. Coach would come to him. He didn't want Saigo driving a car or even moving while he was still high.

Saigo put away his needles and supply, and scrambled to put on a suit. He went to the third floor and waited behind his desk. It felt like hours passed.

He didn't remember Coach entering the room; all he remembered was being slapped across the face and waking up.

Coach was standing in front of the desk, looking down at Saigo, his eyes hidden behind his usual sunglasses. He couldn't understand why Saigo didn't just quit meth. "Hishiyama must be telling you to quit."

Saigo didn't flinch. Saigo wasn't going to listen to Hishiyama. He was a junkie, too. What junkie would listen to another junkie? Coach hadn't been aware of Hishiyama's addiction. He was flummoxed.

"So you're blaming Hishiyama?" Coach asked.

"No," Saigo said. "I'm saying that if you told me to quit, I'd quit. But I'm not going to quit when a meth-head tells me to."

Coach took a seat and ordered Saigo to call Hishiyama into the office. When Hishiyama finally arrived, Coach told him he wouldn't kick him out, but he was setting a bad example. Therefore, Hishiyama wasn't doing his job as an *oyabun*.

Coach motioned to Saigo as he stood up, and tapped Hishiyama on the shoulder. "From today, he's directly under my control."

And with that, the Saigo-gumi was directly under Coach, not Hishiyama, which meant that Saigo and Hishiyama were now on an equal footing. However, in layman's terms, both Hishiyama and Saigo were managing directors under Coach, but they had not been adopted as members of his family. (They were not his *kobun*.)

On the morning of March 28, 1994, a few weeks after Saigo's promotion, Coach called Saigo and ordered him to attend the board meeting that day. Hishiyama was going to make a motion to have him banished. He claimed Saigo was using meth, and that was grounds for dismissal. He had to go, or he'd be fired.

Saigo was as high as a kite. He was coming off a one-week meth binge, and hadn't slept since March 21. He'd barely eaten anything either. He politely declined the "invitation," and told Coach that Hishiyama was a meth-head who should fire himself, too.

Coach wouldn't take no for an answer. This was a serious problem, and he could not miss this meeting.

Saigo thanked Coach for his concern and told him he'd be there. Saigo looked at the clock. It was 11.00 am, and the meeting was at 5.00 pm. He stripped off his pajamas, managed to shave, and put on his suit. Then he crawled back into bed. *Fuck the meeting, and fuck Hishiyama.* He was going to lie in bed until he felt better, then get some more meth, and get moving later. Board meetings were a waste of time. Saigo turned off the light.

At 3.00 pm, Saigo heard a loud knock on his bedroom door.

"Go away," he yelled.

"Hey, open the fucking door."

The door was shaking and rattling. Saigo had locked it. It felt like an earthquake was shaking the building. Suddenly there was an explosion as the door was kicked open.

It was the end. He thought the devil had come for him.

Saigo felt a flashlight shining on his face. He looked up, and was blinded by the incandescent fireball inches from his nose. The blankets were stripped from the bed, and he heard the loud, deep, and slightly nasal voice of Coach.

"Get up. We're going to the meeting."

Saigo couldn't make out any faces. He was in a daze. He looked up and tried to focus his eyes. Looming in his vision, like the harvest moon on a Japanese autumn night, was Coach's angry face. Even in the dark, he was wearing his sunglasses.

Saigo wondered if he was hallucinating. He wasn't even sure it was Coach.

Coach was so close he was practically breathing in Saigo's face. Saigo saw his own sunken and pasty white visage distorted on the surface of Coach's sunglasses. He felt like he was out of his body, staring at some ghost of who he used to be.

Coach slapped him in the face and ordered him to get out of bed.

Saigo refused. He felt like he couldn't move.

Coach took off his sunglasses and turned on a lamp next to the futon. He grabbed Saigo's face by the jowls with one hand, and made him turn to look him in the eyes. "Are you on meth?"

Saigo knew Coach knew the answer.

"You stupid fuck," Coach said as he grabbed Saigo's arm and pulled him off the futon. He kicked him in the ribs, dragged Saigo to the wall, and pulled him up against it until Saigo was half-sitting up.

"Did you hear what I said? I asked you, 'Are you on meth?' Well, are you?"

Saigo began to answer yes, but before he could finish, Coach punched him in the stomach and slapped him in the face. Sometimes, Saigo was too honest for his own good. "The answer today is not: 'Yes, I'm on meth,'" Coach said. "The answer is: 'My high blood pressure is acting up.'"

Coach laid out the plan. They were going to the meeting. He was going to tell everyone about Saigo's high blood pressure, and Saigo was going to say he wasn't feeling well. They would get though the meeting, and Coach would straighten Saigo out, because Coach had promised Saigo's dad he would.

Saigo tried to stand up, but he couldn't. The whole room was spinning. He felt nauseous. He needed some speed. He half-stood, put his back to the wall, slid back down, and ended up lying on his side. He couldn't do anything. He wanted Coach to forget about him and to leave him alone.

Coach reiterated that Saigo had high blood pressure, so they'd get it fixed. He helped Saigo stand up, but Saigo found that he couldn't manage to put one foot in front of the other without losing his balance.

Coach looped Saigo's arm around his neck to support him. They walked to the car, where Coach's soldiers were waiting. He had come in alone because he didn't want anyone else knowing that Saigo was in such a sorry state. Luckily for Coach, he knew there was an easy fix for the problem so it wouldn't happen again in the future — Saigo had to stop taking meth. So, for now, Saigo just had to get through the meeting.

The meeting was in a Western-style room at the Yokosuka-ikka headquarters. They arrived early. Coach sat Saigo down next to him. The rules of the Yokosuka-ikka were written in cursive script on a golden placard and on the wall next to the door. The Inagawa-kai emblem was displayed in a gigantic picture frame in gold and white. Other than the sofa and plush seats on the other side of the room, the room was rather spartan. The room was dominated by a long wooden table, buffed and polished so well that the faces of each member was dimly reflected on the surface. The table could seat up to twenty people. Everyone sat in leather-embossed high-backed chairs.

Coach sat towards the head of the table, along with Saigo, who had moved up in the pecking order for the day.

Before Hishiyama arrived, Coach announced that Saigo had high blood pressure. He had not taken his medication, so he would be leaving early. There were no immediate objections. Then there was a snicker from the back, and one of Hishiyama's associates blurted out, "High blood pressure or just high? He looks high to me."

Coach pounded his fist on the table. "Are you calling me a liar? Is someone else going to call me a goddamn liar?"

The heckler was silent. Coach explained that Saigo didn't look healthy because he had high blood pressure. He didn't exercise or eat right. He needed to, but so did everyone else. They were all lazy-ass yakuza, and they should all be in good-enough shape to fight. Coach motioned for Saigo to speak.

Saigo pushed himself up from his chair and stated, in a monotone voice, "I have high blood pressure. I'm feeling sick right now."

Just then, Hishiyama arrived. Coach immediately asked him to get a car ready for Saigo, as he wasn't feeling well.

Hishiyama was about to explain why when Coach cut him off. He told Hishiyama he knew there was talk about Saigo doing meth, but rumors were just rumors. Of course, they couldn't just ignore them. If you're doing something that makes people doubt you, you're doing something wrong. They all knew it was unacceptable. Plus, if Saigo was really doing meth, due to the Yokosuka-ikka rules, anyone who sold or used the drugs deserved to be expelled. Thus he would be expelled. Foot soldier or gang boss — there were no exceptions.

Hishiyama could see where their conversation might lead.

"So I'm taking charge of Saigo-kun from this day forward. For the time being, Saigo-kun is my driver and my secretary and my responsibility." It was a bit of a backhanded way of making Saigo's promotion public, even if it wouldn't be official for a couple more years.

Coach appointed Yamada as the acting head of Saigo-gumi. He had Saigo put in a car and taken back to his home. Saigo wasn't present for the rest of the meeting, but Coach was. He made sure that Hishiyama didn't have a moment to speak his mind.

Saigo woke up and tried to crawl out of his bed to the dresser where he kept his meth hidden in the bottom drawer, with a few syringes. There was no dresser in the room. He was surprised to find himself not in his own bed, but in a room he clearly recognized as in Coach's house. He was sprawled across a futon, covered in blankets. He felt like hell. His head hurt, and his ears rang. He felt nauseous, cold, and thirsty. There were four glasses of water on a table next to the futon, and a note next to the glasses. He drank three glasses first.

He looked at the note, and recognized his father's handwriting. It was neat, legible, evenly spaced, straight across, although the paper was unlined. He read the note several times, not wanting to believe it.

He had been disowned and kicked out by his parents. Coach was his father now. Saigo remembered vaguely what had happened at the meeting. He had agreed to be Coach's driver from that point on.

Saigo started to absorb everything that had happened as he slumped back into sleep. He didn't have much time to think about it, not until he woke up the next morning — when Coach threw the last cup of iced water into his face at 5.00 am and said, "Saigo! Get up. I'm going to play golf this morning, and you're driving."

Coach added a kick in the ass to emphasize that time was of the essence.

## CHAPTER FOURTEEN

# Driving Mr Baseball—how to be a yakuza

Driving Coach around Tokyo was like being in a crash course on how to be a yakuza boss. For the first few weeks, Saigo lived in Coach's house. He learned to bow properly, greet people, exchange business cards, and shut up. At 3.30 am, he would wake up, get dressed, warm up or cool down the Mercedes, and pick up Coach and take him to play golf.

Coach played golf with doctors, lawyers, prosecutors, heads of national newspapers, politicians, industry magnates, and other yakuza. Saigo slept in the car. Sometimes, Coach bet on the golf games, and he'd come back humming a little tune.

After golf, Coach would usually play mah jong in Tokyo. The venues would vary. Sometimes he'd play in hotels; sometimes, in the offices of listed companies. He would spend the afternoon visiting businesses that he ran, or that were paying tribute money to him or the organization. Sometimes, he'd go to the park and play Shogi (Japanese chess) with an old friend.

Coach was also constantly going to secret gambling events. After most of them, he would sit in the back of the car and count his money. He'd flip through it rapidly once, and then count one bill at a time at rapid speed. The *sa-sa-sa* sound of the money being counted was a pleasant sound for Saigo, because he knew that Coach would probably give him some extra money. He almost always did.

Coach would often attend *giriba* (yakuza events), such as funeral services, succession ceremonies, weddings, and Inagawa-kai committee meetings. So Saigo would drive Coach to those events. The standard apparel was a black suit, a white shirt, and a dark necktie. It was all that Saigo wore for months.

If there was nothing special happening, Saigo would eat dinner at Coach's place with Coach, Coach's wife, and other young members of Coach's group. Sometimes, Saigo's girlfriend would host dinner at his house. It had been about four years since Hiroko had moved in, and although Saigo had vowed to never marry again, they were pretty much married. He considered her his wife.

There was a family dinner almost every night. Saigo and the other senior gang members would usually gather at Coach's house, and Coach's wife would cook them all dinner. She was a good cook, and her evening dinners created a family-like atmosphere in the group; while Coach had no children, Saigo was as close as it came to being his eldest son.

Saigo would occasionally check in with Yamada, but the Saigo-gumi was out of his hands as long as he was serving as Coach's driver. He was eventually given the temporary title of Coach's secretary.

Being made the secretary of the boss above you in yakuza world is a promotion. It gives you access to meeting people way above your pay grade. It allows you to learn by example. The downside is that you don't have the time to manage your organization yourself, and you have to trust everything to your subordinates. However, it's a powerful stepping-stone to eventually occupying the position your boss now holds.

Among other yakuza organizations, the system is different, but within the Inagawa-kai, that was what the Japanese would call the "elite corps." The word "secretary" does not have the negative connotation it has in Western society. Many secretaries of politicians later become politicians in the Diet themselves. And in both cases, not only do you get to meet different people in this position, but the "constituents" get to know you.

He was paid 700,000 yen a month, but was expected to pay for gasoline and tolls out of his own pocket. His salary wasn't quite enough to cover the bills, because the Mercedes ate gasoline at a tremendous pace.

Saigo couldn't ask for more money, because that would be rude, but he figured out how to get Coach to pay for his basic expenses. Saigo would wait until Coach was in the car, and drive up to the toll booth. He'd order a month's worth of toll tickets and then fumble for his wallet. Inevitably, Coach would, in a gesture of generosity, pull out the money himself, and say, "Saigo, I'll get this."

Saigo would apologize and say thank you, over and over, until Coach waved his hand as if to say, "No big deal."

Sometimes, Coach would forget to even pay Saigo his monthly salary. The only way for Saigo to remind him would be for him to say, as they were about to drive somewhere, "I don't have any money for gasoline, boss." The timing was important. He didn't want to say this too soon or too late.

Saigo couldn't actually refer to his job as "work." If he referred to the job that way, Coach would get really angry and yell at him about who he thought he was. Saigo wasn't a salaryman, and he wasn't commuting to an office.

Saigo was a yakuza. To Coach, that didn't constitute work.

Tokyo was a labyrinth of dead ends, one-way streets, and addresses that followed no logical order. The city had been designed to be impenetrable, like a maze. Instead of taking the chance to rebuild the city in some order after the war, General Headquarters and the government of Japan allowed Tokyo to respawn as a gigantic, uncontrolled architectural cancer. Even when you had an address such as Gokudo-ku 1-2-4, it didn't help much. You might find your way to Gokudo-ku 2-1-2 and think it would be right next to Gokudo-ku 1. Unfortunately, the two areas might be blocks away from each other, with no indication of whether to go north, south, east, or west. (If this explanation seems confusing to you, come to Tokyo and walk around. Then you'll understand how difficult it is to understand.)

Saigo didn't know Tokyo very well, and he was forbidden to use a car navigation system. Coach was suspicious of all new technology. He also gave terrible directions. When Saigo asked for guidance, Coach would always tell him to go straight ahead.

Even if Saigo asked him three times, Coach would say the same thing.

Sometimes, after giving directions, he'd have a long phone conversation and then look up to see they were in the middle of a rice field. He'd shake his head and say to Saigo, "You're a rare one. How far do you think straight ahead means?"

There were times when Saigo knew the right way to get there, and Coach did not. So, for example, Coach would tell Saigo to turn left, and Saigo would try to convince his boss otherwise, but he would be obliged to turn left and would end up getting lost. Then Coach would get angry with him. He thought that if Saigo had known Coach was wrong, he should have said so directly, and not turned left.

The alternative would have been to ignore Coach and not take the left turn, but if they had ended up getting lost, Coach would have been even angrier. Whichever way Saigo turned, there was often no way for him to win.

Saigo would often have to park the car, get out, and look for clues to find his destination. This would, of course, infuriate Coach, who'd demand that he be more prepared the next time and use a map.

Saigo accepted Coach's criticism, even though Coach usually didn't tell Saigo where they were going until they got in the car.

Of course, there were times he wanted to look at a map as soon as Coach told him the location, but when he opened the map, Coach would tell him to put it away and listen to his instructions. But if Coach wasn't on the phone, he was reading a book. He read a lot of military history and non-fiction books about war. He never allowed music in the car, because it disturbed his reading. Of course, when he became immersed in his reading, he'd stop giving directions, and, once again, they'd end up in a rice field on the outskirts of Tokyo. It happened so many times that every time Saigo drove through a rice field, he began to experience a sensation of déjà vu.

Sometimes, Coach would get impatient with Saigo's driving and insist on taking control of the car himself. Since he was poor at handling the gears and the left-handed steering wheels on foreign cars, he would drive very slowly or veer dangerously to the right. When he drove slowly, cars would pile up behind them.

Once, on the way to mah jong, Coach caused such a huge traffic jam that the police came by and shouted over their loudspeakers for him to maintain the minimum driving speed on the freeway.

Sometimes, Coach would speed up suddenly or reverse without warning. Saigo would end up holding the strap trying not to get car sick. Other times, Coach would make Saigo stop in the middle of a highway or on a mountaintop, and tell him to get out of the car. The reasons would never be clear. Maybe Coach was going to see a woman, or maybe he just wanted to be alone. Sometimes, he'd hand

Saigo 30,000 yen for a taxi fare. Sometimes, he'd forget to give Saigo the taxi fare.

One time, Saigo had to climb down the bottom of the freeway, and jump from the overpass, approximately 1 meter to the ground, to get to a place where he could call a taxi from. Once, he was dumped on the outskirts of Tokyo with only a couple of hundred yen in his pocket. It took him three hours to walk to a train station.

The mountains, the freeway, an underpass, a tunnel — he'd never know where he might suddenly find himself ejected from the car. It happened so often that he learned to keep a few extra 10,000-yen bills hidden in his wallet, just so he could get home.

Coach would occasionally complain about Saigo's driving. On the way to a golf tournament in the summer of 1995, Coach became gradually irritated as it came closer and closer to the starting time of the event. He kicked Saigo's seat. He thought Saigo had been a *bosozoku* — what happened? Saigo felt his face flushing, and his hands getting tight on the wheel. He revved up the engine, and told Coach to put his seatbelt on.

It was 4.00 am, and the traffic was light. Saigo was driving a Mercedes Benz S-600. It handled well. The gas tank was full.

Within forty-five seconds, Saigo had the car moving at 200 kilometers an hour. The speed meter made clicking sounds as he drove it past its capacity. Coach initially appeared calm. He held his book in one hand while he read. But when Saigo sped, Coach held on to the passenger strap near the door, desperately trying not to sway. His book fell to the floor, and the sound of the wind and engine drowned out his voice. "Saigo. Enough. I get it. Slow down. We're good."

Saigo slowly applied the brakes until they were once again at the upper edges of the speed limit.

186 THE LAST YAKUZA

Coach went back to his book. They arrived fifteen minutes earlier than projected. When Coach stepped out of the car, he smiled, and told Saigo he had done a good job. "At least you can do one thing right."

Saigo's time as Coach's secretary was also a painful period of drug rehabilitation. Coach was constantly checking Saigo for needle marks, and staring at him in the eyes to see if he showed signs of being high. If Saigo drank too much water or downed a bottle of Coca-Cola thirstily, Coach would ask him if he was doing meth again.

Saigo would deny it, and Coach would blow on his fist, as if to warm it up, and then punch him in the head, adding, "If I even think you're doing *shabu*, the next punch is right in your face."

Saigo would rub his head and nod.

There was something fatherly in Coach's punches. They said, *I'm not truly mad at you, but this is the only way you're going to learn.* He never punched with too much force — but it did sting.

Coach was a firm believer in the Japanese sayings *karada de oboeru* (remember with your body) and *tatakinaosu* (beat or hit something with enough force to repair it or fix it). It's a term often used to justify corporal punishment in schools. When yakuza do it to their peers to get them back on the straight and narrow, it's a crime. In fact, it's also a crime when civilians do it, but is rarely punished — especially if the victims are family members: wives and children.

Coach believed that an occasional punch punctuated his verbal lessons better than a shout, and made them easier for Saigo to remember.

One day, while they were in the driveway of Coach's house, Coach gave Saigo an envelope full of cash. He poked one of Saigo's needle-mark scars, and told him to get his name tattooed right there, so every time Saigo thought about shooting up, he'd see Coach's name.

Saigo was wary of getting the tattoo. He didn't even have his girlfriend's name tattooed on his arm. Coach grabbed Saigo's arm, and smacked the area so hard that it stung. "I'm not your girlfriend!" he yelled, then laughed at his own comment. Coach really liked Hiroko, probably more than he liked Saigo. But Saigo's *oyabun* was supposed to be more important to him than his girlfriend.

As Coach saw that Saigo was staying sober, he saw to it that Saigo was promoted within the organization and that the Saigo-gumi was moved underneath Coach's group. This was a big deal. Coach was now the *waka-gashira* in the Yokosuka-ikka. He had lived through the days when the Inagawa-kai and the other yakuza groups were constantly at war, when being a bodyguard meant you were a walking pincushion.

Back in those days, Coach never knew when he was going to be called into action. He was expected to lay down his life without time to prepare.

Coach believed that Saigo should think of driving as part of his yakuza training. Coach considered cars to be great weapons, because they were gigantic blunt instruments and the penalties for using them were a lot less than for using a gun. During a gang war, you could get in your car, wait for the opposition to show up, and just drive into them. When the cops came, you could make up a story about how it had been an accident. Coach was clear that Saigo shouldn't do this if there were civilians anywhere around.

Coach thought yakuza should never use guns. Guns misfire, and they kill innocent people. They draw unwanted attention. Still, one man with a gun could do more damage than a few guys with baseball bats. Even Coach, as convinced as he was that guns would be the undoing of the yakuza, wasn't always consistently opposed to their use. Coach reminisced about this to Saigo while driving home from a general meeting in November 1994.

Suddenly, Coach told Saigo to stop the car. Saigo had the feeling he'd just stepped on a land mine. He pulled the car over to the side of the road where there was a wide shoulder, and got out. They were in Atami on the Tomei Expressway. It was nearly dusk. There was a guardrail, and Saigo looked down to see the violent ocean waves splashing against the cliffs. In the distance, he could see Japan's loftiest peak, Mount Fuji, looking as if it was rising from the deep waters.

He opened Coach's door, and half-expected him to slap him in the face, but Coach did no such thing. He motioned for Saigo to follow him. They stood together and looked at Mount Fuji in the distance; the sound of the waves was all he heard.

"Saigo, have a cigarette. Let's talk."

Saigo took out his Short Hopes, fumbling for his lighter. To his surprise, Coach pulled out a gold-plated lighter and handed it to him. Of course, Coach didn't light the cigarette for Saigo. That would have been too much.

The business of being a yakuza used to be about fighting, Coach said. Fighting for turf, fighting for protection money, fighting because they were being insulted, fighting because they imagined they were being insulted. But fighting was no longer the order of the day. Why? Because gang fights were bad for business. But there would still be times when yakuza would have to fight.

Coach ordered Saigo to never start a fight, but if someone fought with him, he should make sure to finish it. "Don't pull back. You grab your men, your swords, your daggers, your baseball bats, your wooden sword, and you raid the enemy's place and beat the crap out of them." Maybe they'd have guns, but he shouldn't let that stop him.

Saigo nodded, but felt he had to protest. He considered guns a necessary evil. He understood what Coach was saying, but if Saigo and his crew showed up to a gun fight with swords, they were going to get seriously fucked up.

"Then you get fucked up," Coach said.

That was the business. Yakuza should go into battle like goddamn kamikaze. Only one person wins a real fight, Coach said. That's the guy who's not afraid to die. The one who is already dead in his heart.

Coach thought guns were for cowards. A person pulls a trigger, and they're far away. They aren't up close, and that's why people mistakenly shoot the wrong man. They don't see who they're hitting. If the yakuza kept using guns, the police would really start gunning for them. The Coach was sure it would happen. Even then, Japan had a zero-tolerance policy for guns. They didn't want to be like the United States, and have innocent bystanders being shot to death.

If Saigo ever had to make a hit, he should go up to the guy, call him by his name, and make damn sure it was the right person. "You don't just take aim and fire. That's not how it's done."

Saigo thought to himself that Coach's views on the rules of gang-war conduct were out of date. Maybe the old man just didn't understand that technology had improved. Guns were more accurate; swords were hard to get, and hard to use. One man with a gun could take out three men with a sword — any sane man would want the gun.

It would be years later before Saigo realized how prescient the boss really was.

## CHAPTER FIFTEEN

# Less than a beggar, better than a thief

It was August 1994, and a senior gang boss had died. The entire Yokusuka-ikka faction attended the funeral. It took eight buses to get them to the temple and back to the city after the service.

Coach ran the group like he was running a baseball team. He made everyone play by the rules. He was harsh, but fair. He never asked his soldiers to do anything he wouldn't do.

Saigo sat in the back of the bus with Coach. Yamada sat near them, silently reading comics. There was a boss who people called Preacher on the bus as well. He was called Preacher because he was the only active yakuza boss who was a self-confessed Christian. He preached a lot about the power of Jesus Christ and the Lord's forgiveness.

Preacher didn't smoke, so, of course, he chewed gum. The radio made it hard to hear, so Preacher loudly asked for gum. Taro Yamakoshi, a low-ranking member, immediately pulled a pack of Lotte blueberry gum out of his bag and gave it to Preacher. Preacher took a stick and chewed it a few times before making a face and spitting it out into the wrapper. "This is crap. You got anything else?"

Yamakoshi smiled. He had stolen 100 packs of different types of chewing gum from the gas station they had parked at earlier in the trip. He opened his bag to reveal the selection, and put his bag in the aisle. "Help yourself."

Preacher grabbed some Black-Black, pulled out several sticks, and wadded them into his mouth and chewed them contently, his teeth and tongue quickly turning minty black. The other yakuza came over to where he was, grabbing handfuls of gum and passing it around the bus.

Coach suddenly stood up. "Stop the bus."

The driver pulled over to the shoulder of the road and slowed the bus to a stop. Nobody spoke. The only sound was of several people quietly chewing gum, smacking their lips a little.

Coach walked up to the front of the bus, took a wooden sword out of the umbrella stand near the driver's seat, and turned to face the group. He held the sword in his right hand like a baseball bat.

Coach was in good shape. His tailored black suit fit perfectly. Coach usually wore sunglasses. No one knew whether it was for show or whether he had eye problems. You could never be sure if he was watching you or not. It added to his mystique.

Everyone knew that he was angry. They just weren't sure how angry he was.

He pointed at Yamakoshi and asked him where he had got the gum. Yamakoshi admitted that he had stolen it from the gas station.

"You stole it," Coach said. "You stole some fucking gum."

There were nervous laughs among the other yakuza. Coach smacked the sword against his other hand and glared at them. This wasn't funny. He ordered everyone who had taken the gum, chewed the gum, or laughed just then to get off the bus.

Coach motioned to Preacher as well. Preacher looked petrified, but he got up. In all, twenty yakuza got off the bus and lined up outside. Yamakoshi was standing the farthest from the door, near the exhaust pipe. Saigo followed Coach off the bus, taking a wooden sword for himself just in case things got out of hand.

Coach addressed them all. They were yakuza, and they had a code. That code was what separated them from common criminals. They existed in society because their society tolerated them. They tolerated them because, while they might do unsavory things, there were certain things they did not do.

Coach believed that being a yakuza was like being an actor. You had to play a part, but you would always be on stage. You had to become your role; stand tall, sit up straight. You walked with your chest forward and your shoulders back, like you were walking against the wind, firmly, head up, looking straight ahead. You had to project strength and appear unbeatable. If you couldn't intimidate other people, you couldn't be a yakuza.

The best way to win a fight is to not fight. Yakuza should not fight unless they have to. They should especially not fight people within their organization. "Squabbling within the group creates disharmony. Disharmony creates disloyalty. Disloyalty creates conflict. Conflict turns into trouble."

One should never scream, but always speak in a clear, loud voice.

Yakuza should know how to read people. They need to know the rules of a situation and know the odds of winning in any situation.

And, above all else, yakuza shouldn't steal, but they should punish those who did.

The sound of cars passing by punctuated Coach's words. No one with gum still in their mouth was chewing it now.

Coach had every right to expel Yamakoshi. If they had caught him stealing from someone in the neighborhood, not only would they have banished him, but they would have taken a finger in the process. But he confessed, so Coach was going to show him some mercy. "But everyone here who listened to him admit that he stole that gum and not only said nothing but took the gum is just as bad as Yamakoshi is." In Coach's mind, a man who saw another man commit a crime and did nothing about it was even more guilty than the wrongdoer.

Coach turned and broadsided Yamakoshi in the face with the wooden sword. The crack of wood on bone resonated with an echo.

Coach came back to stand in front of Yamakoshi, who was holding his jaw, trying to stay standing up. "Yamakoshi, you think about the high cost of being a thief the next time you're chewing gum or trying to chew it. I should knock your damn teeth out."

Yamakoshi winced, and Coach lifted the sword again. He hit the yakuza standing next to Yomakoshi in the face; not as hard, but enough to sting and possibly crack bone. "You took the gum, even though you know it was stolen," Coach said to the soldier. "That makes you a thief, too. Don't ever steal anything again."

One by one, Coach went down the line, whacking the offenders in the face with the wooden sword.

When he got to Preacher, the collision of the sword against his jawbone made a sickening metallic and yet squishy sound — as a grayish ball of what seemed to be bloody flesh jettisoned from the man's mouth. Saigo figured that the shock had made Preacher bite his own tongue off, and he raced to retrieve it off the road. It was only when Saigo picked it up and got a whiff that he realized it was just the big wad of Black-Black chewing gum.

"We are parasites on society," Coach said. "We live off the good graces of others. We are less than beggars, but better than thieves. Never forget this."

And they all got back on the bus and drove back to the gas station. Coach explained what had happened to the owner, apologized, and put 10,000 yen ($100) on the counter — ten times the value of the stolen gum. They kept the gum. It had been paid for now. Saigo and Coach split what was left between them.

It was an important lesson for Saigo and for all of them.

There were some things that yakuza were not supposed to do — although there was some disagreement about what those things were. While Coach viewed them as parasites, some yakuza were proud of themselves.

In 1995, Takahiko Inoue wrote a memoir of his life, *Going To Shura: the life and times of a yakuza*. It was generally well received. Detective Chiaki Sekiguchi, a senior detective in the Saitama Organized Crime Control Division, praised it as a slightly glorified but good introduction to the yakuza: how they used to be, why they are tolerated, and how they will never be again.

Coach was less enthused by the book. When Inoue brought him a box full of copies, Coach picked one, thumbed through it, and told Inoue, "What is this crap?" He told him to dump the books somewhere. Yakuza weren't supposed to be writers. Writers weren't supposed to be yakuza. "Get your head out of your ass."

Inoue apologized, and took the books back to his office in Shinjuku. He never mentioned the book around Coach again. Coach might have seemed unduly harsh, but he believed that the yakuza should stay in the shadows and shun the spotlight. He refused to do interviews with the yakuza fanzines, and had no desire to be a public figure nor explain himself to the world. He had no use for religion either. There was honor and there was money, and those were the only things that existed in this world.

Inoue saw things differently. Chairman Ishii had been a very religious and superstitious man. When Inoue was his bodyguard, part of his job was driving him to temples and shrines on mini-pilgrimages. Sometimes, Ishii would stop at the side of a country road and pay his respects to the statues of *Jizo*, the Buddhist deity who was the protector of travelers, children, and unborn children. In Buddhist mythology, *Jizo* will sometimes even rescue suffering souls from the depths of Hades. Most of the time, Inoue would watch Ishii put his hands together and pray to the gray stone statues of Jizo. He'd be bored as hell and stifling a yawn, but sometimes it seemed to Inoue that Ishii was actually speaking to *Jizo*, and that the stone statues were speaking back. Extreme boredom could play tricks on a man's eyes.

Under Ishii, Inoue learned to be a civilized person. He still liked to fight, but he also knew how to behave. Ishii had high hopes that Inoue would be the new face of the yakuza: law-abiding, honorable, legitimate. And being the face meant being in public.

Although Coach and Inoue held different beliefs about that, they had similar views of honor. Inoue would never do something as foolish as stealing gum from the locals.

# CHAPTER SIXTEEN

# The white Mercedes of Armageddon

Saigo had a knack for extortion. He was only arrested on extortion charges once in his entire career, even though he probably did it over 100 times. Even then, he was never convicted of it. The best extortionists never are.

Aum Shinrikyo was a new religion founded in February 1984. It espoused a mixture of science, occultism, Buddhism, and new age theology. The founder of the group and its guru, Shoko Asahara, was legally blind, but highly intelligent and charismatic. He recruited the brightest minds he could find and, over the years, began turning the cult into a brutally efficient war machine. They would eventually recruit hundreds of members.

By 1988, the cult was engaging in criminal behavior that caught the attention of those in the legal community.

On November 4, 1989, disciples of Asahara raided the home of Tsutsumi Sakamoto, a lawyer handling complaints against the religious group. They kidnapped his wife and his one-year-old son, killed them elsewhere, and disposed of the bodies. One member of the hit-squad was a former soldier in the Yamaguchi-gumi.

TBS Broadcasting had filmed an interview with the lawyer, Sakamoto, a few weeks prior to the killing in which he discussed his great concerns about the cult and its fanatical tendencies. TBS had shown the tape to Aum Shinrikyo senior members, seeking comment. Tipped off to the problematic interview and increasingly annoyed by Sakamoto's actions, the guru ordered him killed.

Asahara convinced his disciples that anyone opposing the activities of the group was a force of evil, and that killing them would speed their misguided souls onto a new incarnation.

The Kanagawa police did a sloppy investigation, even failing to find an Aum Shinrikyo badge that had fallen at the scene of the crime. Some speculate that their failure may have been partly due to the presence of an Aum sympathizer within the police force.

TBS did not air the interview or alert the police to the fact that they might have given Aum Shinrikyo a reason to abduct the lawyer and his family.

After one set of murders, the leaders of Aum Shinrikyo didn't have qualms about committing a few more. In June 1994, they did a test run of sarin, a deadly nerve gas first developed by the Nazis, in a residential area of Matsumoto City, killing seven people and seriously injuring others. The police arrested a local man for the crimes, and tried to force a confession from him.*

By January 1995, the police were fairly certain that Aum had released the nerve gas in Matsumoto City, but they still did nothing. On March 20, 1995, members of Aum Shinrikyo released sarin gas on the Tokyo subway, killing twelve people and injuring more than 5,000. It was the first case of chemical-weapon mass terrorism in modern history. It caught the police and the nation off guard, although there had been warning signs a year before the attacks.

---

* He was later cleared of all charges.

An organized crime detective, K. Shirakawa, was able to find out that Aum had a helicopter, purchased from Russia, which they were planning to use to spread sarin nerve gas all over the city of Tokyo. The attack would have injured thousands and killed hundreds. This has never been reported. The police knew they did not have much time to move.

On March 22, police launched massive raids on Aum and their facilities.

On March 30, the National Police Agency commissioner-general, Takaji Kunimatsu, was shot and severely wounded in front of his home in Arakawa Ward. Everyone believed that Aum was responsible, but the case was never solved.

For certain yakuza groups, this chain of events was seriously bad news. Especially for the Yamaguchi-gumi.

During the period up to the sarin gas attacks, Aum Shinrikyo needed to collect as much money as they could, and began making methamphetamines. The purity was suspect and the color was red, but it worked. Aum Shinrikyo used their former Yamaguchi-gumi members to connect to the Goto-gumi faction, and began selling drugs, weapons, and powerful incinerators to the Yamaguchi-gumi. It was a good match.

Hideo Murai was one of the chief liaisons to the Yamaguchi-gumi. He had been in charge of designing the cult's chemical weapons compound in the Yamanashi prefecture. As the investigation progressed and the organization feared their connections to the group would be made public knowledge, they decided that Murai would have to go.

On April 23, 1995, Yamaguchi-gumi member Jo Hiroyuki stabbed Murai multiple times in front of a crowd of reporters outside Aum's Tokyo headquarters. Murai died a few days later. Hiroyuki initially insisted that, although he was a South Korean Japanese national, he was also a rightist and had acted on his own. (During his trial, he claimed he had been ordered to make the hit by Kenji Kamimine, a senior leader of the Yamaguchi-gumi Hane-gumi. According to Hiroyuki, they had promised him a great promotion if he did it. The Tokyo High Court cleared Kamimine of his alleged part in the murder.)

The murky links connecting the yakuza to the group, the assassination attempt on the head of the National Police Agency, and the successful assassination of Hideo Murai were a cause of concern to everyone.

Aum Shinrikyo had one of their major headquarters in Fujinomiya city, where the Goto-gumi also had their headquarters. The city had a small population of 100,000 people, and nothing that mattered got done there without the Goto giving permission. Thus the police believed that the Goto-gumi was handling the distribution of the meth and other products created by the cult. They also believed that the Goto-gumi had likely played a role in the attempted assassination of the national police chief.*

However, while the Yamaguchi-gumi faction had been happy to do business with the cult, they probably hadn't known they were dealing with a group of homicidal terrorists. Yet other organizations, including the Inagawa-kai, had refused to deal with the cult.

In May 1995, the *Sankei* newspaper reported that Aum Shinrikyo members had approached the Inagawa-kai, offering to supply them with methamphetamines, but that the Inagawa-kai had turned them down. Then a weekly magazine published an article saying that the police had raided the Yokosuka-ikka headquarters looking for evidence

---

* The senior investigator noted that when the Yamaguchi-gumi assassin finally got out of jail in 2007, he went to work for right-wing groups connected to the Goto-gumi, and worked directly with Goto from 2011 to at least 2014. For a while, Hiroyuki was blogging about his life, but deleted all previous mentions of Goto from his page. His current whereabouts are unknown.

that they had supplied the gun for the attempted assassination of the police commissioner-general.

There was no truth to the second article, and Coach was livid. Coach was well known for his general dislike of all reporters and publicity. Other *oyabun* loved to be interviewed for the yakuza fanzines, but he always refused. That wasn't his style. But Coach was so angry that he ordered Saigo to organize a press conference.

Saigo didn't know how to call a press conference, so he called Detective Lucky, and asked him how to do it. Detective Lucky didn't know, either. However, he knew there was a press club inside the Prefectural police department. The reporters there mostly played mah jong and wrote up police press releases. Sometimes, they actually left the office to do work. Lucky gave Saigo their number.

Saigo called the club, and arranged the impromptu press conference. It was held at the Ikegami Honmonji temple, where Ishii had been buried.

Coach wasn't tall, so Saigo managed to rustle up a beer crate to make a pedestal for him. Coach was dressed to the nines, wearing his signature sunglasses and a brightly colored, almost garish, necktie. To a gaggle of reporters, he read out loud a very flowery, long-winded, and angry speech. He denied that the honorable Yokosuka-ikka had anything to do with Aum Shinrikyo, said they had no part in the assassination attempt, and affirmed that they greatly respected the police.

The press took notes, took some pictures, and adjourned. There were no questions asked.

Saigo had his crew watch all the TV shows that night to see if they'd made the evening news, but they had been politely ignored. However, the spokesman for Aum Shinrikyo and their head of public affairs, also known as the information minister, Fumihiro Joyu, was prominently featured.

Joyu had graduated from an elite university. He was very bright and glib. He was quite fond of arguing with reporters, and often seemed to win the debate. He even developed a cult following of teenage girls who thought he was sexy. He rubbed Saigo the wrong way. And what really pissed off Saigo was watching footage of Joyu driving away from a press conference in a Mercedes. A white Mercedes.

That was a yakuza car. Saigo drove a Mercedes. He was not going to have the leader of some crazy cult driving a Mercedes around Tokyo.

Saigo went to have a chat with Inoue about the whole thing, in his office in the Lion's Mansion in Kabukicho, which was on the seventh floor. Inoue had become a Buddhist priest, and his office was decorated with an imposing statue of *Fudo Myō*, the fierce guardian of hell, who was said to be able to change the hearts of evil demons and make them angels — an iconic figure also carved as a tattoo onto the backs of many yakuza. The statue was the centerpiece of the large Buddhist altar in the room. In front of the statue on the altar was a small incense burner, a candlestick, a flower vase, and a signal bell (*suzu*).

When Saigo entered the room, Inoue was putting his hands together in prayer, having just tapped on the bell with the tiny stick next to it. Saigo didn't say a word, but waited in silence as the clear, reverberating tone of the bell faded into silence and Inoue finished mumbling an incantation. The bell was rung before meditation, or prayer, or the chanting of Buddhist sutras, but for Saigo, who had by now attended many funerals, it wasn't the signal for meditation — it was the sound of death. It always creeped him out a little. The smell of sandalwood from the incense, mixed with the reek of sake and the cigarette smoke, made him feel like he'd walked into a Buddhist theme bar.

Inoue noticed Saigo after a few seconds and stood up to greet him with a smile on his face, and motioned for Saigo to sit down. Saigo told him his plan. Surprisingly, Inoue approved.

Inoue knew a great deal about Aum Shinrikyo. He told Saigo that what he found most troubling about the group was how they had perverted the teachings of Buddha, a religion of peace, into a justification for murder.

Inoue told him the first principle of Buddhism was to cause no harm to others and to love every living creature. This was important in generating good karma. If you hurt others, you were bound to get hurt. Even a five-year-old could understand this.

But the guru of Aum had turned the principle upon its head. Aum Shinrikyo was almost like a yakuza group in which the senior members would beat up the lower-ranking members for any act of insubordination or failure. The group called this "getting rid of bad karma" — a way of getting rid of the spiritual and moral baggage that slowed up a disciple in this life or the next. This was also their justification for killing enemies of the group in a brutal fashion. The Aum Shinrikyo leaders would tell their followers that they were not killing people, but were helping them — by speeding them on their way to their next incarnation, lightened of their false beliefs and karmic baggage. Inoue found the whole concept appalling.

Inoue wished Saigo would give Joyu a stern lecture as well, but Saigo wasn't into wordy sermons; he was more of an action kind of guy.

The next day, Saigo, Yamada, and a few other gang members drove up to the Aum Shinrikyo headquarters and waited for Joyu's car to leave. When it did, Saigo's car blocked the entrance of the driveway, and Saigo got out.

The police who were guarding the area seemed flustered, but didn't do anything. Saigo pounded on the front window. "Get out of the car."

Joyu stayed calm. He stared down Saigo and informed him, in a beatific manner, that he was speaking to a spiritual leader.

In Saigo's mind, he was talking to a pirate and fucking traitor. He wanted to know where Joyu had got the white Mercedes. Saigo said this with such venom and barely controlled anger that Joyu was slightly flustered, but he quickly attempted to take control of the situation.

Joyu told him the car was a present from Yamauchi Taro of the Yamaguchi-gumi, and that Taro had it specially made for him. That was probably a lie, but by telling Saigo this, Joyu was saying he had the Yamaguchi-gumi, Japan's largest organized crime group, backing him up.

Saigo wasn't impressed. The headquarter they were at was in Inagawa-kai territory, and a traitor like Joyu didn't deserve to ride around in a white Mercedes Benz — a car that was basically a yakuza symbol. It disgraced all yakuza.

Saigo thumped on the window as hard as he could with the bottom of his fist. The thick window didn't shake. It was made of bulletproof glass.

"Well, you don't need that. If someone shoots you to death, you deserve it. You're giving us this car."

Joyu was dumbfounded. He looked over at the police, who had all stepped 300 yards to the right. They were standing in a circle smoking cigarettes. Saigo called out to a detective he knew, and asked him if he could hear what he was saying.

The detective shouted that he couldn't hear a thing. None of the cops could. They were all on their cigarette break. "Let us know when you're done."

"Okay," said Saigo, shouting back. "Just wanted to let you know that Joyu-sama is giving us his car for safekeeping."

"That's very nice of him. Congratulations."

It wouldn't have been smart for Saigo to drive off with a car that

Joyu was donating to the Inagawa-kai, so he ordered Joyu to drop it off at a designated intersection that night. Joyu nodded meekly, but the police wouldn't allow him to leave the building. So many people wanted to kill Joyu that the police said they couldn't protect him if he left. In the circumstances, Saigo decided Joyu would have his lawyer drive it over.

Having reached an agreement, Saigo made his parting greetings to the detectives, and took his entourage of thugs back home.

Joyu's lawyer delivered the car ten minutes early. A good source told Saigo that the specially fitted car had cost nearly a quarter of a million dollars. He figured that the resale value would be at least $100,000, but Saigo quickly discovered that no one wanted to buy, drive, or even touch anything related to Joyu.

The white Mercedes turned out to be a giant white elephant in disguise. The Aum cult had failed to do proper maintenance on it, and parts had to be replaced frequently, making the upkeep expensive. All the adjustments that had been made invalidated the warranty. Plus, the retrofitted bulletproof plating made the car so heavy that it ate gas like it was a mini tank. There was some discussion of pressuring the Mercedes Benz dealership to fix it for free, but Mercedes had good connections with the cops, so they nixed the idea.

Saigo considered repainting it, but the car was in such bad shape that he decided it wasn't worth paying for the paint job. Eventually, he ordered one of the foot soldiers to dump it in a parking lot outside Tokyo with the car keys in it. Three days later, the car was gone.

Saigo didn't make any money on the shakedown. In fact, financially, he took a hit. But among cops, right-wingers, and yakuza, he bought himself a huge chunk of credibility, and that was a very hard thing to buy in the underworld.

## CHAPTER SEVENTEEN

# For whom the chimes toll

Some stories are best told from the end. This story ends with the suicide of Kenzo Arai, aged fifty-six, a yakuza boss, and the leader of the Inagawa-gumi Odawarai-gumi Shugetsu family. He blew out his brains and ended his life at his own home around 5.20 pm on October 5, 1995.

In some ways, you could say that Tsunami pulled that trigger and that Coach gave him the orders, but we're getting ahead of ourselves. Tsunami certainly didn't literally pull that trigger. And Arai wasn't the only person to die that day.

Twenty minutes earlier, at 5.00 pm, Arai had shot to death his underboss, Hideyuki Eiri, aged fifty-four, at the gang office, and then driven back to his palatial house.

And an hour before Kenzo Arai aka "Ken-chan" killed his underboss, he had received a visit from another boss of the Inagawa-Kai, at 4.00 pm.

You can guess the name of that boss — and it wasn't Tsunami.

But that's not where this story really starts. It started on a hot night in September that year.

Jiro Kiyota, the head of the Inagawa-kai Yamakawa-ikka (currently the supreme leader of the Inagawa-kai itself), was kidnapped from his home in Kawasaki City on the night of September 6, 1995. It was an audacious crime, considering how powerful the Inagawa-kai was at the time.

Kiyota, ethnically Korean, was a well-respected elder in the organization, and his prematurely white hair gave him an aura of dignity and gravitas.

The kidnappers didn't treat him with any respect. They showed up at his door posing as delivery men, and once inside brutally beat him and dragged him outside into his garden. They not only abducted Kiyota, but also his maid, tying her up with rope and taking her along for the ride. To top it all off, they took several million yen in cash from a safe inside the house.

Kiyota was thrown in the back of a car and driven an hour from his home, blindfolded, and dropped in a room somewhere in an old house. There he was stripped naked and beaten severely, over and over. His kidnappers videotaped the torture, and they sodomized him with a vibrator; they filmed that as well.

The kidnappers sent the tape and the ransom note to the number two in his organization, Kazuo Uchibori, and demanded 50 million yen in ransom money. "Give us the money and you'll get him back alive," they wrote in their ransom note.

They also warned that if the money was not paid, or if there was any attempt to track down the kidnappers, they would release the videotape to the world, humiliating Kiyota forever. In the ultra-macho world of the yakuza, the humiliation was more of a threat than the bodily harm they might inflict on him.

It's well known that Kiyota has been unable to speak for a few years. Some of those in the yakuza world whispered that this is because he screamed so much during his two days of confinement that it ruptured his vocal cords. That is a lie. Kiyota later developed throat cancer, and after an operation was left barely able to speak. But even when he could speak, he was always a man of few words.

Throughout his torture and his beating, Kiyota stayed silent, refusing to beg for his life or to scream. Thus he was beaten severely again and again. The videotape was edited to show the few moments that he did groan or express pain.

The kidnappers were smart, or thought they were. They knew that no yakuza would go to the police, because that would be humiliating and it would also raise questions. Where had the ransom money come from? If the organization had 50 million yen to pay ransom money, had they paid taxes on it? There were one hundred reasons to avoid going to the police, and not a single good reason to ask for their help. The yakuza were essentially perfect victims — they were men with money who could not go to the police.

The number two in Kiyota's organization had no choice but to pay up. Kiyota was not only his *oyabun*, but his own wife was related to Kiyota.

Uchibori delivered the money to the designated spot. A few hours later, Kiyota was released. He was angry and hurt, and at a loss as to what he should do.

The matter required discretion and revenge. He could only think of one person to speak with, and that was his brother in the Inagawa-kai, Nobuyuki Kanazawa — Coach.

Kanazawa was known for his skills in gambling, and also for keeping a stoic calm. Coach promised that he would look into the manner discreetly and efficiently. He chose to call his former bodyguard and now leader of the Saigo-gumi in Machida.

Tsunami showed up at Coach's home and was shown the videotape. There were a few scenes of Kiyota enduring terrible blows; they were hard to watch, as were the scenes intended to humiliate him.

Coach didn't show him the whole videotape. That wasn't necessary.

"What do you want me to do about it, *oyaji*?" Saigo asked.

"I want you to find the people who did it. From the bottom to the top."

Coach had a hunch that the kidnappers had to be other yakuza, probably from a rival gang — or other members of the underworld, people on the periphery. There was even a possibility, although no one wanted to consider it seriously, that the kidnappers might be Inagawa-kai members.

The home addresses of yakuza bosses weren't published on the internet — but in the rosters of the gangs, they were written down. Yakuza bosses from rival gangs also sent each other New Year's cards, as is part of Japanese tradition. A boss from the Sumiyoshi-kai might send greetings to a boss in the Matsuba-kai. Typically, but not always, they would send them to the headquarters. If you weren't plugged into the world of the yakuza, you didn't know those addresses.

Coach had been making discreet enquiries. Kiyota wasn't the only yakuza boss who had been kidnapped. A few months previously, the chairman of the Chojiya-kai, Goro Yoshida, had been kidnapped along with his wife and grandchild when they were on a walk.

Yoshida was a celebrity in the yakuza world, famous for his skills as a master of ceremonies in yakuza rituals. He had a punch perm and thick, gold-rimmed glasses, a wonderful voice, and a command of Shinto lore, real and imagined, that made him the most popular host for yakuza succession ceremonies, funerals, peace treaties, and related activities. It was as if the kidnappers had nabbed the yakuza version of Jimmy Kimmel.

The method of operation had been roughly the same, although Yoshida's grandchild and wife were not touched or harmed.

For Tsunami, it seemed that Coach had given him a mission that he was doomed to fail in. If he could have figured out a way not to take on the job, he would have done it. But he'd been asked to do it, and that was the same as being ordered to do it. And maybe it wasn't hopeless.

They had a clue to work with. An important clue.

Kiyota wasn't stupid. He kept his wits about him. When he was thrown in the trunk of a car, he listened carefully to the noises around him. The driver of the car was using an early car-navigation system, with voice guidance on. Kiyota listened to every notification, every turn, the sounds outside. The car got off at the Hadano Interchange on the National Highway 246, and stopped ten minutes from the interchange. That meant that, in all probability, he was in Hadano City in the Kanagawa prefecture. He was kept in the room for three days — it seemed to be a house. Every day at 5.00 pm, he was served a meal. At 5.00 pm, he heard the distinctive chimes of a school nearby. He was sure that he could recognize if he heard it again.

Most Tokyo wards and towns across Japan have a chime that sounds at exactly 5.00 pm (or earlier, depending on where you live). As the seasons change, some regions adjust the song and time they play, but most keep the same one at five o'clock.

The bells remind kids to get home, but that's not their main purpose. The sound systems are for emergency announcements, and the daily ringing lets the government and people in the area know that everything is fine and dandy. They're like siren tests in France, but in Japan it's a daily occurrence, rather than a weekly one, because of the high earthquake risks and other natural disasters. Due to how often the tests occur, it's thought that it's better to have a nice tune playing than a siren sound, which might alarm people.

And so Tsunami and his crew of about ten other yakuza began to survey the area near the Hadano intersection. They taped the sound of every chime at every school, and brought back the recordings. Kiyota listened to them until he identified the sound of the chime. There was only one school in the area, perhaps in the entire prefecture, using that melody.

Tsunami estimated that the bell could only be heard in a two-kilometer radius. Were there any yakuza living in the area? They began asking around, going house to house, and found one suspect. He was a low-ranking member of the Inagawa-Kai Odawara-gumi Shugetsu family. The family had fifty members and territory in the Tokyo and Kanagawa prefecture.

Tsunami reported back to Coach.

"We have one guy, but I can't say that he's the culprit. He may be completely unrelated. What do you want me to do?"

Coach told him, "Grab him. Bring him in. Get the answers."

Tsunami wasn't sure this was wise.

"What if he has nothing to do with it?"

"Ask him, and see what he does. If his face goes white as a sheet, you've got your man. You're good at reading people. Talk to him."

And so Tsunami went to the young man's house, along with several of his goons, and had them wait outside. It was an old house, not an apartment. It looked more costly than your typical young punk could afford.

Tsunami knew how to conduct an interrogation. At this point in time, nobody knew what had happened outside of the kidnappers, Kiyota, Coach, and Tsunami. That was important.

When Tsunami talked to the man, all the color faded from his face. Before Tsunami had even explained why he was there, the young thug became very nervous. Tsunami pressed him, "Why are you looking so pale?"

"Because I'm suspected of doing something unspeakable," the guy replied.

"Yeah, but there's no evidence. There's nothing linking you to it."

You know what I'm talking about, right?"

The young man nodded. All those years of dealing with the cops had taught Tsunami a few things.

The police always keep out of the papers and the public domain certain details of a crime to help weed out false confessions. This is called *bakuro no himitsu* (the secret that reveals the truth).

In his denials, the young man revealed things about the crime that only the criminal would have known — things that Tsunami hadn't told him.

He called Coach on the phone. He was given permission to apply pressure with extreme prejudice. They kidnapped the young man and took him to an abandoned house nearby, and turned up the heat. He confessed.

"I kidnapped him. I wasn't alone, but I did it. I did it."

When Saigo reported his findings back to Coach, he wasn't as happy as Saigo had imagined he'd be. There were some in the Inagawa-iai Yamakawa-Ikka who had already decided that another former yakuza must have been responsible. They handled it badly.


On September 18, twelve days after Kiyota was kidnapped, members of the Inagawa-kai had grabbed a former yakuza boss, Takeshi Tsukase, aged fifty-eight, and attempted to beat the truth out of him. It was half-baked vigilante justice.

Tsukase had been a member of the Kyokuto-kai crime group years before, when one of his men had broken into the home of a Sumiyoshi-kai boss, stolen the money, killed the boss, and made off with a very rare and expensive wristwatch.

The young yakuza had given the watch to Tsukase, his godfather, as a present, and Tsukase had worn it in public. It was known that there were only four watches of that particular make in Japan, and a

Sumiyoshi-kai member saw the watch. After a violent confrontation, the whole story came out. Tsukase's soldier was dealt with harshly, and Tsukase had to resign from the Kyokuto-kai in disgrace.

Members of the Inagawa-kai reasoned that since Tsukase had played a part in yakuza-on-yakuza crime before, surely he must be responsible for this new similar-seeming crime.

They snatched him from his restaurant in Yokohama, and tortured him. They cut off the middle, ring, and little fingers on his right hand at the first joint, and beat him severely with a baseball bat.

He didn't confess. At around 8.55 pm that day, they dumped him, bleeding and unconscious, in the parking lot of the Daiichi Hospital in Motoki 2-chome, Kawasaki-ku, Kawasaki City. One of the gangsters yelled at the doors of the emergency room, "There's someone dying in the parking lot," and fled.

Tsukase died shortly afterwards.

Tsunami was now telling Coach that the Inagawa-kai had maybe killed the wrong guy. That was bad. And to top it all off, the police had become aware of the kidnappings, and were running their own investigations now. There wasn't a lot of time to solve the case.

Coach told him, "Saigo, don't kill him. Ask him two things — who was the ringleader and who else was involved in the kidnapping. Then let him go."

The young man told Tsunami the truth. The person responsible for the kidnapping and possibly many others was the leader of the Shugetsu family. It was Kenzo Arai — a friend of Coach's. And there was another member of a different crime family involved, a mid-level boss from the Nibiki-Kai, named Kihara.

It turned out that the ex-yakuza, Tsukase, who had been killed had had nothing to do with the kidnappings. The whole thing was becoming very messy.

Coach called over to the offices of the Nibiki-Kai. He spoke to the man in charge. "One of your men, Kihara, has been involved in kidnapping a boss in our organization. That's not acceptable. I want you to grab him and hold him for questioning. I'll explain to you when I get there."

The boss assured Coach that that was exactly what they'd do. They didn't want a war with the Inagawa-Kai. After Coach arrived at the offices and interrogated the accomplice, he knew what he had to do. He was going to pay Kenzo Arai a visit.

At around 4.00 pm on October 5, Coach, accompanied by Tsunami and ten other yakuza, drove up to the office of the Shugetsu family in Odawara City and surrounded the building. They parked several black Mercedes-Benzes in front of, behind, and in the alleys around the office. Coach knocked on the door, and went in to have a talk with his blood brother in the organization.

Coach sat down with Arai and his number two in the organization. Hideyuki Eiri. Eiri, "a straight arrow," had no idea what his boss had been up to these many months.

"Ken-chan," Kanazawa (Coach), said to him, addressing him with familiarity, "the game is up. We all know what you did. We know. Soon the police will know. You kidnapped not only other yakuza, but you kidnapped your own people. There's no life left for you, Ken-chan. Not in this organization. Not in the outside world. Even if the cops get you first, you know that when you get out of jail, you're not going to make it in the straight world. It's all over."

Arai didn't deny anything. He simply nodded his head.

"Consider this the mercy of a samurai," Kanazawa told him. "Clean up your mess. Don't cause trouble to anyone else. You know what needs to be done. You understand, right?"

"I get it," Arai said. "Do me a favor, and spare the young one and Kihara. He was just following orders."

"I'll think about it," Kanazawa promised him. And, with that, he left.

After Coach had left, Eiri and Arai got into a furious argument. Eiri, who had had no part in the kidnappings, was outraged. There were certain things that were forbidden in the Inagawa-kai. Kidnapping? That was out of the question. That was for thugs.

Eiri was relentless, "What were you thinking? How can you even call yourself a yakuza? Kidnapping — that's against the code we have. It's against everything we are. And your own people?"

At 5.00 pm, Arai, at a loss for words, furious with his underling and perhaps disgusted with himself, took a gun out of his desk, and shot Eiri in the chest and then in the temple to finish him off.

Arai summoned his driver and left the headquarters immediately afterwards. When he arrived home, he told his underlings that he would be leaving the house soon, and told them all to wait outside at the front gate.

He made one more phone call to Coach.

"I just want you to know that none of this was done out of a personal grudge. It was all about the money. That's all it was ever about."

Coach told him, "Understood."

Arai didn't apologize, but he asked for a favor. "I'm the person responsible. I take responsibility, and I'm going to pay for it with my life. Let the others live."

Coach promised him that he would honor that request.

"Good," said Arai. "Maybe I'll see you in the next world."

And then he hung up and shot himself in the head with a revolver. When the police arrived minutes later, he was dead, the gun by his side.

The fourth investigative division, which handles organized crime, didn't know what to make of the case at first. However, when they began digging, the facts started coming to light.

In February 1996, the Kanagawa prefectural police arrested eight people for having nabbed Jiro Kiyota , on charges of kidnapping and robbery. The police investigation uncovered several other kidnappings, including one that had been faked by a member of the Nibiki-kai to allay suspicion of his involvement in the kidnappings.

Kenzo Arai was posthumously charged with murder, illegal possession of a firearm, and multiple violations of the guns and swords control act.

In the years that followed, Jiro Kiyota  rose to become the fifth-generation leader of the Inagawa-kai, retiring to his present-day ceremonial post as the supreme leader of the group. Kazuo Uchibori is the current leader of the Inagawa-kai.

There have been many scandals in the world of the yakuza, but this was one that people still fear to mention. Even to this day, the sequence of events is taboo to discuss, and in late 2021, a *kaibunsho*, a scandalous secret document revealing some details of what happened, began to circulate, haunting those who were involved.

The killers of Tsukase have never been caught, and probably never will be. He was collateral damage in a dark and terrible crime. The life of a yakuza is a perilous thing. Tsunami summed it all up the best.

"I read somewhere that when a bell tolls in the west, it means that someone has died. That's not what the chimes at 5.00 pm mean here in Japan, but since 1995, whenever I hear the melody, I can't help but think that someone, somewhere, is going to die. And if I'm not lucky, it might be me."

## CHAPTER EIGHTEEN

# Relapses and the rules of the game

Nineteen ninety-six was a year that had the Japanese people clucking about moral decline — at all levels of society. The newspapers and magazines were full of reports about compensated dating — *enjo kosai* — a euphemism for teenage prostitution. Young girls, mostly high school girls, had discovered they could make good money on the side by going on dates with older men, and even more money by having sex with them. The media portrayed the young women as clueless girls willing to sell their bodies to buy Louis Vuitton bags. It was never clear if this phenomenon was as widespread as originally reported, but the media made such a fuss about it that they may have ended up encouraging the business.

For the yakuza, the government probes into $350 billion worth of bad loans was making them all uncomfortable. In January, the Japanese Diet held hearings on the Ministry of Finance-brokered bailout of Japan's seven insolvent housing-loan corporations known as *jusen*. The *jusen* accounted for $65 billion of the bad loans, which included failed developments of everything from golf courses to apartment complexes.

There were many nervous yakuza fearing the government might come knocking on their door to collect the money that was owed. The bubble had long since burst, but the flood of bad tidings had not yet ceased. The bubble had been one long gambling binge by the entire country, and the yakuza had been playing the role of the house. Sometimes, though, even the house loses. Nobody's luck lasts forever.

Every now and then, Saigo would break down and go on a meth binge. However, his use was infrequent, and Coach would constantly remind him that he'd always be an addict, so "Don't delude yourself and think you can just go on an occasional binge."

That summer, Saigo was sitting in Coach's house after enjoying a nice home-cooked lunch when Coach ordered him to roll up his sleeves. Saigo did as he was told, revealing his tattoos from his elbows to his wrists. There weren't any needle marks, but Coach knew they were somewhere — so he made a bet. If Coach found needle marks, Saigo would give him 10,000 yen.

When the deal was secured, Coach laughed and ordered Saigo to roll up his pants. He immediately spotted the track marks near his feet, and made Saigo hand over 10,000 yen.

Then, very softly, he told Saigo that if he found him shooting up, he was going to snap the needle in half while it was still in Saigo's arm — and it would hurt like hell. He would have Saigo thrown in the trunk of his car that he would drive himself. And, as Saigo knew, Coach was a lousy driver.

Coach ordered Saigo to get new tattoos. The new tattoos would have Coach's name on them, and would be located where Saigo usually shot up. Coach explained his rationale: "Every time you want to shoot up, you'll see my name, and you'll know that you are dishonouring me and shaming yourself. Maybe it will make you think." He threw Saigo a wad of cash, and told him to get it done.

Saigo did as he was told, making his way back to Numazu. However, the tattoos were a little too much — too plain. They looked like stencils. He diplomatically complained to Coach that the tattoos made it look like he was the property of Coach — it was just weird. Saigo asked to blend the pattern in a little bit more with some other tattoo art. Coach agreed.

The little bit turned into a lot. When Coach saw the new tattoos, he was pissed off.

"It defeats the whole goddamn purpose. Go back and get the Inagawa-kai emblem tattooed in the center of your chest. And put my name in the corners of Mount Fuji or someplace. Every time you take off your shirt, I want you to remember who you are and who is counting on you to stay sober and straight."

And so Saigo went back. It's still there today: the Inagawa-kai emblem emblazoned on his chest, slightly covered up in gray chest hair. And if you look closely, you can see Coach's name carved into the landscape.

There were a set of rules that yakuza had to follow. In addition to this set, Coach had his own set of rules, which included no selling, buying, or using drugs. Coach wouldn't stand for it.

Coach asked Saigo if he knew what *ninkyodo* meant. Saigo had the Chinese characters of the word written in black cursive and hanging in a gold frame on his office wall. Still, Saigo hadn't the faintest idea. He felt embarrassed.

*Nin*, Coach explained, is one of the five Confucian virtues. It means to conquer oneself and think of the welfare of others. *Kyo* is the desire to help the weak and fight the strong.

According to Coach, that was what the yakuza were about. You help the weak and fight the strong, because it's the right thing to do. When you're asked to do something, you do it. When people put their trust in you, you don't betray them. That was how you built a reputation as an honorable man — not through guns or weapons.

Coach eyed Saigo. He suspected that Saigo was carrying a *dosu* (short knife), and ordered him to hand it over. Coach turned out to be right. Coach held the knife in his hands, weighing it. He ran his fingers along the grip, and felt the bumpy texture. Then, with a flick of his wrist, he threw it at Saigo. It struck the wall behind him with a thwacking sound, and stuck there. Saigo was frozen in place.

Coach pointed at Saigo and then at the short dagger behind him. The *dosu*, Coach said, was a prop that yakuza should only use if they were dealing with another yakuza or a common crook. It was something to bring to threaten an enemy with, and if the enemy didn't give in, a yakuza could slash their opponent's face with it.

Also, "Try not to get your own face slashed up," Coach advised. Many yakuza thought it was cool to have a scar on their face, because it showed they had had a fight with another yakuza. What Coach saw when he saw a yakuza with a slashed face was that the guy had been too slow to pull out his knife first. Some yakuza slashed their own faces so they would look more like a yakuza — more threatening.* "Your face is frightening enough as it is, though," Coach said.

Yakuza should dress well. Coach thought that if you projected success, you would become successful. He told Saigo to wear a good suit and to keep it pressed. He also needed to buy the best damn shoes he could find. A yakuza with dirty shoes didn't pay attention to detail. Coach offered Saigo a cigarette from the crystal box on the table between them, and Saigo lit up, inhaling deeply. Coach then handed Saigo 40,000 yen and ordered him to buy better shoes, preferably ones without laces. They were in Japan. He couldn't go around tying and untying his shoelaces all the time, or he'd block the door. Saigo was

---

\*   The slashed face of the yakuza had become rather iconic over the years. Many Japanese still refer to the yakuza silently by touching their index finger to their right cheek and drawing a slash mark downward — to show where the scar should be.

walking around in sneakers, and no yakuza bosses wore sneakers.

As Saigo turned to leave, Coach reminded him that his knife was still stuck in the wall, and ordered Saigo to take it with him. Saigo came back to the knife and yanked. He had to struggle a bit to pull it out of the wall.

As he stuffed it back into its holster, Coach said, very quietly, "If you buy any meth while you're out, or shoot up, I'm not going to miss the next time I throw a knife at your head. I know how to throw a strike, and I know how to throw a ball that'll knock your fat head off. If I throw a knife at your ear, I'll slice it off."

This incident marked Saigo's last major relapse. That same year, Hiroko was diagnosed with cancer. They had been together for about six years at this point. He bought her the best treatments he could afford. She was hospitalized frequently, so he would visit her every day, for at least ten to twenty minutes each time. The cancer treatment was supposed to be healing her, but it wasn't. That was the harsh truth of many treatments for cancer at the time — you didn't get better, but you did live longer.

# CHAPTER NINETEEN

# Coronation

Saigo officially became the *kobun* (child) of Coach on June 7, 1998. The Yokosuka-Ikka had their official *sakazuki* cementing father-son ties and creating new relations. For Saigo, it was one of the pinnacles of his life. Coach was now the eighth-generation leader of the Yokosuka-ikka, and, of the over 1,000 members, he was one of only fifteen senior members who could drink directly from the cup of the *oyabun*, elevating him to the upper echelon of the Inagawa-kai. Saigo was an executive director on the Inagawa-kai board and was still serving as Coach's secretary.

During this time, he was also undergoing interferon treatment for his hepatitis C. He'd been diagnosed with it in 1997. He was told that you could get it through blood infections, usually by sharing needles. Whether it was his own meth use or bad hygiene at the tattoo parlor that caused it, he didn't know, but he did know it could shorten your life span. The treatment was brutal; the side effects, significant. The treatment was making his hair fall out a little, but not too much. Interferon was expensive, but it was better than an early death.

Hiroko was still in the hospital as well. Since her diagnosis, she would stay ten months inside the hospital, and come back home for two months, and then go back to the hospital.

So while he felt elated to be attending the ceremony, he didn't feel well physically or mentally.

The lavish ceremony itself was held in the Kanagawa prefecture at an Inagawa-kai-owned event hall. Yoshio Tsunoda, the chairman of the board, presided over the ceremony. The participants, including Coach, were dressed in cream-colored *hakama* with the Inagawa crest on the front of the robe. All the others were in black suits with white shirts.

The ceremony was primarily an in-house event, held in a sixty-tatami-mat hall. The walls were adorned with names of well-wishers, written vertically in Japanese cursive, with the individual's name, rank, and group status clearly written out.

A long white cloth, serving as a red carpet of sorts, divided the room. On both sides, square blue or red pillows were laid out for the guest to sit upon. Yamada was among the attendees, dressed traditionally in a *hakama*. There was also a large notice on the wall that the arrangement was *shihoudouseki*, meaning "the same (level of) seats in four directions." Yakuza are very sensitive to rank, and it had to be clear that there was no pattern or meaning as to who sat where. This had to be done to ensure that no one felt slighted or disrespected. Otherwise, you might have Hishiyama feeling like he'd been called "Hishiyama-kun" because his seat was placed further from the altar than someone else.

At the best-planned yakuza events, every seat was a good seat.

The altar to Amanoterasu Okami was placed at the far end of the room against the wall. There were offerings of two madai fish, two bottles of sake in white porcelain bins, and fruits and vegetables, stacked upon each other or in elaborate displays, including a tower of apples that looked like they would fall over if anyone added a single extra apple. The ritual was conducted with great solemnity and with no talking among the 100 or so people assembled.

It was a religious ritual, and while few people there understood what the ritual meant or why the altar was arranged as it was, they did understand that it was not a jovial occasion. Not until the banquet started.

Saigo tried not to fall asleep as it was happening. Excitement was tinged with the sleepiness and fatigue that interferon treatment brings.

The ceremony was moderated by Akira Otomo, an executive boss in another Inagawa-kai family outside the Yokosuka-ikka. In his opening remarks, he apologized in advance for any slip of the tongue or unintentional rudeness on his part while conducting the proceedings. These prefatory remarks were much like the safety instructions given by flight attendants before a plane lifts off — no one really listens but, in the interests of safety and for CYA purposes, they were absolutely necessary. No matter how many years the emcee has been in the yakuza, he will always say, "I'm new to this business, and please forgive my lack of eloquence and etiquette. Please lend me your ears and support until the end of the ceremony."

Otomo then introduced Coach, noting, "This is the man who will be your parent — the eighth-generation leader of the Inagawa-kai and the board director of the Inagawa-kai advisory committee."

The Inagawa-kai had several committees, like any corporation, and being a director of at least one was important for status and for rising in the organization. Saigo hoped to attain a position sometime soon. Coach closed his eyes and nodded, solemnly, as he was introduced.

The emcee then introduced the Inagawa-kai members who would become the children of the *oyabun*, one by one. Of course, Inoue was there, his black hair now tinged with gray, looking very much like a

Buddhist priest in his traditional Japanese garb. There was no order of introduction, but Saigo was towards the end of the group, and his eyes lit up when his name was called.

The ritual had many honorary participants, including the official mediator, Tsunoda, who was the *waka-gashira* in the Inagawa-kai and the most senior representative at the event. If Yuko Inagawa himself had come, it would have been even more prestigious, but the big boss couldn't make every ceremony. In events like this, the more people who had some sort of title and function in the event, the happier everyone was.

The reading of all the names and honorees itself went on for twenty minutes. Finally, the ritual started, and in a few minutes a large cup of sake in a white porcelain cup, placed on a wooden cup-holder, was brought to Tsunoda, who inspected it and pronounced it "fine." Then it was taken to Coach. He drank from the cup once, gritted his teeth, and returned the cup to the wooden holder, which was then taken back to the presiding Shinto priest. The Shinto priest and Coach made the required exchange of greetings.

A purified bowl of sake was then divided into fifteen cups, brought before the intermediary, Tsunoda, who approved them, and then distributed to "the children."

In the video of the ceremony, made by an Inagawa-kai front company, the distribution of the sake cups is choreographed to mystical Japanese music that soars with drums and the sound of the Japanese flute. Each member sits in the *seiza* position as they adjust their legs and take their sake. The tattoos on Saigo's arms are briefly visible as he reaches for the cup.

The priest addressed them all. "I know that you have all spent years training in your profession. Therefore, no other remarks are needed. Please drink deeply from the sake cup in three sips and then place it within your pockets."

In unison, they all drank their cups dry, to a spattering of applause, and then wrapped the cups within white paper provided and tucked them deep into the inner chest pockets of their robes.

They all turned to face their new *oyabun* and bowed deeply from a seated position, saying, "*Yoroshiku onegai shimasu.*"* Coach bowed back.

It was done. Coach was now Saigo's *oyabun*. He and Inoue were also now both direct *kobun* of the Coach. For a yakuza, Saigo thought, there could be nothing better than an *oyabun* who you truly felt loyal to. Coach had been a strict boss, and would always be a strict boss, but he had gotten Saigo off meth, had never given up on him, and Saigo felt he owed the man his life. He felt he owed Inoue as well. He thought of Inoue as his older brother, and without him he would have never joined the Inagawa-kai.

If it hadn't been for Coach, he would have been kicked out of the Inagawa-kai and ended up either in prison or dead — he was sure of it. It was one of the happiest days of his life.

The banquet was held in the same hall, with a multitude of attractive women in kimonos pouring the beer or sake, and making small talk with the yakuza in attendance. For a few moments, Saigo thought of his first wife and the daughter he hadn't seen in years. Would they be proud to see how far he'd risen? He didn't think about it too much — it made everything taste bitter. He drank as little as possible. It wasn't good for his liver, and it didn't go well with interferon.

As he was leaving the hall, Coach stopped him. He had some good news for Saigo. He was going to grant him more territory to watch over. More territory meant more money.

The after-party was full of good food, and, again, attractive women in kimonos poured beer and sake for the men. He hoped Inoue

---

\* This is a standard Japanese greeting that means anything and everything between "Please help me out" and "Nice to meet you."

would behave himself. When the man got drunk, he was amusing but uncontrollable. However, this time Inoue was well-behaved.

It was an auspicious day indeed.

## CHAPTER TWENTY

# Ice-cream dreams

The summer of 1998 was dominated by news of the poisoned-curry murders in Wakayama City. On July 25, at a summer festival, sixty-seven people who had eaten the curry suffered severe nausea and cramps. Most were taken to a nearby hospital.

Four of them died: a sixty-four-year-old man, a fifty-four-year-old man, a sixteen-year-old girl, and a ten-year-old boy. At first, the local health office thought it was a case of food poisoning. Then the Wakayama Police Department did a forensic analysis of vomit left at the scene, and found that arsenic had been mixed into the curry. Someone had poisoned it.

The incident put a damper on people's enthusiasm for summer festivals and for curry in general. The Japanese are very fond of both. Curry was introduced to Japan before World War II, and was adapted to suit the Japanese palate. It was a household staple. Retro curry lasted forever in sealed vacuum packs. All you had to do was heat it up, open the package, and toss it on rice.

But nobody wants to eat instant poison. Food companies refrained from airing curry commercials. Japan's ubiquitous cooking shows dropped curry from the menu. Even the popular manga about a dysfunctional family in Urayasu-city (*Urayasu Tekkin Zoku*) dropped a storyline that had curry prominently mentioned in it. It would be months before a suspect was even named in the media. To everyone's surprise, the suspect turned out to be a rather portly woman with a history of insurance fraud.

Saigo didn't like curry. But he did like festivals.

Festivals, as noted before, have always been a good source of revenue for *tekiya*, but the association of them with physical illness and death damaged their reputation. Even if no one was serving curry at the festivals, any little incident of food poisoning, funny-tasting food, and/or suspicious behavior was enough to start a news feeding frenzy. People were wary, and stayed away. This meant lower revenue in the form of kickbacks from the *tekiya* was going to be bad for everyone.

The *tekiya* sold cheap toys, plastic samurai swords, candy cigarettes, balloons, and trinkets at festivals, but their real money came from the food stands: fried octopus chunks in batter (*takoyaki*), fried noodles, rice-balls, cotton candy, Japanese pizza (*okonomiyaki*), and curry rice.

If they couldn't sell their food and wares, Saigo couldn't reasonably hope to get a cut of their earnings. He ran the festivals on his turf. The merchants, even if they were members of his own group, had to rent the space. The term for this type of renting was *shobadai*, a deliberately inverted form of the word *bashodai* (rental-space fees). It was a cozy arrangement that the poisoned-curry incident had made relatively unprofitable.

But this year, Saigo was lucky enough to have a new place to try to make some money.

Coach had given Saigo control of Zushi and Hamaya, two prime beach areas in the Kamakura region. Zushi and Hayama had always been part of the Yokosuka-ikka's turf. He needed to make sure it stayed that way.

Kamakura had once been the capital of Japan, and was still blessed with a huge number of Buddhist temples, long-standing wooden buildings, corporate resort hotels, and some of the best beaches in Tokyo. However, even with all the tourists coming to visit each year, and with all the hotels and resorts, it wasn't a great place to make money. The income was very seasonal, and the locals weren't used to paying protection money. Nor were the local police very tolerant of yakuza asking the locals to pay up.

Sooner or later, Saigo knew Coach would want a kickback on any money that Saigo's group made from their turf, and if he wasn't making any money, the new territories would be nothing more than a new financial drain.

Saigo had already had to call in some favors and put ten of his men into an office in the area to make sure their presence was known. Those days, if you didn't tend to your garden, the weeds — the weeds being the Yamaguchi-gumi — would quickly sprout up and take root. That would not do.

In late June, he was driving towards the beach to get a report from his gang when he got caught in a massive traffic jam near Zushi, on the road along the beach.

As he was sitting in the car, thirsty, hungry, hot, and angry, he noticed a kid in opposing traffic happily eating an ice-cream cone. Chocolate ice-cream. It looked damn good.

As he gazed across the ocean of cars in front of him, moving at a snail's pace, it flashed on him: ice-cream. He could sell ice-cream to people caught in traffic jams. Maybe drinks, too. Possibly beer. People would buy. He would have a captive market.

He had his lieutenants locate an ice-cream wholesaler and gather ten motorcycles and riders. The plan was for them to carry the ice-cream in cooler boxes on the motorcycles, and have the riders carry the ice-cream to the cars stuck in the traffic jam. The coolers would also contain cans of soda, water, and beer.

There was some resistance. When he gathered the troops in their makeshift office in Zushi, and had them sit down in the deck chairs assembled in the mostly empty room, the reaction was an overwhelming silence.

The newly designated ice-cream vendors were mostly former motorcycle gang members. Most of them had never worked an honest day in their lives, but that was okay. They had driving skills. You had to be able to drive well to weave in and out of the traffic — it moved suddenly and unpredictably.

Selling things on the streets was a time-honored yakuza tradition. And Saigo thought it was probably illegal to do it, so that was even better. Granted this contradicted his belief that his crew should be on top of the law to find and utilize the loopholes, but sometimes people contradict themselves. His group would probably have to have a license, and they wouldn't bother to get it. After putting some thought into it, he also decided that — in principle — they wouldn't sell cans of beer where there was only one person riding. That would encourage drunk driving. Even yakuza don't like drunk drivers.

The problem was where to store the ice-cream. There was a meatpacking plant on his new turf, and Saigo convinced the owner to let him store the ice-cream there. And that went well at first.

The riders would check into the plant in the morning, load up on ice-cream and drinks, and sell their goods to the drivers of cars stuck in the endless traffic jams along the 10 kilometers between Zushi and Hayama city.

They would slide into the traffic, come up to the side of the cars, gently tap on the windows, and ask the drivers if they cared for some ice-cream. Hanzawa was especially good at this. He liked weaving in and out of traffic. And he was a surprisingly good salesman. Saigo had instructed all of his men to be exceedingly polite and to be careful not to make their words sound like a shakedown. It went surprisingly smoothly.

The problem was that by storing the ice-cream among the frozen flesh, it absorbed some of the smell and taste of meat, and people complained about it.

Clearly, that wouldn't work. Saigo ended up investing in ten large cooler boxes, industrial strength, for each motorcycle. The guys would pick up their ice-cream from a local wholesaler in the morning, put the ice-cream in the oversized boxes, and sell until they ran out.

This went well, and they were making up to $1,000 a day (100,000 yen), but some people wouldn't buy the ice-cream — even though they clearly wanted it. And so Saigo thought about it some more.

What was the problem with ice-cream? It melted. And people feared that when the ice-cream melted, it would get their car dirty, and Japanese people love the interiors of their cars. Even if you licked the cup clean, you'd still have a sticky mess when you were done.

So Saigo decided to hand out small vinyl bags with all the ice-cream.

Sales boomed. Even after expenses and paying salaries, he was bringing in sometimes as much as 300,000 yen ($3,000) a day — in pure profit — from ice-cream sales. It was almost a legitimate job.

The value of drink sales — including canned cocktails — were closing in on another $1,000 a day after a month in business. Saturdays were the best. Revenue would almost double, as many young couples made their way to the beach.

He called his old band member, Maruyama, and had him set up a ramen stand on the beach. Maruyama had been hanging around Saigo's offices more and more, but he wasn't a full-time member of the Saigo-gumi. He was more of a yakuza associate who still worked as a musician.

The ramen was great. Maruyama had really mastered the art of making a good pork-bone broth over the years. He would make three kinds of spicy ramen, including the super gaman ramen special, to which he would add a special Japanese black pepper mix, wasabi, tabasco sauce, Indian curry powder, and chinese peppers. That particular ramen bowl was gross — but also a was a challenge. If you could finish the whole bowl, you didn't have to pay for it. It was a classic appeal to the Japanese love of *gaman kurabe*.

They were creating a little beach-food empire.

Saigo was in good spirits. He'd drive up to the ramen stand, where Maruyama would be playing the hits of the summer, and watch his men selling ice-cream to the passing cars. As he was sitting on a bench near the ramen stand, slurping his noodles, listening to the cheerful sounds of female pop duos, he felt like the world was on one long summer vacation. He wanted to hum along with the music. He liked the lyrics; the whole song was about living life doing things you liked to do, getting by and having fun. He was also visiting Soaplands during this time. Hiroko was in the hospital all the time. He loved her, but he couldn't wait that long to get laid.

The good times didn't last long.

The police began rounding up his salesmen for violating traffic laws. Speeding, weaving in and out of traffic — whatever minor infractions they could come up with. The fines began to add up.

There were problems with the locals as well.

One of his men made the mistake of stopping the car of Chairman Ishii's daughter, and tried to sell her ice-cream. She was not amused.

"What yakuza group are you with?" she immediately demanded as soon as one of the young punks knocked on the window of her foreign car. His man spilled the beans, and a complaint was lodged with headquarters. There was no way for Saigo's underling to know he'd tapped the window of the daughter of a legendary yakuza. But it didn't go over well.

Meanwhile, the police kept amping up the number of arrests. Saigo was still making money, but the losses were mounting each month. As the temperature cooled down, so did the ice-cream sales.

He managed to keep the business running through the entire summer, but then, in early October, he got a call directly from a detective at the police department in Zushi.

The call was short and blunt. The imperial family had a vacation home in Zushi, and the cops were not going to tolerate a bunch of yakuza running an illegal ice-cream business in the area.

He was given an ultimatum: close up shop, or go to jail on whatever charges the police came up with.

And, just like that, Saigo's dreams of running another semi-legitimate business melted away — and so did his revenue of $75,000 to $90,000 a month.

To make matters worse, Coach broadly hinted that he expected a cut of the earnings on the territory — about $2,000 a month. That would have been nothing if the ice-cream business hadn't been liquidated.

Saigo ended up returning the territory to his boss. And Coach was offended. Nobody gave territory back. Coach told Saigo he'd never give him another new piece of turf again.

But that was fine by him. Machida was where he lived, and Machida was enough territory for him. Machida was his home. It was where his family and Hiroko lived. He needed to be with her more than ever.

But even his turf in Machida would go sour in a few years's time — like ice-cream that had been stored in a meat locker for way too long.

# CHAPTER TWENTY-ONE

# Death at a funeral

Two thousand and one should have been a great year for the Inagawa-kai and the Yokosuka-Ikka in particular. The man they had been supporting, Junichiro Koizumi, who had also been born in Yokosuka, became prime minister of Japan. It should be noted that while is not that unusual for Japanese politicians to have yakuza ties, in the good old days, yakuza themselves even served as ministers in Japanese governments. The grandfather of Junichiro Koizumi was a member of a yakuza group later absorbed into the Inagawa-kai as the Yokosuka Ikka. During his term serving as the minister of general affairs, he was lovingly known as Irezumi Daijin, or "the tattooed minister."

The Inagawa-kai played an active part in getting Junichiro Koizumi elected to the National Diet and keeping his scandals in check. No one was surprised in 2004 when the weekly magazine *Friday* revealed that his campaign manager for most of his political career, Kiyoshi Takeuchi, was a former Inagawa-kai member and had been close friends with Susumu Ishii, the second-generation leader of the Inagawa-kai.

Koizumi's political base in Yokosuka was the center of the Yokosuka-ikka's turf. Reportedly, when Koizumi was starting out his political career, a reporter asked him, "Did you receive your political education from your grandfather?" Koiziumi jokingly replied, "No, all I ever learned from him was how to play *Hanafuda*." It was a witty allusion to his grandfather's yakuza past. *Hanafuda* is also the card game that the yakuza love.*

Saigo also did favors for local politicians already in office. Having political connections helped keep the police off their back. In general, their relationship with the local cops was exceptional. Saigo understood that as long as his gang suppressed street crime and didn't engage in it, all was good. Pissing off the cops was bad for *shinogi*.

But killing people, even other yakuza, that was always a bad move. The costs could be exceptionally high.

It was August 18, 2001, and a Saturday night. Saigo could think of other places he'd rather be than at the wake of a Sumiyoshi-kai boss, from the Kogo Mutsumi-kai faction, in the run-down district of Katsushika. There were nearly 700 gangsters in attendance, all cramped into the funeral hall. The area around the Yotsugi Funeral Home was besieged by black cars parked wherever space was available. Their parking lot had long been filled. Some people had come in

---

* Nintendo itself began as a Hanafuda card-maker. Gunpei Yokoi, the famed inventor behind the Game Boy, notes that one his first duties at Nintendo during the 1960s was to check the machines producing hanafuda cards. According to *The History of Nintendo*, Yokoi said, "This duty was important since these cards were often used for gambling." Faulty cards could be used to cheat. According to *The History of Nintendo*, Yokoi said, "People from the local mafia would often come to Nintendo, very angry." The speculation is that they had lost money and were blaming the faulty cards. The Japanese character *Nin* in *Nintendo* may even come from *Nin* in *Ninkyodo* — the noble path espoused by the yakuza.

microbuses. Representatives from every major organized crime group in the country were in attendance.

Death is part and parcel of the yakuza life — and so are funerals. An enormous amount of money and time is spent on them. Perhaps the yakuza's preference for black suits is due to the fact that it remains the appropriate funeral attire. Inagawa-kai boss Kenji Miyamoto once said, "A major part of becoming a full-fledged yakuza executive is learning how to behave at a funeral. To know the customs, the rituals, the right way to light incense, when to bow, and how to stay awake during the services."

Death is in some ways the lifeblood of the yakuza — it keeps the chain of command fresh, and reminds the troops of the cost of failure. Funerals raise funds for the organization, and provide a safe haven for gang members of differing groups to meet. For example, when a Matsuba-kai boss dies, members of the Inagawa-kai, Yamaguchi-gumi, Sumiyoshi-kai, Tosei-kai (Toakai), and other organizations will come to the funeral to pay their respects to the deceased and to each other.

Funerals are demilitarized zones where even warring gang factions can greet each other and thus possibly keep the peace.

The funerals are social occasions, tremendous fundraisers, and displays of power. During a funeral, several hundred high-end automobiles, often black Mercedes, park nearby, while hundreds of thuggish bodyguards stand out the front of the hall. The whole display reminds the world that the yakuza have a small army. Even after the anti-organized crime laws went on the books, the ostentatious ceremonies continued for years.

While the rules of the last rites vary some, they remain remarkably similar across Japanese culture — for civilians and yakuza. In Japan, most funerals are Buddhist, while most weddings are Shinto or pseudo-Christian. The funerals are elaborate ceremonies, often broken up into three parts: a wake, called the *tsuya* ("passing the night"), the actual funeral (*sogi*), and the *kotsuhiroi* (cremation), which involves both the cremation and picking up the bones from the ashes and transferring them into an urn. But even before the funeral, folk tradition dictates a number of esoteric things that must be done.

The prevailing rule of many of these elaborate rituals is *sakasagoto* — things done in reverse. The idea is that since death is the opposite of life, the dead should be treated the opposite of the way they were treated while living. For instance, the futon of the corpse is upside down.

When a person dies, if family members surround them, someone wets the person's lips with a chrysanthemum leaf — or, these days, a cotton ball soaked in water. This is the last drink — the "death water."

Traditionally, the dead are bathed in cold water that is warmed up. The dead body is soaked in a tub, washed clean by the family, and then dressed in white cloth. The ceremony parallels the birth of a child into the world — and marks the sending of the deceased to the new world. In postwar Japan, this ceremony has sometimes been performed by the *kobun* of a yakuza boss, not his own family.

Before putting the man or woman in their final clothes, the body is prepared. A man's face is shaved; a woman has make-up applied. They are dressed in a white kimono, with the left side of the kimono placed under the right — which is the opposite way that living people close their kimonos. When done by the book, a cloth wallet is hung around the neck with six coins inside. This is the fare for crossing the Sanzu River, which runs between this world and the next world. Those who cross it get to heaven or a good place. Those who drift off course end up riding to hell.

Japan has experienced relatively little inflation in recent decades. Even so, it's remarkable that the cost of crossing over has remained at six coins for longer than anyone can remember — or at least anyone under 92.

Sometimes, the white kimono has Buddhist texts written on it — to purify the soul so the person can be reborn in heaven.

Nowadays, many people just dress the deceased in the clothes they most liked when they were still alive. If it's a yakuza boss, they're said to be buried with their favorite weapon, although that's probably an urban legend. The body of the deceased is laid out with their head, resting on a pillow, facing north. Next to the pillow is a small altar where people place an incense burner, food (rice), a bell, water, rice dumplings, lighted candles, and a star anise plant. The rice and water are food for the spirits on their journey to give them strength. The candles light the way. The scent of the anise tree wards off evil spirits that might want to attack the dead on their journey.

The wake is simplified nowadays, and called a *han-tsuya* — a half-wake.* The ceremony lasts for roughly two hours, sometimes more, while a Buddhist priest chants text. People eat, drink, and talk to each other. The mood is relaxed and less solemn.

The traditional full wake (*tsuya*) requires family members to stay awake with their deceased all night, keeping the incense sticks lit, and the room lit up until the funeral services in the morning.

The all-night vigil is a mystery. Anyone who tells you they know the real reason it exists doesn't know what they're talking about. Some believe it's to make sure the deceased are really dead. Some believe it's to make sure evil spirits don't enter the body or disrupt the soul's passage to the next world. Some believe it's a throwback to an ancient ceremony when people would spend days praying for the dead to come back alive and would only accept the reality of the passing when they saw the body began to rot.

For most people, the wake is the preferred venue for paying their respects. It can be done at night after finishing up at the office; coming

---

\* Oddly appropriate, since most people are only half-awake after spending a night at one of these services.

and going is more casual. A funeral eats into the working day.

The funeral and wake have many things in common. You have to bring *koden*, which is an incense offering in the form of money. It's more commonly known as a funeral offering. The visitors give an envelope with cash to a receptionist as they enter, who notes down the name, the amount, and the address of the giver.

The mourners enter the temple room where the body is laid out. They burn incense to pray to the dead or the Buddhas. The incense comes in sticks or powder. A Buddhist priest chants sutras, usually while beating a drum, or while someone else beats a drum, and one by one, starting with immediate family, people go forth and light incense. The last to burn the incense are the friends of the deceased, in order of their closeness to the dead. Figuring out the order of giving incense at a yakuza funeral can be a tremendously complex task.

The way the incense is lit, and the number of times the incense is lit, also depends on the Buddhist sect. Some sects require that mourners sprinkle a pinch of incense powder over a charcoal fire three times. This action symbolizes the three treasures of Buddhism: the Buddha, the teachings, and the brotherhood; and the burning of the three poisons of human existence: desire, anger, and delusion.

The fire of the incense is kept going for hours after the funeral. The Japanese believe that the spirits of the dead take a forty-nine-day trip from our world to the netherworld — and that they are judged during this trip for what they did in this world. The incense keeps the spirits of the dead protected while they are in limbo.

Finally, the body is taken to the crematorium, where it is reduced to chunky ashes. Before the ashes are interned in a grave, the collected family members sort through them and pull out the bone fragments with chopsticks and pass them around, chopstick to chopstick. This practice makes Japanese people reluctant to pass things from chopsticks to chopsticks when eating.

The Japanese funeral and the metaphysical world in Japanese culture reflects a worldview similar to that expressed in *The Tibetan Book of the Dead*, a classic of Tibetan Buddhism — and many places in Asia where Mahayana Buddhism has taken root. Many believe that the last judgment comes on day forty-nine, when Enma, the King of Hell (Supreme Judge) decides where to send the spirit. On this final day, more prayers are held — probably in a last-minute effort to get a lenient sentence. After this, and one more large payment to the Buddhist priest — a sort of backdoor bribe to Enma — the period of mourning is over.

The rules of the traditional ceremony, and the relevant etiquette, are crucial at a funeral, but the most important thing to remember is that, usually, it's all about the money.

If you don't bring money, or don't bring enough money, you're going to leave a bad impression. Death is not cheap, and the priest and the gods must be paid.

Saigo and Coach had each brought envelopes stuffed with cash: Coach, 200,000 yen ($2,000), and Saigo, 100,000 yen. It wasn't one of their own people, after all.

The police were visibly present. Saigo noticed some of the Sumiyoshi-kai members going up to them and making chitchat. "Hey, officer, I legally parked my car there, so don't ticket it." The cops would joke back with them. There was very little tension. The police might as well have been providing security for a rock concert.

The organized crime cops, most of them in plain clothes, were standing near the parking lots, smoking cigarettes, and catching up with some of the mid-level gangsters. Sometimes, the cops lit the cigarettes of the bosses; sometimes, the bosses lit the cigarettes of the cops. There wasn't much meaning in who lit whose cigarette, but later, among themselves, some yakuza would talk of feeling jealous if "their detective" had lit the cigarettes of other yakuza, but not *their* cigarettes. The relationships between the cops and the yakuza sometimes seemed not far removed from the interaction between a hostess and her customer. Depending on how you looked at it, the yakuza were the customer and the police the hostesses. After all, what's an organized crime cop going to do without organized crime cases to investigate?

Back then, the organized crime cops dressed a lot like the yakuza themselves, but you could usually tell them apart by their wristwatches and the cigarettes they were smoking. The cops tended to smoke cheap made-in-Japan brands, such as Mild Seven, Golden Bat, Hope, and Peace. The Yakuza smoked imported brands such as Lucky Strikes, Dunhills, and Marlboro. But, as in everything, people don't always do what they're expected to do. Saigo smoked short Hopes; Lucky smoked Lucky Strikes. The lines between the yakuza cops and the yakuza were often blurry.

This Sumiyoshi-kai boss had died a natural death, and had been in the prime of his career. Saigo and Coach had come to pay their respects. The Sumiyoshi-kai and the Inagawa-kai had been at peace for years, and shared a common enemy: those yakuza barbarians from the west, the Yamaguchi-gumi.

Coach had been in a rather jovial mood on the car ride over. There were too many funerals to get weepy every time. He wore his sunglasses, even though it was already turning to dusk. Saigo saw a cop he knew on the street; they nodded to each other.

Saigo was dressed well. He wore a black suit, silk white shirt, black tie, and good leather shoes that had been made by hand in a little shop in Ginza. His shoes shone brightly enough to refract the candlelight.

Coach had a thing about shiny shoes and footwear maintenance. In Japanese slang, taking the measure of a man and assessing his real value is called *ashimoto wo miru* — to look at the feet (footwear) of a person. Coach would tell you that if a man was wearing cheap or dirty shoes, he had no sense of decorum, didn't pay attention to detail, or had no money. Saigo's older brothers in the gang told him that if you watched someone's feet when they walked or fought, you'd also know how to beat them in combat.

August 2001 was a good time to be a yakuza; their numbers had been rising since 1995. There were now 84,400 yakuza: 43,100 members and 41,300 associates. The Yamaguchi-gumi, the Inagawa-kai, and the Sumiyoshi-kai had 70 percent of them.

Money was good. Saigo's organization had grown to 150 members. He could afford good black-leather shoes. But his shoes weren't as good as Coach's. That would have been disrespectful.

Saigo and Coach entered the Yotsugi facilities together. Coach led and Saigo followed, walking past the lower-level yakuza standing along the road to the main hall. They were all wearing black suits with their organization's pin on their suit pockets. Most of them had short haircuts. Many of them recognized Coach and bowed deeply, muttering "Osu" or another form of greeting. Behind the rows of yakuza, standing towers of flowers lined the path to the hall. They had been sent by yakuza and local merchants as a sign of respect.

As Saigo was looking for a seat in the main hall, he caught a glimpse of Kazumi Yoshikawa, an Inagawa-kai member from the Gunma prefecture. He was with a twenty-nine-year-old gangster named Yoshio from Utsunomiya in the Tochigi prefecture. Both of them were members of the Omaeda-ikka faction, one of the most militant factions in the Inagawa-kai. Saigo hadn't expected to see Yoshikawa at the funeral. Maybe Yoshikawa knew the deceased boss. Saigo walked over to say hello, but Yoshikawa quickly vanished into the crowd, Yoshio with him. Saigo didn't think much of it; he didn't know either of them well.

When it was Saigo and Coach's turn, they went to the altar together. Coach bowed deeply to the family of the Sumiyoshi-kai boss and then to the priest. He bowed once deeply to the altar, put his hands together, picked up a pinch of the powdered incense with one hand, lifted it to eye level, and scattered it on the incense burner three times.

Clearly, the purification only worked for the spirits of the dead, Saigo thought to himself, because while Coach wasn't delusional, he could be a greedy and angry old man.

Saigo sprinkled the incense once and took out his rosary, with the Inagawa-kai emblem, and mumbled a barely remembered Buddhist incantation. He didn't believe in this crap, but Inoue, who was absent that day, did. Saigo had learned all he knew about Buddhism, and more than he wanted to know, from Inoue.

The priests chanted endlessly, the Zen bell with its clear tones and deep bass beat was rung ceaselessly, and the incense wafted from the burners. It was like a Buddhist rave, where everything was done in slow motion. He was used to it.

Another day, another death.

As the two of them left, Saigo saw Yoshikawa near the entrance of the hall. Yoshikawa put his hand over his organization badge on his chest, made eye contact, nodded politely, and stepped back into the hall.

Around 6.00 pm, some senior members of the Sumiyoshi-kai began exiting the hall. There were two bosses in particular whom people seemed to be watching: fifty-two-year-old Ikuo Kumagawa and fifty-seven-year-old Takashi Endo, with their accompanying lackeys.

Kumagawa had just finished lighting incense and paying his respects to the dead, and as he crossed towards the threshold of the hall onto the path to the entrance at approximately 6.10 pm, two people began moving.

As Kumagawa and company stepped outside the hall, Yoshikawa and Yoshio, both wearing black suits and fitted with Sumiyoshi-kai badges — not their Inagawa-kai badges — stepped close, pulled out their guns, and began to fire. Young Yoshio almost fell over from the blowback of the gun, not having much experience of firing one before. The shots were so loud that the chanting stopped. The funeral bell was longer being rung ceaselessly — only the ringing remained, fading into the sounds of the gunshots.

Five shots at close range.

One shot hit Endo fully in the upper right-hand side of his chest, knocking him on his back. The floor below him became a crimson, sticky pool in seconds. He would be dead shortly after midnight. The second shot hit the right knee of Kumagawa's bodyguard, making him fall to the ground. The third went into Kumagawa's right-hand rib cage, causing him to spin around and fall. The fourth shot hit his head. The fifth shot went wild.

Immediately, the other Sumiyoshi-kai members grabbed Yoshikawa and Yoshio, and began beating the crap out of them. Someone grabbed their guns. The two of them were dragged into a car while hordes of other yakuza blocked the police from following.

Within minutes, police cars swarmed to the scene, as did people living in the neighborhood and journalists. One local said, "I thought it was fireworks at first. Then I saw all the yakuza and all the yakuza cars. There were 100 people or so in a circle inside the funeral parlor entrance. Yep. It wasn't fireworks."

The Kogo Mutsumi-kai members dragged the two Inagawa-kai members to a car and took them to the Sumiyoshi-kai Kogomutusmi-kai office in Akasaka. They stripped off their clothes, ripped off their badges, and began interrogating them. They both had tattoos. Yoshikawa had the Inagawa-kai mark emblazoned on his body. At this point, to the Sumiyoshi-kai, this was an act of war.

One of the Sumiyoshi-kai yakuza made a call to Coach. They were brothers, *kyodaibun*. Saigo answered the phone (as that was his job). When he heard the voice of a Sumiyoshi-kai member on the phone, he immediately understood everything.

Yoshikawa and his disciple had snuck into the funeral dressed as mourners — dressed as members of the Sumiyoshi-kai. Whatever had happened, it couldn't have been good.

Saigo handed the phone over to Coach, silently wishing he'd realized what was going on at the time. Coach answered the phone with some puzzlement, and then nodded as he spoke. Saigo looked at his face in the back mirror. The sunglasses may have hidden Coach's eyes, but not his face, which had turned slightly pale — not ghostly pale, but pallid. Saigo couldn't make out what the other boss was saying, but he could hear the anger in the muffled static.

"Look," said Coach, "I understand. Just don't kill them. Beat them half to death, break their arms, break their legs. Do what you want — but if you kill them, we'll never know what happened. And the cops will not be happy either. Turn them over to the police."

The voice on the other end of the phone didn't seem convinced. Coach assured the other party that the men were just the bullets, and what Coach and his caller needed to do was find the person who had really pulled the triggers — who gave the orders. If they killed the men now, they might never know.

That seemed to ring true to the caller, who then promised to turn the two over to the police. And thus a very long night began. It looked like it would be the start of a gang war — an epic gang war between the Sumiyoshi-kai and the Inagawa-kai.

Coach made several calls. Saigo drove him to several places. By midnight, the top executives of the Inagawa-kai had all gathered at their Roppongi headquarters. The discussion as to what to do continued for hours. There was no doubt that the Inagawa-kai, particularly the Omaeda-ikka, was in the wrong.

One executive pointed out that even in war, there are rules. You don't attack ambulances. You don't shoot the Red Cross. Yakuza were not supposed to attack each other at weddings or funerals. It's inauspicious, and it's bad manners.

There was then a long debate about whether shooting a rival yakuza at a wedding was actually unacceptable. However, since there were no women in the yakuza — meaning that the bride was always non-yakuza, and almost all marriage ceremonies included a bride — there was always the danger that the bride or her family or other non-yakuza would be killed, which was unacceptable. This ended the debate.

As they were driving away, Coach went into his familiar lamentations about the evil of *dogu* (tools), yakuza slang for guns.

"Saigo, I'm predicting that guns will bring it all down. We're going to shoot ourselves to death with those things. No yakuza should use a gun."

Saigo protested meekly. If all the other yakuza are using guns, then the team who doesn't will lose the war, he said.

"Then it isn't worth winning," Coach said.

"If you can light a cigarette with a Zippo, you can fire a gun. You point, and you move your finger. That doesn't take courage. It's not hard. The only thing that's hard is getting away. If you're going to take someone's life, it should take more energy than lighting a cigarette. That's what I think."

The Sumiyoshi-kai turned over the two badly beaten Inagawa-kai members to the Kameari police department. The newspapers reported it as if the gangsters had turned themselves in for the killing, but that was not true. They had been turned over. Dropped off like baggage.

The Organized Crime Control Division (known as Investigative Section 4 at the time) came to the station from the Tokyo Metropolitan Police headquarters, and made an emergency arrest for violations of the firearms and sword control laws, murder, and attempted murder.

The two yakuza told the police, "We did it. We shot Kumagawa," but they would not answer why. They claimed to have done it on their own initiative, and didn't explain their motives. The others had been collateral damage, they said.

The settlement was not quickly reached. For several days, tensions were high, and it looked very much like war would break out. Saigo watched Coach 24/7. Coach had close ties with the general director of the Sumiyoshi-kai, which made him a natural as a negotiator. However, being in the position of the negotiator made him a target for disgruntled members of the Sumiyoshi-kai.

While Saigo was driving Coach through Sumiyoshi-kai turf one day, dark-suited Sumiyoshi-kai members suddenly blocked the road and stared at the two of them. There was silence, and then they walked to the side, and Saigo drove on. Even while driving past them, he could visualize one of them pulling out a gun and shooting him in the head at close range.

Coach pretended not to care, and buried his head in the book he was reading.

After they were out of range, Coach said jokingly, "Saigo, don't worry. If anything happens to you or the car, I'll make sure that the Sumiyoshi-kai financially compensates me." Both the car and Saigo were Inagawa-kai property, after all.

The Sumiyoshi-kai and the Inagawa-kai finally agreed to call a truce. The conditions were simple: reparation and appropriate discipline within the Inagawa-kai. No fingers necessary.

Prior to the truce, a senior member of the Yagita-ikka faction spoke up at the Inagawa-kai council meeting and condemned the Omaeda-ikka faction bosses for being greedy in the first place. He didn't believe that the Sumiyoshi-kai had violated Inagawa-kai territory, and that in fact the Omaeda-ikka faction was at fault. The responsibility was clear. The top Omaeda-ikka boss, Yasuo Oda, and his second-in-command, Kunio Goto, would have to step down. Both would be formally excommunicated from the organization.

Saigo and the other Inagawa-kai members were ordered to assemble the reparation money: $1 million in cash.

They stuffed the money in brand-new department store–bought briefcases, and took the cash to the designated Sumiyoshi-kai office in Akasaka. Saigo had never seen so much cash in one place in his life. They were all fresh bills.

A Sumiyoshi-kai boss greeted them while he sat at his desk. He had wanted a gang war; he had wanted revenge. Instead, he got money. It didn't matter to him if it was a rogue faction of the Inagawa-kai and not the Inagawa-kai itself that had started the fight. He had wanted to finish it.

However, calmer heads had prevailed.

There was a long silence in the room as the boss counted the cash, tossing the stacks on the table like they were socks.

"There's 100 million yen here. We have two dead and one wounded. This money won't bring back the dead."

The representative of the Inagawa-kai was silent for a moment.

"It's not enough?"

"It's too much," said the Sumiyoshi-kai boss. "It's too much. It's not the going rate for a life. And sometimes," he added, "it's not about the money. It's not about the money at all. Leave half. Take the rest back."

No one knew what to say.

"I said leave half, and take the rest. And then get out."

Saigo and the Inagawa-kai members scrambled to recount the

money. They put it back in a briefcase, and left as quickly as possible. They were not welcome, and they knew it.

Saigo would tell his underlings that it was one of the most impressive things he'd seen during his time as a yakuza. Mizoguchi didn't get it.

"Why only take half the money? That's not smart," Mizoguchi said.

"Yes, it wasn't smart," Saigo lectured him. "That was the point. That was the old-school yakuza way of saying "Fuck you and fuck your money. You can't solve everything with money." It shouldn't all be about the money. It should be about honor as well. What the Omaeda-ikka did was against the code. Unacceptable. A few years ago, this would have been war. Now, it's a business deal."

But as far as business deals go, it was not entirely successful.

The Sumiyoshi-kai has never been the most disciplined of organizations. For many years, it was the Sumiyoshi-rengo, not an association, but more of a coalition of once-independent organized crime groups. Many were not happy with the deal that had been made.

The Kohei-ikka faction of the Sumiyoshi-kai began to plot their own revenge on Oda, setting up a hit squad. In February 2002, they shot up the home of the former Omaeda-ikka boss. In March, they threw a molotov cocktail into his house, burning it to the ground.

In October 2002, four Sumiyoshi-kai Kohei-ikka yakuza attacked Kunio Goto, who was believed to have orchestrated the funeral hall hit under Oda's orders. They shot him on a road near a golf course in the Gunma prefecture, but he didn't die. The Gunma police offered to put him into protective custody, but he refused.

On a Saturday night, January 25, 2003, at 11.25 pm, Goto was drinking at a bar in Maebashi City. A pair of gunmen shot and killed Goto's bodyguard, who was sitting in his car outside the bar. The gunmen then stormed the bar, apparently targeting the fifty-five-year-old Goto, the former gang leader who was drinking inside.

The Sumiyoshi-kai members fired more than ten shots inside the bar, killing three of the regulars, injuring one customer, and only wounding Goto. He lived. (The incident was later incorporated into the Sega Yakuza video-game series.)

At the trial of the shooters, their lawyers argued that their clients had never intended to kill the other customers — only Goto and Goto's bodyguard — but those good intentions didn't cut much weight with the judges. The Sumiyoshi-kai members were given death sentences.

Kunio Goto is still alive — at least as far as the world knows.

The funeral hall hit in 2001 reverberated for years, in many ways. The blowback was immense. And there is at least one other murder associated with the debacle that remains mysterious.

On February 25, 2002, at 9.10 am at Nippon Medical School Hospital in Tokyo, Sumiyoshi-kai Kohei-ikka boss Takashi Ishizuka had been shot to death through the window while in the hospital's intensive care unit. He'd been shot the day before in the Toshima ward, and was recovering. The police eventually arrested three Sumiyoshi-kai members for his murder.

The police believed that Ishizuka had refused to participate in a plot to kill the former head of Omaeda-ikka in August 2001. The hit might have been to silence him.

It was never clear why his fellow Sumiyoshi-kai members so desperately needed him to keep silent about a failed assassination. Did the killing of Ishizuka pave the way for the Maebashi City massacre in 2003? One Sumiyoshi-kai member alleges that if Ishizuka had been in charge, he would have never approved of the disastrous snack bar assassination attempt.

The two Inagawa-kai funeral shooters were eventually given stiff sentences. The premeditated nature of the crime and the stray bullets did not leave the judge feeling charitable. Yoshikawa, the eldest, was given 'a sentence without end' — Japan's version of life imprisonment. Usually after twenty years, parole was possible. Yoshio, who was twenty-nine, was given twenty years for his part in the crime.

Yoshio told one of his Inagawa-kai brothers before the shooting, "What can I do? It's shoot or be shot. This is what yakuza do. The Sumiyoshi-kai are taking our turf. We have to defend our turf. I'm a soldier, and this is a war."

It was a war that, years before, might have been worth fighting for — there might have been a reward. However, it was a war started only by one faction of the Sumiyoshi-kai, not authorized at the top. So both Yoshikawa and Yoshio were excommunicated from the group.

When Yoshio makes his way back into the world of the civilians, he will not be welcome by the Omaeda-ikka. I don't know what he's up to these days. As for Yoshikawa — he is likely to die in prison, or, depending upon the institutional memory of the Sumiyoshi-kai, is likely to vanish soon after leaving jail.

But there are two things that all the yakuza learned from the whole tragic affair.

Never kill someone at a funeral: it's bad luck for everyone.

And it's not always about the money.

# CHAPTER TWENTY-TWO

# Proper greetings

Saigo was woken by his father knocking on his bedroom door. It was an afternoon in October 2002, and he was taking a nap. Saigo was wearing sweatpants and nothing else. It was still hot, despite being the fall, and he didn't like the feeling of his T-shirt sticking to his sweaty torso.

At first he ignored the knocking, but his father kept politely pounding on the door, gradually with more force. His father finally explained why he was there. There were cops at the front door, and they were threatening to break it down. There were at least fifty of them, and they had a battering ram.

Saigo didn't want to have to buy a new door, so he told his father to ask them what they wanted. His father told him to at least not worry about the door — he had already let them in. So the door would be fine. Then, before Saigo could say another word, his father went downstairs to make some green tea for the police officers.

His father was still keeping the books, managing day-to-day affairs, and Saigo thought the visit by the cops was just a routine greeting or a public performance to show they were cracking down on organized crime. Maybe one of his crew had been arrested. He'd let his father handle it; he was sleepy.

A kick in the ass and the lights being turned on rudely awakened him. He looked up at an old cop, who looked down on him and clicked his tongue in disapproval. The cop was called Inspector Midorigawa aka Greenriver. He had a grizzled beard, and wore a bad suit and an expensive Rolex. Behind him were several young men and women, in bright new blue uniforms, armed with notepads and pencils. One of them was snapping pictures with a compact camera. The older cop asked for the boss.

Saigo, who was just in his pajama bottoms, sat up. "I am the boss."

Greenriver looked down at him. Saigo stood up and came chest to chest with the cop, who was a few inches shorter than him, and moved forward, chest-bumping the detective. Greenriver didn't flinch. He poked Saigo in the chest hard and fast. Saigo was surprised to find that the cop had almost knocked him back down with a single poke. He struggled to stay standing.

Greenriver was a powerful guy.

The cop flashed him a search warrant. They'd heard that Saigo was in violation of the Firearms and Swords Control Act. An anonymous tip had come in, saying that the Suguwara-gumi were holding weapons for the Inagawa-kai. So the police had come to look around.

Saigo was livid. He was about to yell when the cop motioned with one hand for Saigo to shut up, and, to his surprise, Saigo did find himself shutting up.

Greenriver addressed the young cops behind him and held up the search warrant for them to see. "We're here searching for guns or swords. If you find one, yell, and I'll come over. Don't move it or touch it." The young cops all nodded in agreement vigorously. Greenriver then poked Saigo gently in the chest, where the Inagawa-kai symbol was tattooed. Saigo wasn't sure what was going on.

Greenriver traced the pattern in the air. "This is called a *daimon*. The Inagawa-kai *daimon* is the Chinese character for river, *kawa*, made to look like a mountain and rice plants, *ina*, next to it. It's supposed to mean that everything you can see from Mount Fuji is Inagawa-kai territory. It's very artsy."

The students came closer and stared at Saigo's chest. He felt like an animal on display. A young female police officer asked him if the *daimon* on his chest was the same as the one in his office downstairs — and did it have a different meaning if it was colored differently?

Saigo roared at Greenriver. Was he taking the cop kids on a field trip?

In fact, he was. They were collecting data for a study, and Greenriver was teaching them what a yakuza office looked like. The other police officers were still attending the police academy, and this was part of their training.

Saigo told the officer to get the "baby cops" out of his office. Greenriver told him to have some respect for the learning process, and to turn around for a second.

Saigo did as he was told, and the cop poked his back. The skin was slightly raised. Each of the carp's scales were textured.

It all seemed surreal. Saigo turned around and growled. He wanted them out.

Their lesson was over for now. The senior officer told Saigo he would see him later, and he led the kids in blue out of the room. In the hallway, Saigo could hear his voice, pedantically pointing out another *daimon*, the sensors, and the cameras — they were everywhere. He explained to the trainees that yakuza office hallways were often narrow, and sometimes partitioned with iron doors, to slow down an attack from a rival gang.

Saigo got dressed slowly, still half-groggy. He went to the window and opened it up. There were thirty or more police cars parked in front of the house. There were cops everywhere. They were digging up the yard, inspecting his car, looking in the garage.

Saigo wasn't dumb enough to keep guns on his own property. The cops were wasting his time and their own time, but then, without warning, two cops pulled one of his men out of the office. They'd found a sword.

*Damn*, thought Saigo. That wasn't expected.

A minute later, three young cops ran up the stairs and told Saigo that they had just arrested one of Saigo's men for violations of the Firearms and Swords Control Law. They asked Saigo to please come downtown to speak to the inspector in charge as soon as possible.

The cops had nabbed one of his older soldiers. This particular soldier, Yusuke Ikeda, had been planning to leave the organization and go straight. Saigo had given his tacit approval. And now they'd arrested him for possessing a sword. While it was possible to have an antique sword as an art object, it required a lot of paperwork. But possessing a real sword, one that could actually cut and kill, and had no value as an antique, was simply illegal.

It says a lot about Japan that swords and gun are regulated by the same law. The gun and sword control laws are very severe. Yusuke was facing some serious time in jail.

It was a shame.

Saigo was deep in thought when one of the trainees showed him a picture he'd taken off the wall. "This *daimon* is very nice-looking. Did you have it done in gold inlay?"

"Give me that back," Saigo said. He was not about to lose his *kanban* again.

The cop returned it, looking down in shame, perhaps feeling he'd been rude.

Other police trainees were now rifling through his desk and closet. There were close to 100 cops on the property. He called up his crew;

every office and every front company of the group was being raided. It took him an hour to get hold of all his lieutenants. He told his father he'd be going down to the police station to see if he could bail out Yusuke.

They were expecting him at the Machida Police Station. When he came in, he was sent up to the Organized Crime Control Division to see Greenriver. A cop pointed him to the elevator. Saigo took the stairs. In the back of the room, with his feet up on the desk, Greenriver was reading a yakuza fanzine and drinking a cup of coffee.

Greenriver motioned for him to sit down. A year prior, Detective Lucky had taken exams to rise up to sergeant level, and had been sent to the police university for two years of intensive training. Thus Greenriver had been working at the station for over a year as Lucky's replacement, and still hadn't had a formal visit from Saigo. He was offended, and he wasn't necessarily wrong. It was customary to pay greetings to the new sheriff in town.

Saigo did not sit down. Since when was it the law that he had to go and kiss the ass of every new cop in town?

But it was common courtesy. Greenriver was in charge of the organized crime control division in Machida, and Saigo was operating on Greenriver's turf. He had expected a proper greeting.

Saigo was incensed. He pounded his fist on the desk. Greenriver had basically raided his place with 100 cops because he hadn't said hello. Greenriver retorted that there were also rumors that Saigo had guns on his property, but, personally, Greenriver thought the rumors were just that. He hadn't expected to find anything. Finding the sword was a pleasant surprise.

Saigo knew that Yusuke, the retiring underling, was already on a suspended sentence for attempted extortion. This arrest would mean he'd be in jail for quite some time, but what was the point when

Yusuke had planned to leave anyway? Saigo offered to go in his place.

Greenriver took his feet off the desk and put them on the ground, and stared at Saigo "That won't work. It doesn't work like that."

Saigo thought fast. What about the man's fingerprints? If the sword didn't have his fingerprints on it, maybe his subordinate could go home. Greenriver didn't know about that, though. They hadn't given the sword to Forensics yet. So Saigo said it was his. "Arrest me," he said.

Greenriver cocked his head to the right, and stared at him, with a bemused look on his face. Greenriver had met a lot of yakuza in his time. He was impressed.

He decided they would seize the knife and leave the ownership in dispute. Greenriver had a few things to discuss with Saigo, and then they could call it a day.

Saigo was speechless.

"Now," said Greenriver, "would you please sit down and talk to me?" Greenriver was too tired to stand up. He had finished testing for his fourth-degree black belt in karate the day before, and his legs were killing him. The casual mention of a karate black belt would have sounded like bragging from anyone else, but Greenriver was just explaining himself.

When Saigo understood that Greenriver was a karate-ka, some more things made sense to him. Beneath Greenriver's crumpled, ill-fitting suit was a powerful man. He hadn't just poked Saigo at his office, he'd hit him with a *nukite* (spear hand). No wonder he'd almost fallen over. And his chest still hurt. There was more to this old man than met the eye. Greenriver had been busting yakuza for over two decades. Over time, he'd taken on the mannerisms of the people he put in jail. In some odd way, Saigo felt like he was talking to another yakuza boss.

Saigo sat down. Greenriver asked Saigo whether he wanted some green tea. Saigo said no. Greenriver had one of the officers bring some black coffee for both of them. They sat in silence for a bit, both sipping their coffee. Greenriver spoke first.

Saigo's right-wing group and its activities annoyed everyone in the town. It only took one convoy of his right-wing propaganda trucks blaring out through their loudspeakers to generate complaints from 200 people calling 110.* It created a public disturbance every time their trucks did that.

Saigo argued they were just exercising freedom of speech, and Greenriver told him to be a little less free with his speech, or else he'd shut them up completely. He wanted Saigo to reduce the number of trucks. No more running around town in fifteen to twenty truck convoys — five or six would be okay, but no more than once or twice a week.

Saigo agreed to reduce the number. "But you should know," Saigo said, "The Shelter is backed by the Inagawa-kai."

"Ask me if that means shit to me," Greenriver said. Saigo was the Inagawa-kai executive director. So, of course, his group was backed by the Inagawa-kai. And, on that note, Greenriver thought his executive meetings were a nuisance to the neighborhood as well. He didn't care if Saigo had all 150 members of his clan show up, but they needed to car-pool or something. Thirty to fifty Mercedes Benzes, all with the Saigo-gumi standard license plate 3000 on them, intimidated people, blocked the streets, and caused traffic to slow down. It was a pain in the ass for the cops.

Greenriver wasn't saying that Saigo couldn't have meetings at his office anymore; he was just requesting that Saigo reduce the number of guests to ten or twelve people, or get people to share a ride.

That was a lot to ask for, but Saigo would rather do that than go to jail, or have Yusuke go to jail. Those were his choices. Saigo took

---

\*   The 110 phone number is the Japanese equivalent of 911.

a deep breath, held it, and exhaled. He thought it over, and agreed to Greenriver's terms.

They shook hands, and had a deal.


Saigo was smart to take the deal, for, only a couple of months later, Saigo needed Greenriver's help. Hanzawa's meth habit had gotten so bad that Saigo's soldiers were loathe to even let him stay in the office. One morning, Saigo got a phone call from Hanzawa's mother. Hanzawa was home, and on meth again. He was prone to bouts of violence in between catatonic states, and wouldn't listen to reason. She couldn't handle him. Saigo took some men with him, and went straight over.

The entrance of Hanzawa's house was full of broken plates and bloody footprints. Hanzawa was sitting cross-legged and half-naked on a small tea table in the tatami-matted living room. He was trying to cut his hair with a sharp kitchen knife, and his bloody head was completely bare in one spot. He thought there were insects inside his head.

He nodded at Saigo when he came in. Saigo had never seen him so thin. He tried to find out what Hanzawa was doing, but couldn't understand his logic. He told Hanzawa that even if there were bugs inside his head, cutting off all his hair wouldn't get rid of them.

Hanzawa realized that Saigo was right. Then he stuck the tip of the knife in his ear, and prepared to start burrowing into his skull. Saigo shouted at him to stop, and Hanzawa politely warned Saigo that he would stab him if he tried to take his knife.

Saigo tried anyway, and Hanzawa stabbed him in the hand. He backhanded Hanzawa across the face while another soldier grabbed Hanzawa's hand and twisted his wrist back until he dropped the knife. The others joined in and tried to pin Hanzawa down. They managed to tie his hands and feet together with neckties, but he was somehow still moving and violent. The only person that Saigo thought could truly help was the enemy. He dialed Detective Greenriver.

Greenriver answered the phone immediately. Saigo explained the situation, and the detective immediately came over with a patrol car. Hanzawa was now tied to a chair close to the door. Greenriver asked one of the yakuza guys to slap Hanzawa in the face; Hanzawa woke up, and Greenriver checked his pupils. He was definitely high. They wrapped Hanzawa up like a turkey, and tossed him in the back of the car.

Saigo felt a little ashamed of himself. He had called the cops on one of his own men — but he was trying to save this guy's ass. Hanzawa was very, very close to being put in a nuthouse for the rest of his life. If he went to jail instead, he could come back to society after only two years.

As it happened, Hanzawa got out of jail after serving his full time, and was arrested on the usual charges within a month of his release. Some people just can't be healed.

## CHAPTER TWENTY-THREE

# Swimming with sharks

If a patient were dying in the U.S., the doctor would most likely tell the patient directly — but that's not how they handled death in Japan. In fact, Japanese doctors made it a point to not tell cancer patients their diagnosis, and withholding that information was (and still is) completely legal. Saigo thought that maybe doctors were afraid the patient would kill themselves. Or maybe, Saigo thought, they wanted to squeeze as many public healthcare subsidies out of them as they could before they died. But that's a very cynical way of looking at it. Most people see it as not wanting to worry the patient. Doctors don't want their patients to spend their last few months being scared of their imminent death. However, they often tell the families.

Saigo knew it was bad. The chemotherapy had made Hiroko lose all her hair, so she had to wear a wig. She had trouble standing and eating. When Saigo learned that Hiroko only had a year left to live, he told her very indirectly, "You know, we really need to get our lives in order." He had to start arranging for where she would be buried. Her family didn't have a resting place. Her parents had died when she was young, and she still had their ashes. He wanted her and her family to rest in the same area, but it was difficult to bring that up with her without giving away the fact that she was dying.

So he told her that, because he was a yakuza, she wasn't the only one at risk of dying. Who knew when either of them would die?


In November 2003, the Machida Swimming School printed a flyer with the wrong phone number on it — Saigo's. The flyer had been distributed all over the city with the local newspapers. It was a simple mistake; the number of the school and Saigo's home number only differed by one number. He'd yell at the people calling him by mistake, but that didn't stop the calls from coming in.

Saigo had one of his underlings, Soldier 29, call the school and politely ask for a correction. Saigo wasn't really mad. People made mistakes. And that should have been the end of it.

It wasn't.

Soldier 29 saw an opportunity to make some easy money. He called his cousin, and they decided to shake down the school for as much money as they possibly could.

Making sure to roll up his sleeves to show his tattoos, Soldier 29 and his cousin showed up at the school around 2.00 pm on November 23. They made a scene at the reception desk, throwing copies of the ad all over the room, and screaming about what an outrage it was. Their yelling was so loud that the students in the pool next door could hear them. Some came to the window and looked in, only to run away when 29's cousin glared at them. They could see the knife that he had tucked in his belt.

The owner of the school greeted them and apologized profusely. He admitted it was a mistake, and said that they had already corrected it.

Soldier 29 took the lead. He didn't give a shit that they had corrected it. The school had published the home phone number of their boss, Saigo, of the Inagawa-kai Saigo-gumi. Soldier 29 put his business card on the table.

The swim-school owner continued to apologize, but 29 said that wasn't good enough. He claimed that the school owner had pissed off their boss, and because Saigo didn't want to answer his phone, the school owner was interfering with their business. He was causing them great trouble.

The cousin went to the window and looked at the students swimming. They were probably fifth-graders. He patted the owner on the shoulders and whispered in his ear that he, too, was a businessman, so he understood how bad it was to have trouble in a business — such as what would happen if one of his students were to drown. For instance, one night, if one of his students was swimming and got their leg caught in a drain and drowned, it would be horrible — and it would technically be the swim-school owner's fault. He would have to pay damages to the family and close down the school.

The cousin slapped him lightly, and the owner apologized again. But Soldier 29 and his cousin made it clear that words weren't enough. The school owner agreed to pay them 1 million yen in damages. They made him go to the bank with them and take out the money immediately.

Soldier 29 made the owner stamp his seal on a note saying that the money was a settlement for aggravation caused by the printing error. It was a smart move. It would make it hard for the police to treat it as more than a civil dispute.

A few days later, after thinking it over, the school owner went to the Machida police and consulted with them. He was asked to file a criminal complaint, but, at the last minute, he balked. The police pressed him to file charges, but he said he needed time to think it over. They kept his statement, and the business card of Soldier 29, on file.

One of the cops mentioned the incident to a member of the Saigo-gumi, who promptly reported it to his boss. Saigo was outraged. It wasn't just that it was a low-down shakedown of a local business using the Saigo-gumi name, but they hadn't even paid him a cut of their take. It was unethical and disrespectful.

The Saigo-gumi survived in the area because they didn't bother the locals. They didn't pick fights over trivial and honest mistakes. That wasn't how he operated.

He told Mizoguchi to gather four other members and to bring 29 to his office immediately. He was going to have a talk with him. When Soldier 29 was brought into the office, Saigo didn't even look at him. He ordered his crew to pin 29 to his desk so he could ask him some questions.

Saigo fired away, and Soldier 29 denied everything. He said that he had no idea what was going on. Finally, growing impatient, Saigo told Mizoguchi to bring him his Japanese sword from upstairs. Unless he started talking, Saigo was going to cut 29's limbs off until he looked like a *daruma* doll. Mizoguchi brought down the sword. Saigo unsheathed it himself, and held it in both hands. He nodded at Mizoguchi, and explained to him how to use the sword. He'd have to hold it in both hands to get a clean cut. Then he handed the sword to Mizoguchi.

Soldier 29, who had his arms pinned to the table by two men, and his legs held in place by two others, was trying to scream, but one of the men had stuffed a handkerchief in his mouth. He was struggling.

Mizoguchi lifted the sword, right over the left arm, and was getting ready to slice down when Saigo stopped him.

Saigo chuckled to himself. He apologized to the assembled men. He realized that, if he cut off 29's arm at his office, the whole place would be full of blood. So he ordered his men to drag his ass up to the mountains, so they could continue up there. If he still wouldn't talk after he'd lost his first arm, he wanted them to cut off 29's fingers one by one until he did. Then drop him at a hospital somewhere. Maybe he'd live.

Soldier 29 was really screaming now, even though they were muffled screams. Saigo guessed he wanted to talk now.

Soldier 29 told him everything. He told him about his cousin and about how much money they'd made. He apologized for not paying a portion back to Saigo, and Saigo slapped him in the face so hard that it broke the man's nose.

It wasn't about the money. It was about bothering people who they shouldn't have been bothering. Saigo then told 29 what was going to happen: 29 was going to leave his office, gather all the money that was left, and return it to the owner. He was going to apologize and explain that the Saigo-gumi had had nothing to do with the incident. He was going to return to the office to give Saigo his badge, and then he was going to be banished from the organization.

If he didn't come back to the office, they'd come looking for him. Saigo took back the sword from Mizoguchi and pointed it at the man. When Soldier 29 left, he had the sword put back.

It was actually a model sword: a replica of a famous blade from the Tokugawa era. It would have been stupid to keep a real sword on the premises, but Soldier 29 didn't know that, nor did he need to know that. Saigo just needed to make sure he was scared enough to talk.

Unfortunately, Soldier 29 decided to to talk to the wrong people.

Soldier 29 didn't go get the money. He went to the police. He told the Machida police that Saigo had threatened to cut off his arm if he didn't pay 1 million yen to him.

As luck would have it, Detective Greenriver was on duty that day. He heard one of the junior detectives taking down the statement and getting ready to file a criminal complaint. Greenriver interrupted the proceedings, and asked the junior detective to wait about an hour.

Soldier 29 was put in the interrogation room "for his own safety." Then Greenriver called Saigo directly.

Saigo had a feeling that he knew what the call was about. He was on his way to visit his wife in the hospital, but he said he'd wait. Greenriver was there within twenty minutes. He came into Saigo's office and sat down. Greenriver told him that one of Saigo's men had come to the police station and lodged a complaint about a shakedown. Greenriver wanted to know if the story was true.

Saigo confirmed it. Soldier 29 had shaken down a local swimming school and had used Saigo's name, but Greenriver hadn't heard anything about the swimming school. All he had heard was that Saigo had threatened to cut off 29's arm if he didn't pay Saigo 1 million yen.

Saigo brought Greenriver up to speed, even showing him a copy of the mistaken ad. The question now was whether Saigo had threatened 29, and he had. Saigo wasn't going to lie about that. He also wasn't going to lie about asking for the money, although he wanted the money so he could pay back the school. Still, Greenriver could technically arrest him for extortion, and if he did, Saigo wouldn't be around to say goodbye to his wife. It would be stupid to throw away his life over something like this.

Greenriver decided that they didn't have a problem. This was how he was going to handle it: He was going to go back to the station and tell 29 he was ready to arrest Saigo for extortion; but, if he was going to do that, he was also going to arrest his cousin for the same crime. Then he'd offer to let if all slide if 29 paid back the money.

Saigo had threatened 29, though. He tried to remind Greenriver of this, but the detective pretended not to hear him. He told Saigo that he suffered from severe hearing loss when he was tired, and he had just gotten off the night shift. Plus, Greenriver decided that Saigo was just upset because his wife was ill. He was distraught, and not expressing himself well. So Greenriver was going to go back to the station, have a chat with 29, and then go to sleep. He recommended that Saigo go see his wife.

Saigo stood up and bowed deeply. Greenriver got up and bowed as well. He smiled, and let himself out.

Greenriver went back to the police station. In the interrogation room, he had a long talk with Soldier 29. Their talk may or may not have been punctuated with a few punches. It was a closed room.

Soldier 29 dropped the charges. He and his cousin paid back all the money to the school. The owner received his money, plus an apology, and an extra 40,000 yen for damages that he had suffered. He told the police he didn't want to press charges. The police were not unhappy, because while they wanted to bust as many yakuza as possible, everything had been resolved amicably.

And Saigo was able to be with his wife when she needed him the most. During the last few days, she had one beatific vision of a field of flowers. She told him about it. He told her that that must be what heaven was like. He didn't believe this — figuring it was a drug-induced vision, but he told her that because he felt sometimes you lie to the people you love when they need you to the most. He held her hand as she passed. Saigo had a tomb built for her and her parents, under the Saigo family name. There was no obligation for him to do so, because they had never technically been married. Even now, the Saigo tomb is located in Machida city, but there are no Saigo family members in it yet. The only ones in the tomb are Hiroko, her father, and her mother.

Coach mourned her as though she was a member of his own family. He insisted on throwing a lavish funeral in her honor. Over 2,000 people came. It was a huge affair. The money collected went to pay the huge hospital bill and the funeral costs.

# CHAPTER TWENTY-FOUR

# "We once were gamblers ..."

Times change. Bosses die. New bosses are crowned.

Chihiro Inagawa became the third-generation leader of the Inagawa-kai on October 10, 1990, at an elaborate ceremony held at the family headquarters located in Atami. All the leaders of each yakuza group in the country attended, including Yoshinuri Watanabe, the fifth-generation leader of the Yamaguchi-gumi. Watanabe was an imposing figure, very much living up to his nickname "the Gorilla" in his physical features and his almost brutal aura.

At the ceremony, the Inagawa theme song, 'Kanagawa Suikoden', was played. The song's closing lyrics noted that "If you kick down others to climb up the mountain, next it will be your turn to fall." It was almost a prophecy of the ugly succession battle that would occur after Chihiro's death years later.

Seijo Inagawa had entrusted Ishii with raising Chihiro Inagawa to be a good yakuza, and Ishii had done well. He had created the perfect successor. Chihiro Inagawa was handsome, charming, and adept at running the group. Seijo Inagawa was still behind the scenes, living in their family headquarters in Atami, occasionally doing interviews with magazines.

Chihiro Inagawa's son was expected to be the fourth-generation Inagawa-kai leader when Chihiro Inagawa retired or died at a ripe old age. Few people imagined that the founder would outlive his son.

By 2003, Chihiro Inagawa had liver cancer. He needed a liver transplant to survive, and Japan was way behind on transplant surgery. With the strict laws in place, it was unlikely that a yakuza would get to step to the head of the line.

That year was tough — not just for Chihiro Inagawa, but for the whole Inagawa-kai. They were having a bonfire of troubles and bad publicity.

The trouble stemmed from a killing in November 1998, when Inagawa-kai soldiers beat a Japanese *enka* singer to death. He had been playing gigs on their turf in the Saitama prefecture. When the singer stopped by a traditional Japanese pub in Yashio City, the local thugs corralled him. They wanted to know who had given him permission to sing in the area and where was their cut. The local yakuza were "offended" that they hadn't been properly greeted, which was standard practice for the yakuza in that era.

The fifty-six-year-old singer told them to buzz off, so they dragged him out of the pub to their local office, where they beat his head with a wooden chair, kicked him over and over, and killed him. It was the blows to the head that were fatal.

When his widow came to confirm the identity of his body, the internal bleeding had caused the singer's face to swell up and go purple, and his mouth was warped and misshapen. If he'd lived, he might never have been able to sing again. She had rushed to the police station with their four-year-old grandson, whom she often babysat. When the child managed to sneak into the room and saw his grandfather's face, he looked and said, "It's a monster."

The young yakuza responsible turned himself into the police directly after the crime, and was arrested on murder charges. The prosecution didn't believe that there was an intent to kill, and only charged the yakuza with manslaughter. He was sentenced to seven years and six months in prison.

The widow, with the aid of the Saitama Police, sued the Inagawa-kai boss, his *wakagashira*, and the killer, for 160 million yen, asserting that the boss had employer liability for the death of her husband. She spoke to the press.

They had been a happily married couple who together ran a fruit-and-vegetable stand until her husband finally made his debut as a singer. He wasn't a star, but he had done well.

A female police officer, aged thirty-two, who had come to know the widow during the initial investigation, visited her once a month for over a year until she finally convinced the widow to take a stand and sue. The Saitama Center for the Elimination of the Yakuza funded the lawsuit, and the local police patrolled her house every day after she filed.

The Inagawa-kai had bankrolled the defense of the boss — asserting that since the boss had been in jail at the time of the killing, he couldn't be held accountable.

The courts disagreed. In March 2003, the Supreme Court rejected any further appeals, and the case was closed. The sued Inagawa-kai boss declared bankruptcy, and finally agreed to pay a fraction of the payment.

The entire court case had been a huge PR disaster for the group. It certainly didn't illustrate the principle of "not bothering ordinary persons."

On July 9, in Yokohama, which was Yokosuka-ikka territory, two Inagawa-kai members — aged twenty-three and nineteen — got in a fight with a sixty-one-year-old construction worker and his friends. They kicked and punched the older man, leaving him fatally injured. They were both arrested for manslaughter.

The only saving grace for Saigo and Coach was that the two punks responsible were not members of their clan, the Yokosuka-ikka.

But within weeks, the Inagawa-kai heard that the family of the deceased man was considering suing Seijo Inagawa himself for liability. The buck was going all the way to the top.

Coach took it up at the monthly Yokosuka-ikka meeting.


There was comfort and stability in the regular life of a yakuza boss that Saigo had grown to like. The monthly meetings of the Yokosuka-ikka were always introduced with someone reading aloud the *okite* (the rules of the game) in a booming voice. Coach would announce the latest personnel changes. He would often wear his sunglasses during the meeting as well, especially if he didn't have much to say. Some suspected he kept them on to sleep through part of the meetings, which could go on for hours.

Sometimes, a lawyer would come and brief them on how to skirt the most recent changes in the anti-organized crime laws. There would be announcements of who was in jail, who was due to get out of jail, and occasionally new instructions and prohibitions.

Coach opened the meeting the following bombshell: "No more naked sushi. From henceforth, *nyotaimori* is banned at all Inagawa-kai events. That's from the top down." *Nyotaimori* — sometimes translated as "female body arrangement" — is the practice of eating sushi off a woman's naked body.

272 THE LAST YAKUZA

In the spring of 2004, two members of the Inagawa-kai crime syndicate in the Gunma prefecture used a *nyotaimori* show to commemorate a release from prison, and were subsequently arrested for allowing minors to view the proceedings. During the 1990s, Hollywood movies such as *Rising Sun* and scandalous reporting on Japan made it seem like this deviant practice was part and parcel of Japanese culture, but it had never been mainstream — no more mainstream than shabu-shabu restaurants where the floors were mirrored and the waitresses wore skirts with no panties. However, it was something that could spice up yakuza parties, and was still done on occasion. The arrest of the idiots in Gunma did not cast the organization in a good light, and thus the practice was banned.

There were groans or protests from the assembled members. Everyone was aware that it wasn't smart to give the police a reason to crack down on the gang. Coach reminded them that in March, a twenty-six-year-old member of the Inagawa-kai had been arrested for violations of the anti-child prostitution laws after paying 30,000 yen for sex with a thirteen-year-old girl. That was unacceptable, and disgusting as well.

Coach always saved the most important and grave announcements for last, which meant that the meetings usually ended on a somber note. There was something to that strategy. Most yakuza share one thing in common — a poor ability to see into the future and remember what is really important. The last thing they hear is what they remember the most.

Now came the bad news. A few days before the meeting, two members of the Inagawa-kai had killed a regular citizen. There were even rumors that the family of the man was going to Seijo Inagawa and Chihiro Inagawa this time for damages; they would seek to lay responsibility at the top.

As for the two yakuza arrested, they had had been banished

forever — *zetsuen* — and would never return to the organization. It didn't matter if the civilians had started the fight — as yakuza, they should have known when to pull their punches.

"When I started, we were gamblers, we were *bakuto*. And now look at us."

Coach had kept his sunglasses on for the entire meeting, but now he took them off, and rubbed his eyes. They were watery. He looked at Saigo, at Inoue, at each and every member there, one by one.

"At the end of the day, ask yourself whether you're one of the good guys or the bad guys, and if you don't know, then you'd better figure it out. Behave yourselves. The world is watching us, and I'm watching you."

He put his glasses back on, and had Inoue read the rules out one more time. Inoue's voice resonated like a temple bell:

1. It is forbidden to use any form of drugs or deal in them.
2. Theft, robbery, sex crimes, or any activity not in harmony with the noble way is forbidden.
3. It is forbidden to associate with any member expelled from the group.
4. All unnecessary contact with the authorities [the police] is forbidden.
5. Anyone breaking these rules is subject to discipline by the ruling council.
6. Younger members should respect older members; older members should respect younger members, nurture them, and get along for the mutual prosperity of all.
7. Engrave these rules in your heart and follow the noble path (*ninkyodo*)

They had all fallen off the noble path of late. At this rate, Saigo feared that they weren't going to be any better than the Yamaguchi-gumi.

# PART III

# THE BROKEN GATE
# 破門

## CHAPTER TWENTY-FIVE

# One gang to rule them all

Saigo was proud to be a member of the Inagawa-kai. There was only one organization that could compare to the Inagawa-kai, and that was the Yamaguchi-gumi. When he'd joined up, the Inagawa-kai was the more powerful of the two. He disliked the Yamaguchi-gumi vehemently, and had his reasons.

The Yamaguchi-gumi isn't just Japan's largest organized crime group; it's a well-known Japanese corporation, founded in 1915, that engages in a wide array of legitimate and sometimes illegitimate business activity, often with extreme prejudice. Robert Feldman, an analyst at Morgan Stanley Japan, once called them Japan's second-largest private equity group, and he was not incorrect. They are Goldman Sachs with guns — not to mention knives, bazooka launchers, sniper rifles, and assassins.

The Yamaguchi-gumi is a massive organization that employs over 20,000 people full-time. It owns auditing firms, several hundred front operations, and their own network-management and database companies. They control Japan's entertainment industry even now, and over the years have quietly become part of the backbone of several high-profile IT operations — only getting caught once in 2007, when a member of the Kodo-kai faction was revealed to have taken over the equivalent of Japan's "classmates.com" — gaining access to the personal data of 3.2 million people. They own a chain of private detective agencies, and keep tabs on their enemies and their friends better than any intelligence agency in Japan does.

If one were writing a pamphlet on the company to attract young college graduates, this would be the way to say it:

> The Yamaguchi-gumi Corporation, with large, comfortable headquarters in the international city of Kobe and lovely branch offices, complete with swimming pools and gyms in Nagoya and other major cities in Japan, has a proud history of over 100 years of serving the Japanese people. Our construction, real estate, IT, banking, and entertainment businesses are still thriving in a poor economy, and thanks to one of Japan's best R & D sections in any company, we have a treasure trove of personal data on the elite in Japan's business and political world that can be judiciously used for blackmailing such individuals and maintaining maximum leverage in the money markets. Our emphasis on HUMINT and judicious use of force gives us a competitive edge that has given us almost half of the market, while our competitors are gradually being absorbed into the greater operation. We not only offer lifetime employment, but we also offer a generous pension plan.*

The asterisk would serve for the following disclaimer:

> A lifetime in the Yamaguchi-gumi does not preclude the possibility of early death. A "lifetime" may also include time

served in prison, not necessarily for a crime that you committed, but as a designated fall-guy. However, all members serving time in prison can be assured that we will maintain your family's living standards until you return.

The Yamaguchi-gumi had generally been good about keeping their pledges. "Family" included common-law wives and sometimes mistresses; if you went to jail for the team, the team took care of them. If you did survive until retirement, the pension plan wasn't bad. In 2013, the final bonus and severance check for a team member was 50 million yen, according to retired boss Kenji Seiriki. That's almost half a million dollars. The retirement policy was begun decades before when the Yamaguchi-gumi briefly split into two factions. The Yamaguchi-gumi headquarters offered the pension plan as a means of wooing people back. It worked well.

Harukichi Yamaguchi, a dock worker, small-time gangster, and a fearless leader, gathered fifty stevedores and created the Yamaguchi-gumi. The organization primarily functioned as a dispatch service for laborers with a side business promoting *rōkyoku* artists. *Rōkyoku*, also called *naniwa-bushi*, was a type of traditional Japanese narrative singing, generally accompanied by a *shamisen* and often about sad subjects; it was the Japanese version of country and western music. Labor dispatch, dock work, and the entertainment business were staples of the Yamaguchi-gumi from the start.

In 1925, Harukichi Yamaguchi turned the business over to his son, and retired. It was during the reign of the second generation of the Yamaguchi-gumi that Kazuo Taoka, a man who would become "the godfather of godfathers" and a friend of Seiji Inagawa's, joined the Yamaguchi-gumi. He was born on March 28, 1913, in a small mountain village in the Tokushima prefecture. He was the second son, and his father had died before he was born. When he was six, his mother died from overwork, and he was sent to live with his uncle in Kobe. His uncle was violent and abusive, and, in many ways, toughened Taoka up. He learned to fend for himself, and managed to graduate from his school. After graduating, he went to work as a lathe apprentice, but had no patience for the ritual hazing and abuse that was part of traditional Japanese training, and was thrown out for insubordination.

He then became a local ruffian, constantly getting into fights and earning himself the nickname "The Bear" for his fight technique, which was was based on gouging the eyes of his opponent before beating them into submission. He was a feared and notorious troublemaker who was eventually put under the wing of the second Yamaguchi-gumi leader, Noboru Yamaguchi, in January 1936.

The Yamaguchi-gumi was constantly at war with other gangs in their areas, and in 1937 a rival gang leader stormed into their office to take revenge for an attack initially launched by the group. Taoka responded by cutting down the man with a Japanese sword. He was subsequently sentenced to eight years in prison.

It during his prison years that Taoka began to read and study. He was especially interested in the writings of Tōyama Mitsuru, who was a right-wing political leader in early-20th-century Japan and the founder of the Genyosha, a tremendously powerful nationalist group. It may have been Taoka's inspiration for the Yamaguchi-gumi he served to create.

Mitsuru created Genyosha in 1881. It was a secret society and terrorist organization whose members believed the Japanese should expand and conquer all of Asia. The society attracted disaffected ex-samurai and figures involved in organized crime, and waged a campaign of violence against foreigners and liberal politicians. In 1889, Tōyama and the Genyosha were implicated in the attempted assassination of the minister of foreign affairs, Ōkuma Shigenobu. Taoka clearly took notice of Genyosha's practices.

He left prison early, thanks to an imperial pardon, on July 13, 1943. While he was still in prison, his *oyabun* had passed away. There was no third-generation leader of the Yamaguchi-gumi, but the organization still existed. Taoka started his own gang elsewhere in Kobe.

In the aftermath of the war, as he wrote in his bestselling biography, the police weren't much use. Japan was a lawless place following Japan's 1945 defeat. The Korean Japanese, the Taiwanese, and the Chinese, who had been oppressed by the imperial Japanese government and forced to labor for the war effort, made inroads into the underworld.

U.S. occupying forces designated them "third-party nationals," and treated them differently from the defeated Japanese. This gave them access to U.S. military supplies, and enabled them to run the black markets. Gangs of angry foreigners surrounded police stations in Kobe and roamed the streets, taking money and revenge.

In some ways, the 20th-century rebirth of the Yamaguchi-gumi was a response to the domination of the black markets by the Koreans and the resulting disorder. The Koreans had formed their own small gangs, which would rob and pillage from other Japanese, and sell the same goods the next day on the black market. By April 1946, the occupying authorities, known as General Headquarters (GHQ), decreed that everyone residing in Japan had to follow Japanese laws. But the Japanese police found their efforts to crack down on the yakuza hampered by GHQ's decision to decentralize the police.

At the same time, Japanese gangs were fighting over black-market turf with the Koreans. The former began reviving the old yakuza structure and, rather than wage direct war, they began a successful policy of assimilation, and incorporated many Korean Japanese into their ranks. In some cases, the police backed the Yamaguchi-gumi in an effort to restore order and to limit the power and breadth of the Korean gangs.

As a sign of their "respect" for the Yamaguchi-gumi, the Mizukami police station in Kobe allowed Taoka to be the honorary police chief for a day. A photo of him dressed as a police officer being saluted by the uniformed cops was printed in earlier editions of his autobiography.

In October 1946, at the recommendation of the elders in the Yamaguchi-gumi, Taoka took over as the third-generation leader. The time he had spent in prison reading about the exploits of secret societies and books on business inspired by him to issue this order to his new troops: "The yakuza won't be able to survive if all *shinogi* comes from illegal activities. Everyone in this organization needs to have a legitimate job." He was already looking two decades into the future. He revived the construction company set up by his predecessor, Yamaguchi-gumi Construction, and created a Yamaguchi-gumi entertainment division within the company.

By the end of 1945, Yamaguchi-gumi Construction was registered as a joint-stock corporation with 100,000 yen in capital and Taoka as the president. While expanding the business end of the Yamaguchi-gumi, and raking in huge amount of money as the Kobe docks became active during the Korean War, the group began a series of violent gang wars with all the neighboring yakuza in the Kansai area.

Taoka's strategy was to fight, conquer, merge, and grow. If a weaker gang wouldn't fight the Yamaguchi-gumi, they'd start the fight themselves. He was also open to assimilating fearless Korean gangs such as the Yanagawa-gumi in Osaka. The founder of the Yanagawa-gumi, Jiro Yanagawa, was a Korean whose family had served as slave laborers during the war, and he had a chip on his shoulder. He was famous for having taken on 100 yakuza members of rival groups with only eight of his men and a few Japanese swords. That kind of fighting spirit impressed Taoka.

Taoka was also a very smart businessman, as well as an acute strategist. In 1957, he set up and registered Kobe Geinosha (Kobe

Performing Arts Promotion) under his own name. It quickly become the most powerful showbiz broker in Japan. In 1961, the Yamaguchi-gumi Yanagawa-gumi, after successfully managing a pro-wrestling event for former Sumo wrestler Riki Dozan, created its own promotion company, Yanagawa Geinosha (Yanagawa Performing Arts Promotion).

In 1963, Toei films released *Jinsei Gekijo: Hishakaku* (*Theater of Life: Hishakaku*) starting the yakuza film boom, which lasted several years. Taoka is said to have helped finance the first of these films.

Taoka became friends with everyone's favorite insane nationalist, Kodama Yoshio. Taoka and Hisayuki Machii (the head of the Korean mafia, the Toseikai) were elected as board members of the Japan Pro-Wrestling Association. Pro-wrestling had become tremendously popular in Japan, partly due to the influence of the yakuza in promoting it. And even into modern times, promoting sporting events — especially mixed martial arts — has been a lucrative source of revenue for the yakuza. All of this is to say that by 1964, the yakuza weren't outlaws — they were part of the establishment.

But all that fell apart fairly quickly once the first war on the yakuza began. The Liberal Democratic Party had had enough of the yakuza telling them what to do. In 1964, the police launched their first nationwide major offensive on organized crime. Kobe Geinosha was forced out of business. Taoka bought 4,000 shares of a company called Yoshimoto Kogyo under his wife's name, and the Yamaguchi-gumi began to use the firm as a front company. Yoshimoto Kogyo is still one of Japan's major talent agencies. However, the Yamaguchi-gumi's ties to the organization have been a source of major scandal — resulting in "the Ryan Seacrest" of Japan, Shinsuke Shimada, being forced to retire. It was top news for weeks. And once again, in 2019, members of the talent agency were found to have unsavory relationships with Yamaguchi-gumi members.

The police put tremendous pressure on Taoka to dissolve the Yamaguchi-gumi. The Sumiyoshi-kai, the Inagawa-kai, and almost all the other yakuza groups made a show of dissolving their groups to let the police save face. Machii's group, the Toseika, dissolved as a yakuza group, and reformed under a new name as The East Asian Love and Friendship Business Enterprise. However, Taoka, now in poor health due to a heart condition and the stress of the crackdown, refused to budge.

He told the police, "I won't dissolve the group, even if I'm the only man remaining."

The gang wars among the yakuza had spurned part of the police crackdown, and there was a growing consensus that gang war would benefit no one. The Professor, Susumu Ishii, knowing full well that the Yamaguchi-gumi would eventually try to expand into the the Tokyo area, had the prescience to become friends with Taoka's number two, Kenji Yamamoto, in the organization circa 1971. Seijo Inagawa was in jail for gambling violations, and Ishii was running the organization. Yamamoto contacted Ishii, saying that when he was supposed to leave prison in January 1972, he wanted to greet Inagawa himself — with Yamamoto's entourage of a few hundred Yamaguchi-gumi members. It was meant as a gesture of goodwill. But when Ishii passed the message along, Inagawa refused, saying, "A gambler like me shouldn't have a fuss made about his return from prison." However, the goodwill gesture was appreciated.

A few months after getting out of jail, as scheduled, Inagawa visited Taoka in the hospital, and the two struck up an agreement. They defined their terms and their territory, and all seemed good.

In October 1972, Susumu Ishii, the chairman of the board, and the number two in the Inagawa-kai, and Kenji Yamamoto, the second-in-command of the Yamaguchi-gumi, performed the ritual exchange of sake, becoming brothers on equal terms. Haruki Sho, the only Taiwanese yakuza at the top level of the Inagawa-kai, also became a brother with another Yamaguchi-gumi member. The two groups had reached a peace of sorts.

Taoka wrote his autobiography, which sold reasonably well. It was made into a film starring everyone's favourite yakuza actor, Ken Takakura, in 1973, entitled *The Third-Generation Leader of the Yamaguchi-gumi*. Taoka visited the set of the film and gave Takakura advice.

The Yamaguchi-gumi continued its efforts to achieve a state of legitimacy. In 1975, they published their own internal newspaper — with haiku, photos, and essays. The newspaper contained the credo of the Yamaguchi-gumi, printed on the inside front cover:

> The Yamaguchi-gumi pledges to contribute to the prosperity of the national body based on the spirit of chivalry. Therefore, gang members are required to embody each clause below:
> Esteem highly friendship and unity in order to strengthen the group.
> Value fidelity and feel love when in contact with outsiders.
> Understand that elders come first and always show courtesy.
> When dealing with the world, remember who you are and do not invite criticism.
> Learn from the experiences of those who came before you and strive to improve your character.

It seems like an exemplary creed at first glance, but when compared to the credo and rules of the Yokosuka-ikka, something important was missing and is still missing: nothing is banned; everything goes. The credo sounded great and was beautiful, but meant little.

The Yamaguchi-gumi succession wars after Taoka were long, bloody, and brutal. In what almost seems like high comedy now, the

Yamaguchi-gumi would occasionally have televised press conferences to announce the end of a gang war or deliver a sort of mid-term report. They were as legitimate as the Tokyo Electric Power Company.

By the time the emperor had died, and the Heisei era had begun in 1989, the Yamaguchi-gumi had become a ruthless, powerful gang with offices almost everywhere in Japan. They aspired to be the one gang that ruled over all. The Yamaguchi-gumi was taken over by the fifth-generation leader, Yoshinori Watanabe, on July 20. Seijo Inagawa was the official "guardian" of the ceremony — an honorary position that also showed the relative strengths of yakuza groups.

Watanabe was not a man of high moral principles. Under him, the Yamaguchi-gumi terrorized anyone in their way, and his second-in-command, Masaru Takumi, rivaled Ishii in his financial wizardry, and certainly excelled Ishii in cunning. He was the yakuza boss who told his men, "From now on, the first thing a yakuza needs to do when he gets up in the morning is read the Japan economic trade newspapers."

The Yamaguchi-gumi aggressively expanded into Tokyo, with the Goto-gumi paving the way via a labyrinth of front companies and political groups. This helped spur the first anti-organized crime laws to go on the books and the first film to portray the yakuza as they had become. They did not "Esteem highly friendship and unity in order to strengthen the group," or "Value fidelity and feel love when in contact with outsiders," and they definitely were not courteous.

When Juzo Itami, the film director, parodied the Goto-gumi in his film *The Gentle Art of Japanese Extortion*, whose original title meant something closer to *The Intervention in Civil Affairs by the Yakuza*, the reaction was brutal. Thugs sliced up his face as he was leaving his house. The world was appalled. Goto, who denied any knowledge of ordering the attack, but approved of it because "Itami deserved it for making fun of us", wasn't touched at all by the police investigation. The message of the film had been that if you were a civilian bothered by the yakuza, you could work with the police and lawyers to fight them, and you could win. Justice would prevail. But that was not the case.

In 2005, Watanabe was deposed in a bloodless coup, and Shinobu Tsukasa, from the Kodo-kai faction, one of the largest factions in the group, and the most violent, took over the Yamaguchi-gumi and set it on a course that would spur a third wave of police crackdowns.

The sixth-generation head of the Yamaguchi-gumi is known as Shinobu Tsukasa. His real name is Kenichi Shinoda. His yakuza name, said in the proper Japanese way (family name first, and first name last) is Tsukasa Shinobu. It is written with two kanji characters: one meaning "to rule, to govern over all" and the next "to endure, stealthily approach." The kanji for his name is also the first character for ninja. Everyone knows his name and who he is, so at this point in his career he'd make an unlikely ninja.

A few months after Tsukasa took over, the Yamaguchi-gumi merged with a smaller organized crime group in Tokyo, the Kokusui-kai, and now had a permanent foothold in the area. It rewrote the yakuza map of Japan. The Yamaguchi-gumi was now inside Tokyo, and they would not leave. The Sumiyoshi-kai was not pleased with the new arrangements, and intermittent gang war broke out.

The head of the Kokusui-kai, Kazuyoshi Kudo, was someone that Saigo had met at the usual yakuza gatherings over the years. Kudo seemed very pleased with himself — as a reward for joining the Yamaguchi-gumi, he had been made a senior advisor. When he realised that the role was ceremonial and that the Kokusui-kai had no independence, he became bitter.

In late 2006, there were rumours that the Kokusui-kai might go independent again. In February 2007, Kudo was found in his home with a plastic bag wrapped around what was left of his head. He had a gun clasped in his hand. The police ruled it a suicide. One of the detectives who was at the scene says, "Normally, if you blow out your brains, the gun doesn't stay neatly in your hand — the recoil snaps it out of your hand. Maybe wrapping the plastic bag around his head was meant to be out of consideration for others — not make a mess. But was it a suicide? We all had doubts, but the gun was in his hand. There you go."

Meanwhile, the group also took advantage of a succession battle within the Inagawa-kai to cement their power over the Inagawa-kai as well.

Saigo's junior, Kazuo Uchibori, in the Yamakawa Ikka faction, became a blood brother to Teruaki Takeuchi, a senior member of the Yamaguchi-gumi Kodo-kai.

Tsukasa was not in power for long before losing an appeal in a court case involving arms violations, which resulted in him being sent to prison. His ruthless number two, Kiyoshi Takayama, took over the group, and changed years of previous policy by openly challenging the police, not cooperating with them, and even investigating the investigators — hoping to find materials that could be used to blackmail or intimidate the police into leaving the organization alone.

With the backing of the Kodo-kai, Uchibori also began to rise up the Inagawa-kai food chain, soon surpassing Saigo.

These days, the Yamaguchi-gumi, with the Inagawa-kai effectively under their control, has become essentially the one gang that rules them all.

The yakuza have a saying: "The Yamaguchi-gumi could cost you your life; the Inagawa-kai will cost you your life savings; and the Sumiyoshi-kai is all talk."

Kudo would have agreed with the first part, as would have many other deceased members of the Yamaguchi-gumi, and those killed by them. Saigo would certainly come to agree with the second part of the saying, and the Sumiyoshi-kai — they would violently disagree.

But probably verbally rather than physically, although they have been known to hold their own in a gang war.

What Saigo didn't like about the Yamaguchi-gumi was their arrogance. Despite their fancy credo, it seemed like there was nothing they would not do for money: human trafficking, fraud, theft, armed robbery, murder. That was the Yamaguchi-gumi he knew. He might be a gangster, but he was an Inagawa-kai gangster. They had standards.

At least, he hoped they did.

# CHAPTER TWENTY-SIX

# Taxing matters

Ishii had once famously admonished an Inagawa-kai member to become a "yakuza who pays taxes." However, he'd never said that he should become a yakuza who steals taxes.

Saigo had a problem with a deal that Mizoguchi was bringing to him. Governor Shintaro Ishihara of Tokyo had set up a bank, ShinGin Tokyo Limited, ostensibly to help fund small businesses and venture projects that the mega-banks wouldn't touch. Governor Ishihara was a former novelist, a flaming nationalist and racist, and very close to the political arm of the Sumiyoshi-kai, known as the Nihonseinensha.

The Sumiyoshi-kai had already borrowed so much money under dubious pretenses and "paper companies" that they were willing to share the wealth for a kickback. They had a person in place within the bank, and they were looking for yakuza who would borrow money from the bank and give them a cut on any loan. This would bring huge profits to both the Sumiyoshi-kai and any yakuza who worked with them.

According to Mizoguchi, the bank was practically giving away the money. All a yakuza needed was a front company and their personal seal. The checks on the borrowers were practically non-existent.

The deal was simple: set up a company, approach the designated loan officer, borrow as much as reasonably possible, kick back 25 percent to the Sumiyoshi-kai, and make at least four payments on the loan before defaulting.

Mizoguchi was going to set up a 100-yen shop — the Japanese equivalent of a dollar store. They would purchase their merchandise from a Sumiyoshi-kai supplier at inflated rates, and this would cover up the kickback. If all went as planned, when the shop eventually went bankrupt, Mizoguchi would sell the merchandise back to the Sumiyoshi-kai supplier at an inflated rate, thus creating more losses on the balance sheets, and the Sumiyoshi-kai would give him a small kickback from that as well. Then the whole process would start over — another company, another 100-yen shop.

It seemed very much like a foolproof plan.

Yet if the bank crashed, taxpayers' money would be used to bail it out. Saigo had mixed feelings about this. It was like stealing money from honest people, in a way. So he decided not to personally join the scheme, but he wasn't going to stop Mizoguchi from going through with it. Instead, he requested a 25 percent kickback on all profits that Mizoguchi and his crew made, and to be kept in the dark.

It worked out. Mizoguchi scored a $250,000 loan a few weeks after applying. About $100,000 of it went into Saigo's pocket, and he gave $50,000 of his share to Coach. Mizoguchi set up several different companies, one of which would later back a politician who briefly served as the country's finance minister. Without lifting a finger, Saigo pulled in nearly $300,000 that year, even after tithing to Coach. His conscience was relatively clear, for a while.

Mizoguchi, flush with money, was happy as well.

When a yakuza has established himself, it's all about finding new ways to make money and rise up the ladder. That's the game. There was always some scheme, some new con, some easy way to make money in the yakuza world — sometimes, even by legitimate means.

However, while Saigo was doing well, he wasn't doing as well as some of the other bosses. He heard Yohei Nakamori, the head of the Nakamori-gumi, bragging at a succession ceremony about selling off a property in Ginza for 4,400 million yen (about $44 million). Plus, he'd done the whole real estate deal via a dummy company, and hadn't paid a dime in taxes. Tax evasion, Saigo thought, was almost as bad as stealing — except, of course, when Saigo did that himself. (Like many yakuza, he was blind to the contradictions between what he professed and what he did.)

He asked Nakamori how he did it, and Nakamori explained it to him in detail. Actually, "bragged about it" would probably be the appropriate term. In October 1999, at the height of Japan's economic depression, Nakamori used his front company, Bunkyo Development, to start buying up the famous five-storey Tokunaga Building in the center of Ginza — he had some leverage on the owners that helped him cinch the deal. The rental laws in Japan favored the rights of the tenant, so acquiring all the rights to the property took time, up until 2004.

The building had been built in 1948, housed an art gallery and a German restaurant, and was well known as an example of Japan's best modern architecture. For a time, Nakamori was happy to just collect rent as well as run some dubious clubs in the building, and to use it as a base of operations. In 2005, the real estate market boomed again, creating a mini-bubble. Foreign funds and investors were snapping up land right and left. The yakuza quickly got in on the business, and some foreign firms were quite happy to do business with them.

Everyone was getting in on the new real estate bubble, especially the Goto-gumi. Saigo had bumped heads with Goto over some real estate transactions himself. He didn't like the man. There was a twelve-storey building worth over 2 billion yen ($20 million) in the Shibuya ward, part of which Inagawa-kai members had illegally taken over and then sold to a company affiliated with the Goto-gumi in February 2005, without the consent of the owner. The building was two-thirds owned by a family-run real estate company. The family hired Kazuoki Nozaki, who was fifty-eight at the time, as a consultant, and put him in charge of clearing out people illegally occupying the building, which included Goto-gumi members.

Nozaki was stubborn and persistent. He consulted with a legendary detective in the Tokyo Metropolitan Police Organized Crime Task Force (Investigative Division 4), and asked for help in solving the problem.

Saigo knew all about it, because one of his Inagawa-kai associates had been involved in the original deal. It had been a dirty transaction. The gangster involved had gotten a younger member of the family owning the building hooked on methamphetamines, and had convinced him to sign over his rights for a few bags of crystal. Then they gave the young man some meth so pure that it almost killed him. The kid ended up in a mental hospital somewhere.

The Inagawa-kai and the Yamaguchi-gumi were on friendly terms, so technically there was nothing wrong with the Inagawa-kai members selling the property indirectly to Goto, but the whole deal was foul, and Saigo did not approve of the way that Goto did business.

There were already rumors going around that Goto was going to have Nozaki killed. Saigo wouldn't put it past the man. He knew Goto. He was a new type of yakuza who thought nothing of killing or injuring any civilian who got in the way of him and his money. To him, Nakamori and Goto weren't so far apart.

When Nakamori saw that the real estate market was starting to boom again, he evicted all the tenants of the Ginza building. Some were paid off; others were forced out. Nakamori excelled at evicting people. Nakamori sold the building to another real estate agency in December 2005, using a dummy company, Tokyo Koei, and padded the expenses, thus hiding $26 million worth of profit and evading $8 million worth of taxes on the transaction. It had gone smoothly. Nakamori ran the company, but was nowhere on the books. A couple of the tenants took him to court for wrongful eviction, but he knew that even if the courts ruled against him, there would be no way the courts could force him to pay back the money. Civil damages were a joke to him. Even if he lost, he still won — because he just wouldn't pay the money.

Saigo jokingly said that the tenants could maybe hire some yakuza to collect the compensation. Then they might actually get something. Nakamori frowned at the idea.

"Who would be dumb enough to do that?" he asked.

"I might," Saigo said. "If the price was right."

There was a long silence. Then Nakamori laughed nervously, and that was the end of the conversation.

Saigo did feel more than a twinge of professional jealousy. Forty-four million dollars. If he had $44 million, he'd get out of the business. He'd give half to Coach, put half of his share in the bank, another half in stocks, and then …

He wasn't sure what he'd do then. Play guitar? Get the band back together? He had no hobbies and nothing he enjoyed, other than playing in a band and listening to music. He had no retirement plan.

Saigo was smart. He wasn't as smart as Nakamori, but he had a hard time admitting that. Nakamori was Korean, so Saigo wanted to chalk it up to Koreans being better at making money, rather than admit that Nakamori was brighter than him. He tried to console himself by thinking that maybe Nakamori just hired smart people, or maybe he was just greedier than Saigo.

Saigo didn't consider himself greedy; he liked money, but it didn't rule his life. He only needed one fancy car, didn't like to gamble, didn't want a mistress or a series of mistresses, nor did he particularly enjoy hostess clubs.

He was making good money, though. He now had seven organizations under him, including the Shelter and 150 fully fledged members and 100 associate members — "part-time yakuza." If you included the Saigo-gumi headquarters, it was eight groups.

For him, money was a means to an end, the end being rising up the yakuza ladder. He wanted everyone to know his name. He wanted to be told that his "face was wide" — that everyone knew who he was and that his "face worked", that he had power and influence. He didn't understand it himself, but he craved recognition from the world and his peers. Not necessarily admiration from everyone, but recognition.

He had reached the status of managing director in the Inagawa-kai, putting him in the top 100 of a 10,000-member organization. With a little luck, he'd become committee chairman one day. He was secretly delighted to see his name published in the August edition of the yakuza fanzine, *Jitsuwa Bull*.

He was well known locally, for sure.


On a cold morning in October 2006, Saigo was in his office, reading manga about yakuza and going over the books, when Shinji Maruyama knocked on the door and walked into the office. There was a man, a woman, and a baby waiting for him downstairs. They wanted to talk to him. They wouldn't explain why.

Maruyama was now living on the first floor of the gang's headquarters, in the room for new members. He had joined the Saigo-gumi, not because he wanted to be a yakuza, but because he wanted to get out of his contract with Sony Records.

Once Maruyama was a fully fledged yakuza, he figured that Sony would beg to release him from the contract. In those days, being a member of a yakuza wasn't something that could void a contract, but it would be damn embarrassing for Sony to have a fully sworn-in yakuza member on their label as a rock musician. The police wouldn't like it, and the shareholders probably wouldn't either. Maruyama was counting on getting out of his contract and getting a substantial hush-money payment in the process.

Saigo had agreed to take him on as yakuza brother, partly out of friendship, partly out of a promise to get a share of the severance fees, and partly to say "fuck you" to the record industry for having forced him out of the band so many years before. In his mind, they had made him a yakuza, and they might as well pay for it sooner or later.

The only problem with Maruyama was that he didn't take the business of being a yakuza very seriously. He was only in it for the short term, and was still the obnoxious, practical joke–loving clown he had always been. Thus the *oyabun/kobun* relationship, the absolute bonds of loyalty and foundation of the yakuza hierarchy, didn't register in his brain. Saigo had no choice but to treat Maruyama as more or less his equivalent, which didn't sit well with some other gang members. But Saigo was the *oyabun*, so those grievances were never openly aired.

Saigo asked Maruyama to describe the couple. Maruyama told him the man was dressed in a navy-blue suit, wearing a tie, no wristwatch, and scuffed business shoes. The woman was wearing a dress and an overcoat, and holding a baby, maybe six months old. The baby was crying.

Saigo asked Maruyama if he had any idea why they were here. Maruyama wasn't sure, but then asked if, by any chance, Saigo had knocked up the guy's wife.

Saigo threw the manga at Maruyama, and missed. He told

Maruyama to invite them in and sit them in the reception area, and to shut the door.

When he got downstairs, the couple and their child were sitting on the sofa on the far side of the door. The man was wearing thick glasses and had a thick head of unkempt hair. His wife, or who Saigo assumed was his wife, would have been beautiful when she was younger. Her hair was black, straight, and long — almost coming down to her breasts.

Saigo spoke first. He politely asked them why they were there.

The man explained that their son had a heart problem and that they were going to need surgery for him. The surgery was not covered by national health insurance, so they had pay for it out of their own pockets. The wife said nothing, just trying to quiet the child. The man started to explain the details of his son's condition and the medical procedure, but Saigo wasn't interested in that. As the man started talking about valves and ventricles, Saigo interrupted him. He wasn't a doctor, but he did instinctively believe the man. So he wanted him to get to the point.

The man needed money, and had heard Saigo might lend it to him. He heard he was generous.

Saigo wasn't sure who would say that about him, but it was flattering to hear. It was good to be generous. And Seijo Inagawa was indeed generous. He had once handed a $1,000 tip, in cash, to each of the flight attendants on a plane. Generosity was good; it was manly.

The man asked for $10,000. Saigo told him to wait there. He called Maruyama back to the room, and asked him to bring him a fat envelope and to wait for Saigo in the room. And also to bring the family some green tea.

Saigo went up to the safe in his office and took out the yen equivalent of $20,000. Downstairs, in front of Maruyama and the family, he counted out the money, had Maruyama stuff it in the envelope and hand it to him, and handed it to the father.

The man took the money, and was about to get on his hands and knees and bow on all fours, but Saigo motioned for him to stay put. The father tried to speak, but Saigo cut him off.

Saigo had given him twice what he had asked for. It wasn't a loan, but a gift. If they could pay it or some of it back someday, that would be fine. Saigo wouldn't say no. All he asked was that when their son got better, it would be nice if they came by and said hello.

The father reached into his pocket and pulled out his business card, and offered it to Saigo. It had all of his contact information. Saigo motioned for him to put away the card. He assured the man that he wasn't going to come looking for the money or for him. They knew where Saigo was. He just requested that they not tell people he had given them money, because he wasn't running a charity.

There was a long silence. The husband and wife stood up, and bowed deeply.

Saigo felt good about it. He could see that the man wanted to know why Saigo was lending him the money, but had decided not to ask why. Saigo figured that any man who came to a yakuza boss for a loan was either a fool or desperate. This man was desperate.


If you're going to talk the yakuza talk about helping the weak and fighting the strong, sometimes your actions have to match your words.

Saigo instructed Maruyama to drive the couple to the closest train station — not to their house. Saigo reasoned that the couple would become paranoid if Saigo knew where they lived. He didn't want to know. He didn't want to know the man's name, either. Because if he did, when times got tough, he might feel tempted to ask for the money back. He knew himself.

Maruyama nodded silently, and escorted the couple to the car parked next to the compound, and drove them to the station.

Upon returning, he smoked a cigarette in the empty room and, being a little lazy, drank the rest of the green tea the father had left behind.

As for Saigo, what was $20,000? Nothing. It was the equivalent of one good business deal. He could borrow the money from Shingin Tokyo and never return it. It wasn't like losing anything at all. So he told himself.

Now, of course, he had told the couple to keep quiet about this singular act of generosity, but he hadn't said as much to Maruyama. Maruyama would talk. Other yakuza would know.

And that was good.

What was the point of doing something nice if it didn't at least buy you some good PR?

## CHAPTER TWENTY-SEVEN

# The one-digit solution

Saigo had always been friends with the members of the local band Rapper Orchestra, which had become one of Japan's premiere rap groups before dissolving in 2004. The lead vocalist, Barbarian, and he had become pals. There was a point in time when Saigo had beaten the crap out of Barbarian — because Barbarian had been peddling pot in Machida, Saigo's turf, without permission — but after the beating and his escape from Machida, he came back and patched up things with Saigo.

Barbarian and his crew were fun, and while Saigo had no use for pot, he didn't consider it a hard drug. In fact, in Japan, using the drug isn't a crime — just possession of it. So he turned a blind eye to Barbarian's dealings, and the two became friends. And Barbarian brought in a little cash now and then. Saigo would also go watch Barbarian perform as a solo artist, and while he preferred rock and roll to rap, some of Barbarian's lyrics were pretty funny. Years later, Barbarian wrote a song about Saigo beating him up. Saigo shows up in the video as himself — in a wrestling mask, re-enacting the worst days of Barbarian's life. Art does imitate life, sometimes.

One particularly lucrative new source of income came from peddling uncensored adult films. Due to strict obscenity laws in Japan, the juicy bits in the movies are blurred out. The uncensored copies, only available on the black market, command a higher price. Saigo was able to obtain the original tapes from a producer friend in the porn industry, and, armed with eight video decks, good advertising, and the complicity of the local police, managed to maintain a tolerable business.

His father was still doing the books, making sure that revenues and expenditures worked out so that the business was perpetually in the black. He was paying association dues of nearly $30,000 a month and not even feeling pinched by it.

He even met a beautiful woman who his troops liked. Saigo met Yuriko at a hostess club in Tokyo. She had a long history of encounters with the police, and Saigo felt like he could straighten her out. In some ways, he needed someone who he felt was more screwed up than himself. At the time, she was dating a member of the Yamaguchi-gumi Kodo-kai. He decided he needed to be with her, so he whisked her away. He took malicious pleasure in knowing that he was stealing the woman of a Kodo-kai man. It was a terrible reason for choosing a mate, but Saigo excelled at making terrible choices in his personal life. Still, it helped him on a professional level, and kept him happy.

But it only took one screw-up for everything go haywire, and that screw-up was Mizoguchi.

Mizoguchi was acting as a collector for the group, collecting debts, rent, and protection money. He borrowed 2 million yen (roughly $25,000) from Baraki Tetsu, a loan shark associated with the Inagawa-kai Kumaya-gumi. The problem was, Mizoguchi was behind on his payments, and Tetsu had allegedly been short on capital when he'd made the loan — and thus had also borrowed money from Charlie, a member of the Yamaguchi-gumi Rachi-gumi. Although Mizoguchi had only directly borrowed from Tetsu, in the yakuza world, the money trail is followed beyond the initial two parties. In short, Saigo's foot soldier owed money to both another faction of the Inagawa-kai and the rival Yamaguchi-gumi at the same time.

Unlike Saigo's crew, Preacher's crew was dealing drugs and was involved in brothels — not just taking a cut of brothel profits, but running the whorehouses down in Kawasaki City. He owned the rights to two soapland parlors as well, The 7th Gate and Paradise Pleasure Palace. Most of the women working there were also buying *shabu* from Preacher at the same time, so he was able to keep his expenses low. North Korean meth was much better than the shit stuff they sold in the U.S. and called meth. It was more organic — made primarily from the ephedra plant.

It seemed like a dubious business for a Christian to be in, but Preacher said that every day he repented for the sins of his flock and his own — and that the more you sinned, the more Jesus forgave you. It sounded like a lot of bullshit to Saigo, but almost all religion sounded like bullshit to him. If the afterlife was so wonderful, he figured that Preacher should just shoot himself in the head and rise up like an angel to a better place, but Preacher wasn't keen to do that. For all his talk of the wonders of the Lord and the glories of heaven, he seemed much more interested in his own kingdom on earth. He was also notoriously tight-fisted about money. So when Tetsu, who was Preacher's corporate blood brother (*kigyoshatei*), complained that Saigo's soldier Mizoguchi was behind on his debts, he didn't take it lightly.

The first word of the problem came by a phone call. Preacher called Saigo directly. The two had entered the organization around the same time, so they were on friendly terms. After chit-chatting,

Preacher got to the point. He had a problem. Preacher explained the situation, and Saigo got a sinking feeling when Preacher mentioned the Yamaguchi-gumi's involvement.

He could understand one of his men borrowing money from a loan shark, although he wished Mizoguchi had come to him first. But he didn't quite believe that a loan shark tied to the Inagawa-kai would need to borrow money from the Yamaguchi-gumi. It strained credulity.

It should have been simple, but it was already complicated. Preacher made it clear that it was more than just a matter of late loan payments. Mizoguchi was one of Saigo's soldiers. He had borrowed from one of Preacher's loan sharks, who had borrowed money from the Yamaguchi-gumi Rachi-gumi. Because Mizoguchi hadn't repaid what he owed, Tetsu lost face, Charlie lost face, and, ultimately, Preacher lost face. It made him look bad to the Yamaguchi-gumi.

Saigo promised to have a talk with Tetsu and Mizoguchi to clear things up. Altogether, including interest, the amount was maybe 3.5 million yen ($40,000).

Saigo had his driver take him to Tetsu's office. He didn't make an appointment.

Tetsu had an office on the second floor of an office building near Yokohama station. It was ostensibly the premises of Roses Real Estate; but, of course, almost no legitimate real estate office operates on the second floor of a building where foot traffic is unlikely.

The office was large. There was a reception area in the front, where two women and a man sat behind a long counter. Behind that was Tetsu's private office. There was also another room next to it that appeared to be connected.

Saigo had his bodyguard come with him. Ignoring the wailing staff members trying to bar them, they stormed into the ornate private office, which was surprisingly well decorated for your standard loan shark. Tetsu was dressed in a dark navy-blue suit, sitting behind a large oak desk with a marble top, leaning back in a leather chair. His black-and-gray hair was slicked back, accenting his oval face and tiny, mole-like eyes.

He was wearing a purple-tinted Armani shirt, much too tight for his slightly pudgy body, and a paisley patterned bright-red tie. He didn't stand up to greet Saigo when he came in. He didn't have a bodyguard in the room, but there was a camera embedded in the ceiling. Saigo was fairly certain that there were several thugs waiting in the adjoining room, and that Tetsu had a gun under his desk that he could reach quickly.

The conversation did not go very well. Tetsu was arrogant. He made an off-color remark implying that Saigo was "the bottom" in a homosexual relationship with his *oyabun*. The comment angered Saigo so much that he came close to smashing the man's face in on the spot. He seemed to know exactly what buttons to press to make Saigo reach his full storm potential. Before he knew it, Saigo was saying things he had sworn he wouldn't say. He felt like he was driving a truck whose brakes had failed while he was going downhill.

By the time the conversation was over, Tetsu had assailed Saigo for his failure to adequately govern his subordinates and had implied that he would be taking up the matter with Saigo's boss and possibly the Yamaguchi-gumi as well.

What had stung the most was Tetsu's parting shot: "Your people come to borrow money from me because you're such an arrogant asshole that no one wants to deal with you." Tetsu called Saigo a cheap bastard, and said that was why people called him the "Jew of the Inagawa-kai."

"You know what?" Saigo said. "I'd rather be a cheap Jew than make my living sucking Yamaguchi-gumi cock for cash."

That line hadn't gone over very well. Tetsu stood up, and the side door of his office opened, his goons emerging from inside. Saigo's bodyguard immediately moved close enough to Tetsu that it was clear he could stab the man to death before his hired hands could stop him. No one apologized, and Saigo held his ground until Tetsu's men went back into the other room.

Tetsu told Saigo to tell Mizoguchi to pay up, or he'd collect the money himself. Saigo told Tetsu that he'd deal with him. And that was where things stood.

Saigo sent Maruyama to pick up Mizoguchi. Saigo trusted Mizoguchi very much. Instinctively, he knew that this wasn't just about late payments. There was more to it; he just couldn't see all the angles yet. It was like trying to thread a needle while looking at the string through a fishbowl.

When Mizoguchi came into the room, Saigo motioned for him to sit down in the tatami room for guests. He nodded to Maruyama, who slid the paper doors shut behind them when they sat down. For everyone's sake, the fewer people who knew about these problems, the better. Mizoguchi had been with Saigo a long time. He was fond of the guy, but that didn't mean he completely trusted him. Only a fool trusted someone 100 percent. Sometimes, Saigo didn't even trust himself.

Saigo knew Mizoguchi owed 3.5 million yen. Mizoguchi said he hadn't paid it back because he didn't have the money. Saigo asked why he had borrowed it, but Mizoguchi didn't want to say. That answer caught Saigo by surprise.

He didn't want to answer because he thought Saigo would be very angry if he told him the truth.

Any other person would have just lied, but Mizoguchi just didn't seem to be capable of lying. *Baka-shojiki,* "stupidly honest," was the term for people like him. It made him trustworthy, but it also made it hard to entrust him with some jobs. He wouldn't lie to the cops. He would keep silent, though. Maybe that was better than someone who would lie without a moment's hesitation.

Saigo splayed his fingers on the short table in front of him, tapping them, thinking. He stood up, went to the corner of the room, and pulled a wooden sword from the umbrella rack. He walked back to where he had been sitting, lifted the sword above his head, and ordered Mizoguchi to put his left arm on the table.

Mizoguchi did as he was told, leaning forward and putting his arm on the table. His whole body shook violently.

Saigo brought down the sword so quickly and powerfully that he could feel the air fly against his face. The sword came down with a nasty snap — cracking the table right next to Mizoguchi's arm. An inch to the left, and it would have shattered the man's elbow. But Saigo didn't believe in pointless violence.

Saigo raised the sword again, holding it right over Mizoguchi's arm. He wanted answers.

Mizoguchi told him to break his arm, because he didn't want to say.

Saigo threw down the sword. "Goddammit!"

They sat in silence for a minute. Saigo pulled a cigarette out of the crystal cigarette-holder on the table, chewed on the end, and lit up. He blew out smoke, and sighed. After thinking it through, Saigo promised that no matter what Mizoguchi told him, he wouldn't cripple him, banish him, or kill him — so he needed to tell him.

Mizoguchi nodded. He was heavily into *shabu*. He couldn't get enough, and he had started borrowing money to get some.

Saigo backhanded Mizoguchi so hard that his face turned 90 degrees, and bloodied his mouth. Mizoguchi, like a punching bag, rocked back to his previous position, his head bowed in shame. The Saigo-gumi had a zero-tolerance policy towards methamphetamines. He knew where it led.

Saigo had promised not to cripple him. He hadn't promised not to beat him up. Saigo asked if he was still using, but Mizoguchi said he had been clean for three months. Saigo made sure. He had him roll up his shirtsleeves; the tattoos disguised the needle marks, but he could make them out in the areas where the flesh wasn't fully inked. Saigo couldn't see any fresh marks.

Saigo kept his word. He wasn't going to banish Mizoguchi, but if he touched the stuff again — bought, sold, or used it — he'd break his fucking arms and banish him from the organization.

Mizoguchi understood. Then Saigo asked him why he hadn't come to him for the loan instead of going to that asshole loan shark Testu. In a sense, Mizoguchi explained, it was because he knew better. Saigo would have asked him why he needed the money, and then would have beaten the crap out of him. As for why Mizoguchi went to Tetsu, and not someone else, it was because Tetsu was a dealer, too. Charlie supplied him with meth, and when Mizoguchi didn't have enough to buy any more meth, he could borrow money from Tetsu to buy more. They were supplying the money and the drugs.

Now Saigo understood. He thanked Mizoguchi for telling him the truth, and decided he would pay off his debt.

Mizoguchi put both his hands on the table and lowered his forehead to the surface, prostrating himself as low he possibly could go. That was when Saigo noticed the rubber band wrapped tightly around Mizoguchi's left finger. The blood had already drained out of it.

In a calm, low voice, he told his foot soldier that he was not going to chop off his finger. It wasn't necessary, and he forbade it. Saigo ordered Mizoguchi to give him the knife.

There were not many ways to atone for a screw-up of the caliber that his soldier had made. Mizoguchi had broken the code. He'd disgraced his boss, and he owed serious money. In those days, in the yakuza world, that kind of atonement, if it wasn't paid in huge wads of cash, could only by paid in single digits: one amputated pinkie. But this wasn't one of those times, Saigo decided. Not for his soldier, at least.

Mizoguchi sat up, looking shocked. He pulled a short knife from inside his jacket and handed it over to his boss. Saigo made his soldier hand over the white handkerchief, too. He took both items and laid them on the table. He nodded to Mizoguchi, and told him he was not to speak about what had happened to anyone, and, in the future, he was not to borrow money from anyone other than Saigo personally.

*Yubizume* means "to shorten the finger." It's a yakuza euphemism for chopping part of it off. Traditionally, the first joint of the pinkie was more than enough to indicate great regret or to make absolution for your screw-ups or the screw-ups of your friends. There are any number of explanations of how the practice began and what it means, though no one seems to know the truth. Some assert that in the days when the sword was the yakuza weapon of choice, cutting off the tip of the pinkie weakened one's grip and thus showed submission and sacrifice.

In the postwar yakuza world, where killing an enemy up-close with a knife was considered the manly way to finish off an opponent, the lack of a pinkie was also a liability. That was because, if you wanted to stab someone to death, you had to jab them in the gut deeply, and then turn the knife. That would cause so much pain they couldn't fight back, and would most certainly kill them. With no pinkie, turning the knife was a serious challenge — much harder to do.

In other words, the chopping off of part of the finger, wrapping it in a white handkerchief, and offering it to the one who had been offended was much like a dog showing its neck to the victor in a dog fight.

In the old days, there were very few yakuza lucky enough to rise up the ladder without losing one or two fingers in the process. Usually, some trouble or grievance arose that necessitated the procedure. To make the cut, you had to make "the cut", so to speak. It wasn't uncommon for some bosses to reach the top missing two or three fingers. One legendary boss in the Sumiyoshi-kai was called Kani-san (Mr Crab) because a lifelong series of screw-ups had left him with only the thumb and index fingers of both hands.

Saigo understood that his time had come. It was part of the life, but if he was going to have to lose a finger, he was going to make sure he gained something in return. He wasn't like the other yakuza who thought nothing of chopping off their fingers — as though it was a fashion statement. Even among the top echelon of the yakuza, not everyone held the practice in esteem. For one thing, it easily identified the individual as a yakuza, and that wasn't a plus as they began moving into more corporate-type activities. A missing finger was even more obvious than a tattoo. Still, for his generation, there was a time when that was the only solution.

According to a police study circa 1992, roughly 40 percent of all yakuza had chopped off a finger or partially amputated one. Of those who had performed *yubizume*, 60 percent had done the deed while still a low-ranking yakuza member. When asked how they came to lose their finger, eight out of ten yakuza replied that it was "an expression of apology," and the rest that it was to "show sincerity." The most common reasons given for performing yubizume were 1) money troubles; 2) women troubles; 3) causing problems to the organization; 4) causing trouble to a brother; and 5) to remain in the organization or to leave it. The most uncommon reason was "to take responsibility for the mistakes of an underling", which was about 5 percent of the total.

The ritual was most often done in the home (40 percent) and other places such as the gang office, a soldier's home, or in the woods.

Saigo's motivations were unusual, but he chose a common place: in his kitchen at home. He had everything he needed there to do the job right; but, as it turned out, amputating his own finger was not easily done.

Most yakuza, when they're being honest, will tell you that *yubizume* is not a solo job. One mid-level boss explained, "If you ask me, the 88 percent of the yakuza who said they did it all by themselves are lying out their ass. It's not as easy as you'd think. Some yakuza even call a doctor to come do the deed for them; there is less infection, the cut is cleaner, and there's not so much of a problem with nerve damage and phantom limbs later. Probably hurts less, too. So I hear."

Saigo didn't call a doctor for help, or anyone, for that matter — at least, not at first. He decided to call Yuriko, on her cell phone. She was out shopping. He asked her to buy him a sashimi knife and to bring it home immediately. He had some serious crap to clean up.

Yuriko asked whether he was going to kill someone or chop off a finger. He was honest with her, and she was happy that at least he wasn't going to kill anyone. If he did that, he would definitely go to jail. She double-checked with him and he said he wouldn't kill someone if he didn't have to, and again asked her to bring home a sashimi knife.

Saigo had to get prepared. Yuriko told him the rubber bands were in the kitchen. She knew the drill. Her previous boyfriend had been a yakuza as well, and a screw-up. He was down to eight fingers when she left him.

She had one more question: "Don't you think a saw would be better?" Saigo thought about it. No. Saws made huge messes — he'd get a jagged and sloppy cut.

He hung up. He took out the rubber bands and sat at the kitchen table. He wrapped one around the base of his left little finger as tightly as he could, looping it repeatedly.

At first, the finger got slightly black as it filled up with blood, the white of his fingernail becoming whiter, almost glowing. After a while, the pinkie became swollen, full of blood that couldn't leave, and then it suddenly turned white. He smashed his right fist on the finger to check — no sensitivity at all. His little finger was effectively numb to the world.

He knew a yakuza boss that actually had a surgeon do the procedure. He'd thought about that, but it seemed unmanly. And if word got out — well, then you would become a first-class joke in the yakuza world. You might as well slit your wrists if you were going to have a surgeon cut off your pinkie. Doctors talked.

Actually, he was lucky. He's seen guys who'd had to cut off their fingers right there on the spot, with no time to prep or buy the sharpest of knives. That always resulted in a bloody, painful mess.

Yuriko came back with a bag of groceries and a sashimi knife. In another bag, she brought a white handkerchief, some rubbing alcohol, and a Kero Kero the Frog set of Band-Aids.

Good god, he thought to himself. He wasn't putting a fucking Band-Aid on his amputated finger. And if he did, it would definitely not be some cute smiling frog. But he didn't say anything about it.

He took out the knife from its box and held it up to the light, eyeing it. She'd gotten a good knife. It had a black neo-ivory handle, and a blade that looked like folded steel. There was a pattern on the cutting edge made of delicate swirls. It had almost no curve.

Yuriko stood next to the refrigerator, keeping her distance. In the back room, he could hear the sound of Maruyama snoring.

He motioned to Yuriko with his jaw. She brought over the cutting board, and dropped it on the table with a big thud.

She pursed her lips. She didn't want him to use that cutting board, she said. Ideally, she'd prepare dinner on it. Salads and stuff.

Saigo knew better. She'd never chopped a vegetable in her entire life, nor made a salad. But she argued she might start, and then she wouldn't have a clean cutting board. Saigo said he'd wash it when he was done, but Yuriko knew that was a lie. He'd only have one hand for a few days. How was he going to wash a cutting board?

They stared at each other. She could sense that Saigo wanted her to leave. She gave him a gentle squeeze on his shoulder, went into his office, closed the door behind her, and left him alone. He knew he could call her if he needed anything.

There he was at the kitchen table — a knife in one hand, and his other hand splayed out on the white cutting board. Four of his fingers were flesh colored. His pinkie was now as white as the cutting board. It almost blended in. That was probably the root of the mistake.

He stood the knife up almost vertically, the blade edge facing towards his finger, and pulled it down hard. But he hadn't been careful enough, and cut right into the second joint.

He had meant to only sever the tip. He'd cut two joints down. There was nothing to do but keep cutting. However, to his surprise, the finger was enormously sinewy. And the blood made traction difficult.

"Yuriko!"

She came running, saw the mess, and put her hands over her mouth, sucking in air. The knife wouldn't cut anymore. He needed her help, but she wasn't sure what he wanted her to do.

He thought about it. He told her to take the doorstop and pound on the knife.

She ran to the entrance and brought back a heavy brick. Saigo gritted his teeth as she brought it down hard on the top of the knife — and nothing happened.

She did it again, and this time missed the knife and hit the tip of his middle finger.

He swore up a storm. At this point, Maruyama woke up and opened his door. He was in green pajamas. He took in the scene, and his mouth opened wide.

Saigo didn't have the time for Maruyama to gape. He needed a hand. He walked over to the table and stared at Saigo's finger, pinned under the knife. Saigo explained that he couldn't cut his finger off. Maruyama stroked his goatee. Then he motioned for Saigo to turn his hand over.

Saigo pulled out the knife and did as much, his palm now facing up. Maruyama took the knife, positioned it over the joint, and held it in place. He motioned Yuriko to hand him the brick. Knife in place and brick in hand, he brought it down on the back of the blade with controlled impact, and with a rubbery snap the finger severed.

Saigo instinctively pulled his hand away. He stared at the little bloody nub of flesh sitting there, and went over to the sink to wash his hand. He told Maruyama to take care of his finger — and, seriously, not to lose it.

Maruyama told him to trust him — he could handle it — but his voice sounded a little strange. Almost nasally. Was he crying? Fuck. Saigo didn't need that.

Saigo looked at Maruyama, and saw that he had stuffed the severed finger joint up his nose. He smiled. "See? Safe and sound. It's right under my nose."

In spite of himself, Saigo laughed. He thought it wasn't the time to be making jokes, but Maruyama felt the exact opposite. If he thought about what had just happened, he'd go crazy. "Dude, we just chopped off your pinkie."

Saigo gawked. We?

Okay, Maruyama admitted. Saigo had done at least 90 percent of the work, but it wouldn't have been severed if he hadn't been there to help finish the job. It was that less than 10 percent that was important. "*Aikawarazu tsume ga amai ne,*" Maruyama said.

The saying is understood to mean, "To overconfidently do something half-assed and fail to fully complete it," but it literally means "Poorly compacted." The work *tsume* means "to pack in, to shorten," and the word for chopping off your finger in yakuza slang is "*yubi* (finger) *tsume*". The joke may translate poorly, but it was quite witty at the time.

It was a wonderfully morbid and appropriate pun. Even Yuriko laughed at this one. They were all laughing now. Maruyama laughed so hard at his own joke that he blew the finger out of his nose and then caught it quickly in one hand.

He showed it to Saigo and gave him a thumbs-up with it. They couldn't stop laughing at the whole situation. Eventually, Maruyama held out the finger.

Saigo reluctantly took it back and wrapped it in the white handkerchief. He was starting to feel some pain. The two of them got in his car and headed towards Shinjuku. They were going to meet Charlie and Tetsu at the Furinkaikan Coffee Shop in Kabukicho. It was neutral territory.

Saigo had a plan. He was going to pay the debts and come back with five times what he was going to pay in cash there. He was going to give the two of them the finger, both literally and metaphorically. Sometimes, he thought, the Japanese saying is true: losing is victory.

The coffee shop was in yakuza central: Kabukicho. The place was nearly empty that afternoon.

At the table in the back were Charlie and Tetsu. Saigo had summoned them there. Saigo walked up to Tetsu and pulled a handkerchief out of his pocket, and then unwrapped his bloody finger and held it up for Tetsu to see, straight up.

Saigo gave him the finger. He didn't need to say, "Fuck you." Sign language was working for him quite well. That should settle their debts. He had cash in his bag and a finger for Tetsu's troubles.

Tetsu was shocked. He didn't know what to do with it. The proper ritual would have been to hand Tetsu the finger, wrapped in a white cloth, bowing and murmuring apologies. But Saigo was in a bad mood, and was feeling more pain. "Why don't you put it in your coffee?" he suggested. "It'll add some flavor."

So Saigo just dropped the finger in the man's coffee cup, where it quickly floated to the surface, turning red. Tetsu turned very pale. Charlie didn't say anything.

Tetsu tried to take the finger out of his coffee with a spoon, as his coffee with cream started turning a darker shade of brown, thanks to the faint amount of blood oozing from the finger.

Saigo mocked him. Tetsu was a yakuza. The least he could do was touch the piece of flesh with his own hands. "Take the finger."

Saigo hadn't been to the doctor yet, so there was now blood oozing from the joint where he'd severed his finger.

He pointed at the floating finger, and joked about how it sort of looked like a wiener. Tetsu looked like he was going to throw up. He tried to pull out the finger, but the coffee was so hot, he burnt his own fingers and dropped the finger as soon as he pulled it out. The finger rolled off the table onto the floor. The waiter, unperturbed, scooped it up deftly, wrapped it in a napkin that was on the table, and pushed it towards Tetsu.

The two of them were now completely silent.

"Take the damn finger," growled Saigo. From out of his bag, he took an envelope of cash and tossed it in the lap of Tetsu. "And the money."

Now he had control of the conversation. Saigo's subordinate had owed Tetsu money, and now he was paying it back. But because Tetsu had made a scene about it, Saigo had felt he had to cut off his finger, too. Tetsu looked at Charlie, who immediately excused himself to the restroom.

Tetsu apologized extensively. He hadn't meant to make so much trouble — but words were cheap. Saigo wanted him to show his sincerity in the form of 7 million yen. That was twice the amount that Saigo had just thrown in his lap. Tetsu wasn't counting the money, though.

"It'll take me until next week."

"Bullshit," Saigo said. "You'll bring it to my office tomorrow." He ordered the money in cash, and told him to bring it sooner, if he had any decency. Saigo knew that, when closing a deal, especially one that was pretty much extortion, you never wanted to give the person time to think it over. Give someone too much time, and they might talk to the cops. They might have second thoughts.

Tetsu started protesting feebly, but Saigo pounded the table with one hand and pointed his amputated finger at Tetsu. He took the wet napkin with his finger inside it, and stuffed it into Tetsu's inner coat pocket.

Tetsu had until the next night, at the latest. And he was never allowed to lend money to Saigo's people again.

Maruyama drove Saigo to the closest hospital. He told the doctor that he'd slammed the door on his hand while driving down the freeway, and his finger had flown off and was lost on the expressway. Of course, the doctor didn't believe him.

Since there was no finger to reattach, the doctor severed the nerves as best he could, and sewed up the wound. He didn't use much anesthetic. When Saigo got home that night, one of Tetsu's emissaries was waiting for him with the money — 7 million yen in cash.

He would have counted the money himself, but his hand hurt too much. He had Maruyama do it.

Once the money was counted, Maruyama and Saigo sat down to smoke. Saigo didn't feel like talking much. He was really feeling the pain now.

Maruyama was optimistic.

"Saigo-san, it's not so bad. You came out of this with 3.5 million yen."

"Yeah," Saigo said, "but I lost a finger."

"Yeah, but now that you only have nine fingers, you can park in the handicapped zone."

It was true. After having applied his one-digit solution, he never had trouble getting a parking space. Technically, he should have applied for a handicapped person's benefit card, but showing the parking attendant his hand usually did the trick.


Over the years, before chopping off his own finger, there had been a couple of screw-ups who'd offered their fingers up to him as penance. Saigo used to keep the jars on display in the house, but the cops started to use them against him. So he started to bury them in his backyard, but he could never remember their exact locations.

## CHAPTER TWENTY-EIGHT

# Refrigerator Man and the honest yakuza

In January 2006, Purple came to Saigo with a problem. A member of his gang, Jo Yabe, was addicted to meth and wouldn't get clean. He had taken Purple's prized Cadillac for a joyride without a license. If Purple told his *oyabun*, he'd have to kick Yabe out. So he was wondering if Saigo could possibly beat some sense into the guy for him.

If Purple beat Yabe up himself, the organization would question why he did it — and then he'd get into trouble for not having told his *oyabun* about Yabe's meth problem. However, if Saigo beat up Yabe, people would think he'd just lost his temper over some trivial thing, and wouldn't even question it.

Plus, Purple knew that Saigo had been a meth addict himself. And he'd been given a second chance. His brother was asking him, and he didn't feel like he could refuse. So he ordered Maruyama to bring some men with him and to fetch Yabe.

Yabe was still asleep, even though it was four in the afternoon.

They dragged him out of bed, took back the Cadillac, and shoved Yabe in the trunk.

When they got to the office, they took Yabe upstairs to Saigo's main office. He was forced to sit in the *seiza* position on the tatami-mat floor while Saigo interrogated him. Saigo asked him again and again if he was on meth, and Yabe denied it. Maruyama slapped him across the face.

Saigo's thought was, first, that he had to get the addict to admit he had a problem. If he wouldn't admit it, Saigo would hit him until he did. Saigo's men pinned Yabe down and rolled up his sleeves. He had the needle marks of an addict.

He gave Yabe an ultimatum: give up the drugs, or be kicked out of the organization. And if they caught him doing meth again, they'd really hurt him.

Yabe confessed to everything.

Saigo made a great show of calling Purple on the phone in front of Yabe. Purple pretended to demand Yabe be expelled from the organization. Saigo argued against it. Finally, the phone conversation ended. Saigo turned back to Yabe.

"You're going to promise to get off the shit," Saigo said. "And you have to get a beating for this. Otherwise, you won't learn." Saigo gave him a choice: Saigo could beat him up, or the Inagawa-kai could beat him up.

Yabe chose Saigo.

Saigo thought about punching him out, but Yabe was still sitting in the *seiza* position on the floor, so it was easier to kick him. He kicked him twice, once in the face, and once in the chest. He had a wooden sword lying close by, and he thought about whacking Yabe with it a few times, but decided that smacking him with it once was more than enough. It made a hell of a sound as it swooshed through the air, but Saigo pulled back a few millimeters before it hit. The blow resulted in a smacking sound, but made no real damage.

They made Yabe show them where he had hidden his drugs, and flushed all the meth down the toilet. They found his syringe, cut it up with scissors, and flushed it down the toilet, too. They found drugs hidden in the Cadillac, and they flushed those down the toilet as well.

Yabe was put on suspension, his return to the organization being contingent upon him staying clean.

That should have been the end of it, but it wasn't. Saigo had not followed the wisdom of Purple — he'd left very visible marks on his victim. Detective Kenji Muraki of the Kanagawa Police Department noticed Yabe's puffed-up face when he met up with him "to catch up" a few days later.

Muraki was a cop in the police force who was legendary for being corrupt. The yakuza hated him, and the other cops disliked him. He always wore an oversized black suit. He must have owned seven or eight copies of the same suit. He always shaved his head like a Buddhist priest, and wore a pair of thick gold-rimmed glasses. He was a former judo champion, stocky and strong, and his ears, from being thrown onto the mats many times, looked like crumpled pieces of paper — dumpling ears.

He asked Yabe what had happened, and why his face was puffed up. Yabe didn't want to talk about it, but Muraki was insistent. When Muraki heard the whole story, he was delighted.

"So he beats you up, and you get suspended," Muraki confirmed. "That's fucked up. I'll get a warrant, and we'll arrest the bastard for assault. Did he do anything else?"

Yabe said he didn't want to press charges and that nothing else had happened. Yabe had paid back some money he owed to Saigo after his beating, but that was money he had borrowed.

He was told to come into the Kanagawa Police Department headquarters for further investigation. He went reluctantly, and was taken to the interrogation room. It was a drab place. It had a desk and two metals chairs with plastic seats. There were no windows, no wallpaper, and no glass on the door. There was an ashtray and a black lamp on the table. On the wall was a 'Wanted' poster for a missing member of the Aum Shinrikyo cult.

Muraki explained where things stood. He hadn't done shit that year. He'd had no good cases or good busts. He wanted to arrest a few of the Inagawa-kai bosses and score some points with the top brass. The Inagawa-kai was about to change chairmmen, so the timing was good.

"I need your help to make this bust."

There had been nine or ten Saigo-gumi members in the office when Saigo had dragged Yabe in for their talk. Muraki figured he could arrest them all. The charges might only stick for a few of them, but a large-scale raid and arrest like that would practically guarantee him a promotion, or at least a pat on the back and a reward within the department.

Muraki ordered Detective Lucky to take down the confession. Neither Lucky nor Yabe was very happy about this latest turn of events. As Lucky came into the room, Muraki said loudly to him, so that Yabe could hear him, "If this guy doesn't feel like talking about what happened to him, ask him if he's been using meth. He's either a crime victim or a criminal. His choice."

Even Yabe, not the brightest of guys, understood the subtext: cooperate with the investigation of Saigo for assault, or go to jail for using methamphetamines.

The whole time, Lucky was thinking to himself that Yabe was blessed to have a yakuza boss like Saigo looking after him. He would later tell a junior detective, "If you are a yakuza and your *oyabun* beats you up because you're doing drugs, you should write a thank-you note, not file a criminal complaint.'"

Once they started the paperwork, an arrest was inevitable. Lucky wasn't pleased with how the case was shaping up. It wasn't just a simple assault case now. Muraki had turned it into an assault-and-extortion case.

A week or so before Muraki was ready to request an arrest warrant, the news leaked to Saigo. Kanagawa police information always leaked to Saigo. He would know a week in advance when they'd be making a raid — even when they didn't schedule an appointment.

Saigo called up Muraki directly; he had Muraki's cell phone number.

"I hear you're coming to arrest me for beating up Yabe. I won't deny anything. I'll turn myself in. Don't touch anyone else in the organization."

Muraki was shocked.

"How did you find out? You can't turn yourself in now. We haven't asked for an arrest warrant. It'll look like information is leaking."

"It doesn't just look that way. It is. It's always that way with you guys. I'm turning myself in. I'm not waiting for you to come raid my place and arrest me in front of the television cameras."

"Let's talk this over. Right now, I'm going to have to arrest you and nine others. I'm sure you don't want everyone going to jail."

Saigo definitely didn't want that. The cost of taking care of ten court cases — that could be expensive indeed, and it would be his duty and obligation to do so. Muraki hinted that he could work something out with Saigo.

The next morning, Muraki showed up at his office with a vase full of chrysanthemums and a young police officer next to him. Saigo understood what that meant. There was a blank envelope inside the flowers. Saigo took it to the other room, quickly put 200,000 yen in cash (roughly $2,000) into the envelope, came back to his office, and handed the flowers back to Muraki, saying, "I appreciate the gesture, but couldn't accept these. I'm not very good with flowers. They wouldn't survive long."

Saigo took Muraki's choice of flowers as both a snub and a threat. Chrysanthemums were usually reserved for funeral arrangements. Perhaps the message was, "Fill up the envelope and hand back the flowers, or it will be your funeral."

Subtle.

Muraki took back the flowers and glanced at the envelope.

"Yabe says you beat him up and you made him pay you 120,000 yen to leave the group."

That wasn't what what had happened, but that's what the cops were going to say had happened.

"We're going to raid your office in the next few days, and I'm going to arrest everyone who was in the office that day."

Saigo glared at him and nodded towards the flowers.

"You can arrest as many as you like — I want an assurance I'm the only one going to jail."

"I can't guarantee that, but I can pretty much promise that only you will be prosecuted. They might hold the others for a while."

Saigo knew he couldn't beat the charges but could minimize the damages, and that's what they were negotiating. It was true that he'd hit Yabe, and even if it was for all the right reasons, the law was not on his side.

They set the time for the raid and the arrests.

On September 2, the police raided Saigo's place, and he, along with nine others, was arrested. The prosecution decided not to charge the nine of them, but Saigo was held in custody, bail was denied, and the prosecution asked for his time in custody to be extended twice.

He was looking at twenty-three days in preliminary detention. If the charges stuck, he faced years in jail.

In Japan, the accused doesn't have the right to have a lawyer present during his interrogation. Although Saigo did have a very good lawyer, there was no way he could beat this rap.

Detective Lucky was in charge of his interrogation on and off during the holding period. Saigo wouldn't admit anything. He did say, "As I was speaking to Yabe, maybe I bumped into him. I don't remember. I didn't lay a finger on him."

On Saigo's twenty-first day in custody, Lucky sat across from the table and made him an offer.

"It would be a shame to go to jail for this one. Extortion is a serious felony. What do you say you admit to hitting the guy, and we'll just file it with the prosecutors as simple assault? You'll get a fine, maybe $5,000. That's nothing to you. You admit to hitting him, pay your fine, and go home. You save face, we save face, justice is served. The timing is right, too."

Saigo thought it over, rubbing his forehead with his index finger and his thumb. It seemed like a good deal, so he took it.

Within about thirty minutes, Lucky had prepared the statement, writing it in the first person as if he was Saigo himself, and Saigo signed it. He was then escorted to the prosecutor's office. There was little time left: the prosecutor would either have to file charges or let Saigo go.

Saigo sat down at a table in a brightly lit room while the prosecutor went over the paperwork. The prosecutor read through the document a few times, nodding. He spoke to Detective Lucky.

"Well, he admits to hitting the guy. Seems pretty cut-and-dry."

"Yep," responded Lucky.

But then the prosecutor paused. He looked at the attached documents and scratched his head.

"He was arrested on charges of extortion. There's not a single word about extortion in this statement. What kind of investigation is this? What happened to the extortion bit? I'm a little —

Saigo interrupted him, "I didn't extort anything. I just hit him."

Lucky nodded in affirmation.

The prosecutor looked at both of them and back at the statement. He sighed.

"There's not enough time to do this over. All right. Fine. Simple assault. Summary prosecution, and you pay a fine."

And that was that. Saigo pled guilty and paid 500,000 yen ($5,000) in cash. It was one more mark on his criminal record, but it wasn't jail time, and that was better than he'd hoped for.

Later, Lucky admitted, over coffee at his office, he'd made sure they held Saigo the whole time, just to force the prosecutor's hand. After all, Lucky thought Saigo had done the right thing, and he was sorry he had gotten arrested.

"Although, technically, you can't go around beating up people."

Saigo was grateful for the kind words, but also slightly miffed. If that was the plan from the start, he could've told him.

Lucky clarified the matter. It wasn't really a plan. And if he'd told him the plan, it would have been like plea-bargaining. And they didn't do that.

"You know," Saigo said, "I was telling the truth in my initial statement when I said I never laid a hand on the guy."

Lucky choked on his coffee.

"I kicked him and hit him with a wooden sword, but I never laid a hand on him. Literally, that's true."

"You're the most honest yakuza I've ever met. In a lying, duplicitous sort of way."

"Thank you. You're the most honest cop I know. You may be the only honest cop I know."

"Well, thank you. There are others, you know."

"I don't know of any."

"Then you're not paying attention. Try to stay out of trouble."

"I will."


Saigo didn't stay out of trouble for very long.

And, in the end, Muraki didn't stay out of trouble either. On March 2, 2010, the *Asahi Shimbun* published a long exposé of Muraki, pointing out that he had borrowed a refrigerator from a member of the Inagawa-kai during an investigation in 2007 — and that it had been used at the police department ever since. The "scoop" also noted that Muraki, who wasn't specifically named in the report, had been disciplined for sexual harassment of a police employee, and was being investigated for skipping work and going to a sports club while on duty.

Even with violation after violation, the Kanagawa Police Department would not fire him. After all, he produced results. The newspaper article helped him earn the nickname Refrigerator Man within the department, and the name lasted until his mandatory retirement a couple of years later. He retired with full benefits and a significant amount of savings he had gained over the years via flower bribes.

While Saigo was grateful to Lucky for having kept him out of jail, the legal costs and his twenty-one-day absence from work created a huge dent in the group's finances.

He was in poor shape for the bullets that would soon be fired into his world.

## CHAPTER TWENTY-NINE
# One thing leads to another

Two thousand and six wasn't a bad year for everyone. In 2006, Shinzo Abe, the grandson of the incredibly mobbed-up former prime minister Kishi Nobosuke, decided that he wanted to be the next prime minister of Japan. He was part of a political dynasty. His grandfather, an accused war criminal, freed by the U.S. authorities in the so-called "reverse course", would frequently attend yakuza weddings, especially those of the Yamaguchi-gumi, and during his time in office had been willing to use the yakuza to suppress the student uprisings protesting the renewal of the U.S.-Japan Security Treaty.

Nobosuke had also been instrumental in asking the Inagawa-kai to form a second police force for President Dwight D. Eisenhower's planned visit on June 19, 1960. There were not enough Japanese police to handle the ever-growing number of anti-treaty protestors. On June 10, 1960, an aide of Eisenhower's had arrived at Haneda airport, only to find the entire airport surrounded by demonstrators. He had been put on a helicopter and flown to his destination.

The original plan was for Eisenhower and the emperor to ride in an open car from the airport to the Imperial Palace with an eighteen-kilometer parade. The Liberal Democratic Party and Kishi reached out to Yoshio Kodama, who called for the help of right-wing groups, the Inagawa-kai and other yakuza, as well as yakuza-backed right-wing groups. The Inagawa-kai promised to provide roughly 10,000 men for extra security, and prepared a helicopter and a Cessna (a light aircraft) for an emergency. However, the trip was cancelled, and the yakuza welcome never materialized.

Tokutaro Kimura, the Liberal Democratic Party member who had come up with the brilliant idea of using the right wing and the yakuza as a second security force, was also the chairman of the LDP Countermeasures Against Boryokudan (Yakuza) Committee.

In Japan, there's a joke that runs like this:

*Q: What is the difference between an LDP member and a yakuza?*
*A: They have different badges.*

It's well known that Junichiro Koizumi, former prime minister and member of parliament, had been elected with the aid of the Inagawa-kai, which held a lot of power in the LDP. Abe had served as Koizumi's chief cabinet secretary and had his support, but that in no way guaranteed that the Inagawa-kai would put their weight behind Abe. However, Abe's family had long been connected to the Yamaguchi-gumi out of Kansai.

There is some evidence that (with or without his knowledge) the Yamaguchi-gumi lent Abe a hand in achieving his prime ministerial ambitions. To be the prime minister of Japan meant first being elected the top dog of the Liberal Democratic Party, which was determined by the prefectural offices of the LDP. As it turns out, the Yamaguchi-gumi had a heavy influence over these offices.

Abe needed a clear majority of the votes of party legislators and rank-and-file members because many felt that, at the tender age of fifty-two, he was too young for the job. Quietly, many ridiculed his lack of intelligence and common sense, referring to him as *Abe-*

*bon-bon*. *Bon-bon* means "spoiled rich brat," and is generally used to refer to the sons of the wealthy who inherit their money and power. Abe needed to beat the minister of foreign affairs, Taro Aso, and the minister of finance, Sadakazu Tanigaki, for the job of running what was at the time the the world's second-largest economy.

According to Inagawa-kai members and Yamaguchi-gumi members, as Abe lobbied to succeed Koizumi, Icchu Nagamoto, a Yamaguchi-gumi boss and financier, visited all the local yakuza in Kanto, carrying Abe's business card and asking them to ensure that the politicians in their pocket voted for Abe in the party elections. Nagamoto met with Coach, who told him bluntly, "I don't get involved in politics. Take your business card and go home."

It was insulting to the Inagawa-kai to perceive that a politician would use the Yamaguchi-gumi to curry their favor, rather than come to them directly. However, the power balance was already shifting.

In the end, by winning 66 percent of the votes as party president, Abe became Japan's 57th prime minister because of the LDP's parliamentary majority. He didn't last long, not quite having the stomach for the job. It's hard to say how much influence Nagamoto had on Abe's first run as prime minister, and certainly Abe never admitted to knowing him. There is a picture of them shaking hands in 2007 that appeared in a weekly magazine. It could very well be that Nagamoto was simply claiming to know Abe, though that seems like an odd move when there was no profit for him in doing so.

Two thousand and six wasn't a bad year for Kazuo Uchibori in the Inagawa-kai Yamakawa-ikka, either. He became brother (*kyodai*) with a rising star in the Yamaguchi-gumi Kodo-kai, Teruaki Takeuchi. He had the Yamaguchi-gumi backing him now in the shadows.

For Saigo, business wasn't bad; revenue had fallen, but was constant.

However, there are things that you can control and things you can't control, and even the smartest yakuza boss can't always see what's coming up ahead.

On April 17, 2007, Nagasaki mayor Itcho Ito was gunned down by a Yamaguchi-gumi member during his reelection campaign.

Only three days later, Saigo was in his office when reports of another shooting started to filter in. A Kinbara-gumi gangster, Madoka Yokoyama, had been fatally shot in a parking lot in Sagamihara, in the Kanagawa prefecture.

Saigo had a bad feeling about it. Of course, it only took an hour for the police to raid his offices. If a Kinbara-gumi member got shot up, Saigo and his crew automatically became suspects.

When it became apparent that Yokoyama had been killed by another Kinbara-gumi member, Yuji Takeshita, who was allegedly high on meth, the police politely recused themselves from searching his offices, and headed to the crime scene.

Takahiko Inoue called Saigo on his cell phone. He could tell the shooting would be trouble for them. The world outside the yakuza didn't know the difference between the Kyokuto-kai and the Inagawa-kai. They were all the same to them. After the police raided the Kyokuto-kai offices in Kabukicho, they came by Inoue's office. Overall, there had been too much gun violence, and the Inagawa-kai needed to prepare for the crackdown ahead. Inoue believed there would be a zero-tolerance policy in Machida for yakuza.

Saigo knew Takeshita from his motorcycle-gang days. He couldn't say that they were best friends, but he wondered what had motivated the kid to shoot his boss and barricade himself in an apartment, firing at the cops. That was suicidal and stupid.

He turned on the television to see if anything was happening. There was live coverage of the event, and it was becoming a huge spectacle. Saigo figured it would be over in a few hours. He was wrong.

That very same night, he got a call in his office. It was Takeshita. He vented to Saigo about how he had killed Yokohama because of association dues. Yokoyama was Takeshita's *aniki* (older brother) in the organization, and he'd demanded that Takeshita pay a hefty fee. Takeshita's earning had been bad, and he was way behind on his payments.

There's a Japanese saying, "The end of the money is the end of the relationship" (*kane no kirime ga en no kirime*), and it was definitely true for the Kyokuto-kai Kinbara-gumi. You could do just about anything in that organization: rob, steal, defraud, sell drugs, use drugs, and it wouldn't get you banished. But there was one unforgivable sin, and that was not paying your association dues.

Takeshita told Saigo he knew that if he didn't pay up this time, Yokoyama would beat the crap out of him; Yokoyama had a violent temper. Takeshita worried that Yokoyama might even beat him to death — it was a real possibility. He was afraid. He had no money, no future, no hope.

That day, Yokoyama had summoned him to the parking lot and ordered him to pay the money. Takeshita didn't have it. He did have a gun, though. As soon as Yokoyama got out of his car, Takeshita shot him.

Yokoyama died almost instantly. Takeshita walked over to his body and called his name. He apologized, and meant it. He had already decided that he'd kill Yokoyama and then himself. But he didn't want to die in a parking lot. He wanted to die in his own home. He was on his way home when he realized that the cops were following him. He panicked, and he fired some shots. And that's where he was now. In his house, trying to figure out what to do and calling Saigo for advice.

Saigo asked him why he wasn't calling Kinbara and asking him for advice.

Takeshita said that the only person more cold-hearted than his *aniki* was Kinbara. He was hoping that Saigo would have some advice.

"If you're not going to kill yourself, then turn yourself in. Say it was self-defense."

Takeshita thanked him profusely and apologized profusely for having to cut the phone call short.

Saigo didn't get much sleep that night. A few hours after Takeshita called, he got a call from Kinbara. He wanted Saigo to talk Takeshita into surrendering.

Saigo refused. Yes, Takeshita was his junior, but trying to talk down a guy who was whacked out on meth — no, thank you. It was too much to ask.

There was a long silence. Kinbara made a second proposal. Maybe Saigo could kill him. No one would have to know — people would think it was the cops. The whole situation was getting embarrassing for Kinbara. He offered to get Saigo a sniper rifle, if he didn't have one, and possibly pay him to do the job.

Saigo was dumbfounded. He felt like he should be angry, but instead he was amused. He laughed. There was no way he was going to clean up Kinbara's mess.

Kinbara snapped back that it was his problem, too. Just as Inoue had said: it was going to be a problem for all of them. The heat after this was going to melt down the yakuza business, and they'd all be screwed.

Saigo didn't agree, but he did agree to take a look the next day. A local detective was there, along with the whole organized crime squad. Maybe, by making an appearance, he could score some favor with the local cops.

When Saigo arrived in the morning, the stakeout was still going on. He had called ahead, and the detective waved hello as he arrived.

There were three police vans and a few squad cars parked outside the building. The SWAT team was on the roof. The entire area was cordoned off with the usual "Do Not Enter" yellow tape, and beyond the tape were hordes of reporters and photographers with telephoto lenses hoping to get some snaps.

It was a stand-off between an armed yakuza and the entire local police force — like something right out of an American movie. *Dog Day Afternoon: Japan.*

Saigo was offered a chance to take the microphone. He politely declined, but was allowed to come near the inner circle, where an ever-changing parade of speakers were given the megaphone and tried to talk Takeshita into throwing down his arms and turning himself in.

Takeshita's mother and father took the megaphone, speaking in turn. They urged him to stop before anyone else got hurt. His mother told him not to do anything stupid. His father told him to stop bringing more shame to the family and to just come down and turn himself in.

There was no visible reaction.

In a moment of inspiration, or insanity, the police turned the megaphone over to Kinbara, who grabbed it with his thick hands and shook it while screaming at his former soldier. He shook the megaphone so hard that he was unintelligible — so someone gave him a wired microphone hooked up to colossal speakers. It looked like the whole set-up had been salvaged from a right-wing van.

Kinbara had always been something of a show-off. He was a flamboyant fellow, and with a captive audience and a metaphorically captive audience listening in to him, he played the role of the angry yakuza *oyabun* to the hilt. It was an amazing, shocking, and darkly comic performance. If Saigo hadn't seen Takeshita's parents still hanging around, he might have laughed.

Kinbara got right to the point.

"Hey, Takeshita! Are you listening? Die, damn it, just die! You're a yakuza, right? Then die. You're a pain in the ass. You're bothering everyone. Come out with guns blazing and get shot to death — "

At this urging, the police took away the mic from Kinbara for a few seconds, and there was a muffled murmur as the cops clarified what they wanted Takeshita to do. Clearly, Saigo guessed, they didn't want to participate in a "suicide by cop," and they didn't want Takeshita to come out with his guns blazing.

Kinbara took the mic back and cleared his throat. "Takeshita! Never mind what I just said. Only a coward gets shot to death. Kill yourself like a man. Just die, you stupid fucker. You've got a pistol? Shoot yourself with it. If you don't shoot, we'll shoot."

The cops next to him nodded their heads, but not very enthusiastically.

Kinbara continued.

"Takeshita! If you've got no bullets for the gun left, just tell me. We'll throw some onto the balcony! I can get you bullets!"

Saigo was trying not to laugh. Kinbara was practically inviting the cops to search his place for illegal ammunition. Just having a bullet, in and of itself, could result in up to five years in prison. Kinbara was an idiot, but the cops didn't seem to mind his rhetoric. Off to the side, he could hear two cops speculating as to whether or not it would be kosher to get bullets delivered to the suspect. They decided that it wouldn't be legal to do it themselves. But if someone from the Kyokuto-kai tossed them onto the balcony — that would probably be okay.

Kinbara kept pressing for an answer. Did Takeshita have bullets, or not? Because if he didn't have bullets, he needed to tell them. He had to communicate.

Kinbara appealed to his sense of decency. He told Takeshita that he understood where he was coming from. Yokohama probably had it coming. But shooting at a cop was bad. It was a problem for everyone, and no one could go home because of him. There were murmurs of agreement from the police assembled, some of who had been there for over twenty-four hours.

There was a way to solve the problem, "and that's for you to die," Kinbara said. That would solve everything.

When Saigo left, a new detective was trying his best to convince the man to come down. He wasn't even sure that Takeshita was listening.

In the end, the police raided the place after pumping in tear gas. Takeshita shot himself as they entered, according to popular accounts. However, some have always insisted that the SWAT team shot him before they entered. It didn't really matter who shot him, in the end; he didn't die. The bullet blew out his eyes, but not his brains. He was blind, but alive. He was given a prison term without end. It's hard to imagine what a blind ex-yakuza could find to do in the straight world.

As always, Inoue was right. By the end of the month, the police were cracking down on the Saigo-gumi as though they were Red Army terrorists. It wasn't just the Tokyo police, the Kanagawa prefectural police joined the fray as well. Every front company, every office, every associate member's office got raided. The police put pressure on all the local businesses to stop paying protection money. Many did.

Members of the Saigo-gumi were arrested on any charges that the police could come up with. The Kinbara-gumi had it even tougher, but the cops and the world didn't see any difference between one yakuza group and another.

Coach had been right, too. Guns were weapons of self-destruction for the yakuza. A few shots fired into a public space, and suddenly years of tacit tolerance for them in Machida was gone. Saigo himself was followed by the police wherever he went.

Revenues dropped. So did the number of his soldiers. Even his *wakagashira* left. Yamada's wife had developed cancer, so Saigo let him retire with a generous pension, and promoted Mizoguchi in his place.

In the midst of this, Saigo also found out that Yuriko was pregnant. At first, it was a shock. Saigo believed that, because of the interferon treatments over the years, he was sterile. But he was ecstatic when he found out she was having a son. He had always wanted a son. He was born on October 12, 2008. Saigo gave his son the name Makasu, which is the first Japanese character in *ninkyodo*. Saigo and Yuriko officially got married on October 21, the same day they turned in the registration of his son's birth at city hall.

He was delighted to have a son and a wife, but everything else was going wrong. He was increasingly finding it harder to pay his association dues, and he was heavily in debt.

It had been a crappy couple of months. Business had dried up. Younger members of the group, now unable to collect any protection money, were quitting in droves.

Every time he came home, there were cops waiting for him — either at the front of the house or at the back. They would do a body check; they were looking for guns and meth. They knew there was no way he would be stupid enough to carry those on his own person, so they checked his driver as well. They would search the trunk of the car, the hubcaps, the glove compartment, the seats, and his bag.

On March 17, 2008, while on his way to an Inagawa-kai meeting, Saigo stopped at a convenience store with Yuriko. He was in a rush, and she was reading magazines and refusing to leave. They began to quarrel. Within minutes, the police showed up. Saigo told the police officer to butt out, and quickly found himself under arrest. The charge was obstruction of public duty, which was punishable by up to three years in prison or a fine of up to 500,000 yen ($5,000).

He had to hire himself a lawyer. He was again held for the entire twenty-three days that the Japanese police and prosecutor are allowed to keep someone before they are set free. He was able to see his lawyer, but only at the discretion of the police.

He was lucky to have Detective Lucky in charge of his interrogation. At least it was an old, familiar face. At the same time, there was something that seemed sad about it all.

Confessional statements in Japan are always written in the first person. The detective may prompt the confessor, and sometimes the whole process ends in someone confessing to a crime they didn't commit, just following the script they are given.

In Saigo's case, his statement to police became his official "Confessions of a Yakuza." He was forced to make an accounting of his entire life up to then, and, upon further reflection, he wondered if he had really made the right choices. Maybe he had not.

## CHAPTER THIRTY

# Goodbye and get out

In 2007, the police were raiding Saigo's offices right and left. The Tokyo and Kanagawa cops were going from shop to shop to inform business owners and merchants that they would protect them from the yakuza, but if the shop kept paying protection money, the police would view them as yakuza associates. And if the police viewed them as yakuza associates, that meant getting harassed by the police, the local officials, and possible even the National Tax Agency.

So his customers stopped paying. Maybe it was because the economy wasn't looking like it would pick up, or because profits were low for everyone and Saigo's services didn't seem worth the extra money. Either way, Saigo's revenue dried up — and many people left. Maruyama went back to music. There were no hard feelings.

The association dues to the Inagawa-kai were still around $20,000 a month, and he couldn't pay them.* He started borrowing money from other yakuza to pay his dues. If he didn't pay his dues, he couldn't keep the organization running, which meant he couldn't pay

---

*    Figure according to police records at the time.

back the loans he'd taken out to pay the association dues in the first place. The business model had worked when there was money left over after the dues had been paid, but revenue had dropped while the dues remained the same.

By January 2008, he was heavily in debt and dissatisfied with the direction that the organization was taking. There were unspoken standing orders to yield to the Yamaguchi-gumi in any conflict. If the Yamaguchi-gumi opened an office in your turf, you were supposed to keep your mouth shut and look the other way. While chairman Tsunoda was still running the show, more and more power was passing to the Inagawa-kai Yamakawa-ikka. Kazuo Uchibori was the silent ruler of the organization, and he was under the thumb of the Yamaguchi-gumi Kodo-kai.

At a meeting of the Inagawa-kai executives, Saigo lost his temper. He had joined the Inagawa-kai, and had fought and lived for the Inagawa-kai crest. He had never joined the Yamaguchi-gumi. They didn't have a code, and his turf was not supposed to be their turf. He didn't work for them.

Everyone understood that the Inagawa-kai was falling under the control of the Yamaguchi-gumi, but no one dared say it. Perhaps Hanzawa would have said something, but his uncontrollable meth addiction had led to him being institutionalized.

Some of the upper management began to see Saigo as a problem. He had the potential to rally the anti-Yamaguchi-gumi factions in the organization and to stir up trouble. Not to mention, there was rivalry within the Yokosuka-ikka itself.

The organization had grown weak under Coach's command, not entirely because of Coach's lack of leadership, but because Coach was not Yamaguchi-gumi friendly.

The organization, which had 3,000 members in its heyday, was down to under 1,000 members.

One of Coach's sub-bosses, Takaya Aishima, was vying for power. Although this boss was Coach's second-in-command, he didn't particularly love Coach. Instead, he was rooting for Uchibori.

Aishima had quietly taken several other Yokosuka-ikka members as his *shatei* (disciples). He even approached Saigo, who refused to pledge allegiance to him. Saigo tried to warn Coach about what was going on, but he couldn't figure out how to do it without being a snitch.

Coach only half-listened to what Saigo was telling him. Sometimes people rise so high they don't see the earth anymore. They say in Japan that "a lighthouse is darkest at the base," and that seemed apt to Saigo. Coach was well aware of what was happening in the world outside the organization, but he was blind to what was happening beneath his feet.

Inoue was having trouble as well. He was supposed to be next in line to replace Coach, but Uchibori didn't like him, nor did Aishima. The factions loyal to Uchibori in the Yokosuka-ikka began reporting Inoue's activities to Uchibori and Aishima. At Yokosuka-ikka meetings, if Coach wasn't there, Saigo and Inoue were treated like problem children.

In May 2008, Saigo turned off his phone. He had begun receiving calls from the Yokosuka-ikka head office. He knew why they were calling. He owed money to them.

Saigo simply couldn't borrow any more money. He couldn't pay his dues. So he unplugged his phone from his office wall and skipped his board meetings. He'd instead just sit in his office, smoking, and looking at magazines and old photos. He didn't have any hobbies, and he didn't drink. He didn't know what to do with himself.

Saigo had another headache in that the owner of the land his house was built on was now asserting that Saigo had no right to live there. That meant "the compound" might be impounded. He was probably going to be evicted from his home. Even if Saigo was legally in the right, what judge would take the side of a yakuza? His parents still had the family home outside Tokyo, but it was a small place.

If he had to move, what would he do with all the jars of fingers buried in the hills behind his house?

Inoue called Saigo a few times, but he wasn't answering. Finally, Inoue managed to get hold of him at his home. He warned him that the situation was serious. Saigo was on the verge of being kicked out.

"I don't care," Saigo told him. "Let them kick me out. They can kick me out, or I'll quit. Either way, I'm done."

Rumors about Saigo were flying around. Some people said he was back on meth, and that was why he'd been behaving erratically. His own underling, Mizoguchi, was saying it was time for Saigo to go. Saigo could sense the discontent within his own troops.

He was irritable all the time. He was nagging his underlings to pay their association dues to him, but he understood that the money was drying up for them as well. When he thought about how much money he owed, it made his stomach hurt. Every funeral, wedding ceremony, or succession ceremony he had to attend was more money he had to spend that he didn't have. If no one could contact him, at least he'd stop bleeding money for a while. He just needed some time and luck. Something would come up. If he could increase his revenue stream, he could stay as a yakuza boss. However, without his position and the backing of the Inagawa-kai, there would be no way to pay back the money he owed already just to stay where he was — balancing on the edge of fiscal ruin.

On the afternoon of June 7, Inoue called Saigo to tell him that the end was near. That evening, Coach called him as well. Saigo expected to be yelled at, screamed at, and lectured. Instead, Coach was apologetic and even sad.

⁓

*Kane no kireme ga en to kireme* — when the money ends, the relationship ends. There are many ways to leave the yakuza, but there is one definite method of getting kicked out: stop paying your dues. The association dues, *jonokin*, are in a sense licensing fees. You pay the money, and you get to use the corporate emblem and the influence that comes with it. An individual boss in the Inagawa-kai doesn't just represent his own organization, which might have ten people or 150 people — he represents the Inagawa-kai, which means there are 10,000 yakuza backing him up.

Saigo stopped paying his dues, so the Yokosuka-ikka's ruling council decided to expel him from the group. Coach didn't authorize it. In fact, he argued against it, but Saigo had set a poor example. No one could reach him for two weeks, and that was unacceptable.

Coach half-heartedly lectured him. In the yakuza world, the boss had to be on duty 24/7. This was why the men at the top of the echelon usually stopped drinking. You never knew when you would need to be sober.

What if a gang war broke out and Saigo wasn't around? Who would give orders to the men? Who would mobilize the troops? What would happen if other Inagawa-kai members stopped answering their phones?

Coach did what he could, but it wasn't his decision, and he couldn't change it. The *hamonjo* (notice of banishment) would be issued the following day. Saigo would have to find a better job and move. As his land troubles were going on in civil court, he'd set up a temporary office that was now the property of the Inagawa-kai, since he was no longer a member.

If Saigo behaved himself, and some changes at the top of the Inagawa-kai or Yokosuka-ikka were made, Coach would be in a better bargaining position to get Saigo back into the fold. From there, it would probably take Coach a year to convince them. Until then, Saigo would have to find a new way to make a living. He was no longer a boss. His men were no longer his men, and someone else would be taking over the group. The name Saigo-gumi would probably vanish as well.

Saigo phoned Purple. Purple had already heard. Saigo was hoping that Purple could help him out, but Purple was surprisingly unsympathetic. He called Saigo a pariah, and told him there was nothing he could do for him. "Why do you have to fuck everything up?"

Saigo didn't see it that way. He'd been off comms, sure, but that wasn't a reason to banish someone. There were other reasons, Saigo insisted. Purple agreed, partly, but he was not sympathetic. As far as Purple was concerned, Saigo had simply self-destructed. He didn't want to be in the radius of the bomb blast.

Saigo had expected more support than that, but he wasn't going to get it. Reluctantly, he still had to beg Purple for help. Saigo needed help moving. He needed to find someplace to stay.

There were many reasons he needed to get the hell out of Machida. It wouldn't take long for word to get out that he'd been kicked out of the Inagawa-kai, and that meant more trouble. The people he owed money to would know that he couldn't possibly pay it off now, not in the near future, and possibly never. He owed a lot of people. There would be a scramble to collect what money he had left first. He was no longer under the protection of the Inagawa-kai, either, which meant that Kinbara might decide he could settle some old grudges against Saigo with impunity.

Saigo felt surrounded. He had to go somewhere, but he had nowhere to go. He felt like a dead man standing on the edge of the Sanzu River without enough coins to cross over. He was going to be washed down the river straight to hell.

He did actually have enough money to cross over with, but his bank account was practically empty. It only contained a couple of thousand dollars. He'd once had over $1 million in the bank. He'd bought a Mercedes Benz for $300,000 in cash just a few years before. He'd bought one for his boss as well. And now? Now he wasn't sure he'd have enough to put up the deposit and the honorarium necessary to rent an apartment in Tokyo.

Purple called back and said he'd try to find Saigo a place to stay. Saigo tried reaching Inoue, but he wasn't picking up his phone, either.

A banished yakuza is immediately treated like a leper. The rules of banishment prohibit other members from associating with the individual. Thus everyone avoids him. Your closest friend doesn't know you within hours after you've been kicked out.

He told Yuriko to pack their bags. They were going on a long trip. While they were packing, he got a visit from the rapper Barbarian. He'd heard what had happened.

He'd brought Saigo a bag of cash — the equivalent of a couple of thousand dollars. Saigo didn't know what to say. Yamajin told Saigo that he didn't have to pay it back. Saigo was like his older brother. He had helped Yamajin before. He'd also kicked the crap out of him before, but that was besides the point. Saigo needed the money, and he had to take it.

Saigo's face crinkled. His eyes watered. Twenty years in the yakuza, and this was how it ended: kicked out, broke, and the only person who had his back wasn't even a real yakuza. He was a rapper, a punk, a civilian. They weren't even *kyodai*.

Yamajin offered him some pot, and Saigo thought about smoking it, but he declined and sent Yamajin on his way.

Coach hadn't abandoned him entirely. He sent one of his direct underlings to Saigo's home with 1.5 million yen ($15,000), who gave it to Saigo's wife with clear instructions: pay back the debts he owed to loan sharks as much as he could, and get out of town.

Coach hadn't told Saigo that he was going to give him money. He just did it. Saigo found out when his wife, Yuriko, called him and told him the news. But it was only a fraction of what he owed.

Saigo had to think clearly. He could sell his solid-gold Rolex at a pawn shop. That might be worth something. He had a friend in the Sumiyoshi-kai who owned a moving service. He could store the bulk of his possessions at his in-laws' home, and move the essentials to a new place — if he could find a new place. The Saigo-gumi *kanban* — he would take that with him.

The only other condolence call he got was from Detective Lucky. Lucky didn't offer any help, but did offer some advice — the same advice that everyone was giving him: get the hell out of town. Even Lucky knew that Saigo owed money to a lot of people. Saigo thought he'd been good at keeping his perilous financial situation quiet, but apparently that wasn't the case. Yakuza talk.

On June 8, 2008, the Inagawa-kai officially expelled Saigo. The *hamonjo* was circulated to all yakuza offices in the Kanto and Kansai area as a postcard, a fax, and possibly even as an email. Coach's name was not on the notice — a highly unusual situation. Saigo had been banished by the Yokosuka-ikka executive committee. His *oyabun* hadn't been able to save him from expulsion, but he had at least not condoned it. There was some comfort in that.

His parents moved back to their family home.

Purple hadn't abandoned him completely, either. He called up a journalist they both knew, Tomohiko Suzuki. Suzuki would make sure that Saigo had a place to stay.

## CHAPTER THIRTY-ONE

# Haunted houses and hearty homes

People don't like having demons or yakuza for neighbors, and there aren't many landlords who will rent to a yakuza, or even to an ex-yakuza. The neighbors at his old home had seen his tattoos. The used black Mercedes Benz he'd bought from his *kyodai* only confirmed their worst suspicions. They raised hell with the landlord, and the landlord gave the Saigo family a week to leave.

No regular real estate agent would give him the time of day, so he reached out to a friend and was introduced to Kenji Sakamoto, a shady real estate agent. (In a way, he was lucky to have had already left the yakuza by that date. If he'd tried finding an apartment in 2012, it's unlikely that anyone would have rented to him.)

Sakamoto was a gang boss for a faction within the Yamaguchi-gumi and a part-time real estate dealer, until resigning in 2006 to take responsibility for a terrible lapse in judgment. At a post-succession ceremony party, he pulled the lace panties off a hostess and put them on the head of his boss. He was drunk, and his boss had a poor sense of humor. He'd been a full-time real estate broker ever since.

The day Saigo went to see him, Sakamoto was wearing his usual outfit: a jet-black hand-tailored suit, made in Japan, a gray dress shirt, and a red tie. He wore his signature made-in-China fedora and a tasteful, thin gold Patek Philippe watch. Only the small badge on his lapel displaying the crest of his former crime group would tell you that he worked in the underworld and not at a high-end bank.

There was already an elderly man in the real estate office talking to him. There were three of them in the room: Saigo, Sakamoto, and the elderly man.

Sakamoto talked to the elderly client as though Saigo wasn't even in the room; it made Saigo feel like the invisible man or a ghost. The sixty-to-seventy-year-old man was wearing a pair of jeans, a dark-gray sweater, and tortoiseshell glasses. His semi-long hair was still black, although the stubble on his face was tinged with gray. He was no longer living in Tokyo; he had come to the meeting all the way from Southern Japan, where he retired to after working for a mid-sized bank for several years. Saigo wasn't even sure why he had been invited to the meeting.

The old man had been renting his former house to a young man in a residential area in Tokyo. The tenant had committed suicide, and although it didn't make the papers, it seemed like everyone in the neighborhood knew about it. Nobody in Japan wanted to live in a place where other people had died — especially when that person had killed himself. No one was going to rent his place, "except maybe some gaijin or a yakuza," Sakamoto said, nodding to Saigo.

The old man was listening intently. Sakamoto smiled as he lit a cigarette.

Seeing that he had the man's attention, Sakamoto told him that he knew one person who'd buy it, but for half the original price. "I'm going to make you an offer — take it or leave it. You get one chance. Turn it down, and you're stuck paying property taxes on a place that no one will rent. It's a money pit."

Sakamoto pulled a large envelope from his leather briefcase. It was filled with the equivalent of $250,000 in cash. He put it on the *chabudai* (low-standing table).

The elderly man looked at it and hesitated, but only for a few seconds. He held the money in his hands, weighing as if he was weighing his decision as well. He put it in his small black-leather bag, and bowed deeply. Then the paperwork began.

In the Japanese underworld, brokers of *jikobukken* (tainted properties) are called *jikenya*. Sakamoto had been a *jikenya* for over a decade. He said his income was roughly $400,000 a year, and that was him being humble.

The first thing you have to know to be a real estate broker who specializes in *jikobukken* is that no one wants to live in a *jikobukken*.

According to an article in Japan's *Yomiuri Shinbun*, *jikobukken* were so bad for business that unscrupulous real estate agencies would even sue family members of those who had killed themselves for property damages caused by the suicide.* For example, in Miyagi prefecture, a real estate agency interrupted the cremation services of a girl who had killed herself in a rented apartment to demand compensation of more than $60,000 from her bereaved parents.

The second thing you have to know is that Japanese law requires all real estate agents to inform buyers of any "important problems" with a property. That includes whether someone committed suicide or was murdered there, or whether a yakuza lives in the building or near it. If you fail to meet that obligation, you can be sued, the contract can be declared invalid, and, in a worst-case scenario, you could be arrested for fraud.

---

\* Published on September 27, 2010.

So it's important not to be the one left holding the bag at the end of the day. If you play your cards right, you can make a very good living off the misfortunes of others.

According to Christopher Dillon, author of *Landed: The Guide to Buying Property in Japan*, there are large discounts applied to places where there has been a murder, suicide, death, rape, or other crime. After two title transfers or two years, real estate agents are no longer required to disclose this information to prospective buyers. It's within that window of opportunity that Sakamoto made his money.

Sakamoto had a network of real estate agents, yakuza, ex-yakuza, and informants who kept him posted on problem properties. The biggest money was made on houses or condominiums. A suicide on the premises could reduce the value of a house by about half. There were a number of ways to acquire those places for even less and to sell them for a huge profit. Of course, you needed an unscrupulous licensed real estate agent to make it work.

As soon as he got wind of a *jikobukken* up for sale, Sakamoto did his due diligence, tried to find out if the owner was in debt, assessed how well known the suicide was in the neighborhood, and found out what he needed for leverage. Then he had a proxy pose as a potential buyer and directly approach the seller.

In one such case, Sakamoto's proxy, posing as a wealthy housewife shopping for a family place, showed wild enthusiasm and made an appointment to close the deal. The owner foolishly failed to disclose what had happened. In this case, when the proxy showed up the next week, she feigned anger, hysteria, and indignation. She claimed she didn't want anything to do with it, and the "deal" was terminated.

Sakamoto then directly approached the owner himself. He used the suicide to drive down the price. It was a house worth roughly $900,000 to $1 million. By offering to pay for it in cash, right there on the spot, in his office, he sealed the deal.

Of course, Sakamoto promised he would tell the buyer that there had been a suicide on the premises. However, what often happened in such cases was that the real estate agency didn't disclose the information to the next buyer. If the buyer discovered it and complained to the agency, they'd respond by telling them that the person who handled the account had left the firm — and they'd get back to them. They'd stall for time, and hopefully the person would forget or not care enough to take action. If it appeared that the buyer was going to take legal action, the real estate agency would file for bankruptcy and dissolve. It would then move on to create another real estate agency.

Of course, legitimate real estate agencies always inform prospective buyers of the property's past. Sometimes, they will hire an exorcist (*kitoshi*) to come and purify the property as part of the transaction.

Another breadwinner for Sakamoto were properties located next to yakuza offices or homes. Not many people wanted to live next to a yakuza. There was always a chance that a stray bullet might hit them. That really drove the housing prices down.

When Sakamoto heard that a yakuza had moved into a neighborhood, he would buy the adjoining property at a steal. If he and the yakuza worked together, he could help them find a new place, and offer them a fee for moving out. In a few months, after the property's value recovered to its previous level, he'd make a killing.

Homicide sites were the most difficult of all to handle, because word got out very quickly. Sakamoto had been able to profit from homicide sites before, but even he was a little creeped out by them. Japanese people believe that the angry spirits of the murdered, known as *onryo*, haunt the places where they were killed.

Saigo needed a piece of property to haunt. He told Sakamoto that he didn't care how old the place was, who had died there before, or if footless ghosts roamed the halls at night. Saigo just wanted a place he could afford, and maybe a place close to a park so his son could have someplace to play.

Sakamoto thought about this for a bit, and grinned.

Saigo could almost envision the lightbulb going off in Sakamoto's head as he came back and pointed to a condominium about fifteen minutes from the office where Saigo would be working. He showed Saigo photos of the interior and the layout. The price was very reasonable, and he offered him a very good deal: no deposit, no key money, and no questions.

Saigo only had one other question, and it had nothing to do with the history of the place. Was there a parking space big enough for a Mercedes Benz?

Sakamoto assured him that there was. In fact, "The parking space is so big you could fit a Mercedes Benz and a bike in it. Even a hearse."

Saigo took the apartment.

## CHAPTER THIRTY-TWO

# Hotel Gokudo

Saigo felt that if the post-yakuza life could be captured in a song, Hotel California would be apt. You'd have to change the title to something like *Hotel Gokudo* or *Hotel Yakuza*, but the closing lines, written by The Eagles, were so fitting: "You can check out anytime you like, but you can never leave."

It didn't matter that he was no longer a yakuza. As far as the world was concerned, he was still a thug, a criminal, and a gangster. The missing finger and his tattoos didn't help. He looked like a yakuza, and he talked like one, so it wasn't unnatural that people would assume he still was one.

It made staying straight a nearly impossible task. He couldn't lose his temper. He went to a local Korean barbecue, and they served him a plate of meat that was already discolored. In the old days, he would have complained. He might have even demanded compensation. As it was, he just cooked it himself and ate it. He didn't get food poisoning, so that was a victory.

He had to pay an additional $150 every month to a guarantor for his apartment. Without a guarantor, no one would rent to him. It was irksome that the company providing the guarantee was run by the Yamaguchi-gumi, which everyone probably knew, but the company had the veneer of legitimacy.

It wasn't easy making an honest living. He worked for a real estate company, did some chauffeuring and bodyguard work, and whatever else he could find. The real estate job, finding *jikobukken*, paid the bills, but he never knew much how money he'd have at the end of the month. He'd give his wife whatever he earned, and she'd never give him a dime back. He was always broke.

He wasn't a yakuza, but when any of his old friends died, he'd get invited to the funeral. There was practically a funeral every month. He couldn't not go — that would be disrespectful. He thought about changing his phone number so people couldn't reach him; he could save face and money if he didn't know about the ceremonies. The cost of shelling out at funerals alone was killing him.

He had options, but not very good ones. There were people in the Inagawa-kai asking him to come back, but if he came back, what was there waiting for him? There was no future in the yakuza. He could see the signs.

On October 1, 2011, Tokyo finally passed an exclusionary ordinance against organized crime. It promulgated a number of matters, but it principally made paying off the yakuza or working with them a crime. That had never been done before — not across the board.

There was a serious problem in Japan beforehand, in that because there was no penalty for those who used the yakuza to solve problems, the yakuza stayed in business. Getting paid off was how they earned money. For example, from 2005, Suruga Corporation, a company listed on the stock exchange, paid over $100 million to a Goto-gumi front company to evict tenants from properties they wanted to acquire and to resell at huge profits. The yakuza who hounded out the tenants by killing their pets, making threats, and performing other unpleasant acts were arrested by the police on minor charges in 2008; however, no one from the corporation was arrested or punished. After all, it wasn't a crime to hire the yakuza. The police realized that in order to put the yakuza out of business, they also had to punish those who did business with them — and the 2011 ordinances made that principle systematic and universal.

If people don't pay the yakuza or hire them, their income dries up significantly.

There were similar ordinances enacted in every prefecture in Japan. The laws varied in their details, but they all criminalized sharing profits with the yakuza or paying them off.

In other words, if you paid protection money to the yakuza, or used them to facilitate your business affairs, you would be treated as a criminal. You might be warned once, but if you persisted in doing business with the yakuza, you might have your name released to the public, be fined, be imprisoned, or all of the above.

What was particularly vexing to the yakuza, however, was that any payments to them were now criminalized. For example, if the yakuza were blackmailing you or extorting cash from you, and you paid them off, you were no longer a victim under the new laws — you were also a criminal. Thus, for most people, the benefits of throwing yen at the yakuza to keep them quiet faded quickly.

For years, blackmail and extortion had been the bread and butter of the mob. In 2010, roughly 45 percent of all the people arrested for the crime of extortion in Japan were yakuza members. But hush money can be a big business only when people will pay you to hush up. When they start going to the police as soon as you try to shake them down, the business model falls apart.

A retired police detective explained the changes in the law very simply: The new laws make the price of paying off the yakuza, in loss of face and in penalties, much more expensive than the cash payments. It highly incentivized firms not to cooperate or collude with organized crime, much as the revisions to the commerce law in December 1997 made it unacceptable for large listed companies to pay off *sokaiya*. After a few major company executives were arrested, along with the bad guys, for *riekiyoyo*, the payoffs drastically declined, as did the number of *sokaiya*.

The price for being publicly linked to the yakuza was not only public humiliation, increased police scrutiny, and possible punishment, but it could mean a huge loss of revenue. Businesses would suffer cashflow problems when banks refused to lend them money. They could suffer the revocation of their business licenses and possible termination of rental agreements for office space. For any small business, being outed as a yakuza front company was more than likely to result in bankruptcy or eviction. On an individual level, it meant being fired or being forced to resign from your occupation, as was the case with popular comedian and TV host Shimda Shinsuke.

The new ordinances did not exempt foreign firms, either. There was no *gaijin* escape clause. They obligated all companies operating within Tokyo to follow the ordinance by inserting organized crime exclusionary clauses into their contracts and making an effort not to do business with the yakuza and/or other anti-social forces. The Tokyo ordinance was unusual in that it included, a "Do tell and we won't ask" escape clause. If you went to the police before they came to you, and confessed that you had been working with the yakuza, the police would exempt you from the ordinance and help you sever relations. This did not apply if you had been using the yakuza to threaten people.

The Tokyo Metropolitan Police Department assembled a cross-divisional team of over 100 officers to put the new laws into effect. As one police source put it, there was only one *daimon* that was allowed in Tokyo now, and that was the police crest (the *sakura-mon*).

Even abroad, times were getting tough for the yakuza. In July 2011, President Obama, in an executive order, declared the yakuza a threat to the national security of the United States and the world, and authorized the seizure and freezing of any yakuza-related assets in the U.S.

As far as Saigo was concerned, the twilight of the yakuza started on October 1. The final sunset was on the way. The yakuza were being forced out of Japanese society, and they were given a choice: walk out or be carried out.

It didn't take long for the effects to sink in.

Purple had phoned him in early spring. An employee of Kamakura Credit Union, where Purple had his bank account, had showed up at his house with a police officer. The message was this: you can no longer bank with us. They asked Purple to dissolve his account and pay back all outstanding loans, and they would never open an account with him or lend him money again. Purple argued that he was running a legitimate business, but the cops and the bank didn't agree. What was he supposed to do without a bank account? How could he pay his bills? Could he sue the bank?

Saigo called his lawyer. The lawyer talked with Purple. The conclusion was that Purple's bank account predated the ordinance, but the contract had a renewal clause that kicked in after two years. After that, he'd have to sign a new contract — a contract with a clause prohibiting transactions with yakuza members. On the contract, he'd have to check a box saying that he, Purple, was not a member of an organized crime group — but the second he signed the paperwork, he'd be committing fraud and would be arrested.

In Kobe, that year, an upper-echelon Yamaguchi-gumi boss, Masaki Usuha, was arrested for hiding his yakuza affiliation when he joined a gym. The unlucky fellow had joined a sports club in Kobe in December 2009. On the application there was a stipulated regulation that no yakuza member could join the gym. He signed anyway. He had therefore obtained membership under false pretenses — that was fraud. All over the country, yakuza were getting busted for violations like this.

Golf clubs, hotels, banks, insurance companies, real estate agencies, rental car shops — they all now had contracts excluding yakuza. If you signed the contract, you were a criminal. If you didn't sign a contract, you couldn't do any of the things that normal people did in their day-to-day lives.

Saigo tried to enroll in a class to learn how to use computers and how to type on a keyboard — application rejected. He went to the local police and asked for them to intercede, and, surprisingly, they did — but the computer school still refused. They also argued he'd scare the other students and that they couldn't teach a nine-fingered man to type.

What made it even worse was that, even if you left the yakuza, the police kept you on the books for five years. He hadn't been out for five years yet.

Periodically, he'd be pulled over. It didn't help that he was still driving a Mercedes Benz (a used one), which was the iconic, classic yakuza car. The cops would run a check, ask to see if he had any meth, and look through the car. It would take twenty minutes to an hour for them to get verification that he was no longer a gangster.

In essence, it was like being in a permanent state of yakuza parole: presumed gangster until proven civilian.

The police rationale for the five-year rule was simple: they didn't believe the yakuza were really leaving, and in some cases they were right. The organizations were drawing up fake letters of expulsion and still keeping their members on the payroll. The Yamaguchi-gumi had for years kept expulsion letters for members ready to go, so as soon as one of their members got caught, they'd take the letter to the police. Thus the newspapers would often run articles on the arrest of "a former yakuza," but, after a while, the police ignored the expulsion letters.

It pissed him off. The cops were tightening the screws and encouraging everyone to leave the yakuza, but there was no safety net. How were they supposed to make a living? How were they supposed to fit back into the *katagi* world? For almost sixteen years, ever since the organized crime laws went on the books, the number of yakuza had hovered around 80,000. But by the end of 2011, membership was down to 70,300 members. By the end of 2012, there were only 63,200 of them. Where were all the yakuza going?

The National Center for the Elimination of Boryokudan had been set up by the government to help organized crime members in starting their lives over and facilitating their return to normal society. It was supposed to help them find work. The results were dismal. The Tokyo headquarters only managed to find jobs for fewer than ten people in 2011.

Most of the yakuza Saigo knew who left their organization were lucky if they found any work. If they did, it was usually in construction or transportation. A lot of them killed themselves. That seemed to be the retirement plan most favored by former mobsters. Some were forming new groups and dealing in crimes that no "real" yakuza would ever touch — fraud, theft, armed robbery, investment fraud.

Saigo had his own worries. He'd noticed unmarked cars parked near his house. He felt that he was being followed. Then, on June 18, 2012, he went out to his car and found himself surrounded by what looked like very angry and fierce yakuza.

It was only when they told him he was under arrest that he realized they were cops from Nishi-Shibuya. (He now lived in Setagaya.)

He was taken to the Nishi-Shibuya police station, his cell phone was confiscated, and he was led into the interrogation room. No one would tell him what he was being charged with.

The young detective who entered the room called him *"Kumicho."* It had been a while since he'd been referred to that way. He didn't mind it much. He did mind, though, being held without knowing what crime he'd committed. He told the cop that he'd left the yakuza in 2008 and that he was a civilian.

The cop wasn't buying it. They were almost sure he was a top member of the Inagawa-kai who was opening up a branch on their turf.

Saigo wouldn't admit to something that wasn't true. He didn't say a word. He just let the detective talk. After a while, he began to understand what had happened. Someone had told the cops that there was a yakuza in their neighborhood, but they hadn't talked with the local cops in his area — because if they had, the local cops would have assured the Nishi-Shibuya police that Saigo was on the up and up.

Saigo knew if he opened his mouth that he'd lose his temper. So he just shut up. The cop eventually got to the point.

They saw him driving an Iranian all over the place — to Kabukicho, Roppongi, Shubuya. They knew who he was and what he and the Iranian were doing. He was a drug dealer, and Saigo was helping him make deliveries.

Saigo laughed. He chuckled quietly at first, and then the silliness of the whole thing overwhelmed him, and he burst out in loud guffaws.

"You're wrong," said Saigo, "he's not an Iranian. He's a Jew. He's a reporter. He's a Jewish American reporter." He reached into his bag and pulled out the business card, adding that he was also under police protection, by orders of the National Police Agency. If they called the number on the business card, the police would confirm that Saigo was just his driver and his bodyguard. They could even Google him.

The young detective took the card and stared at it.

An hour passed. This time, the detective came in with an older detective, a middle-aged guy with a crew cut and a heavy build. The detective, from the organized crime control division, sat down across from Saigo, introduced himself, bowed slightly, and handed Saigo his card.

"This is a little embarrassing," he said. "You're here because you're living in the Setagaya-ward, but you haven't changed the address on your license. Technically, that's a crime."

That was true. It was also a crime that hundreds and maybe thousands of people in Tokyo were guilty of committing.

The detective had assumed that Saigo was still a yakuza operating in their area, but his story checked out. Unfortunately, since they had already arrested him, his minuscule crime was a problem. They asked him to call someone to let them know where he was.

He handed Saigo back his cell phone. Saigo made a few calls. He called Detective Greenriver, who was now retired. He called a lawyer. He called one of his employers. The people he called made calls.

A few hours later, Saigo was released.

The senior detective apologized to him as he left. Saigo accepted the apology, but added that he wasn't happy about what happened. He was trying to make a fresh start, and while he was in the wrong, because technically he should have changed his address, he had no intent to do anything illegal.

The cop nodded. They understood, and agreed to talk to the prosecutor. They requested that he ask his boss to vouch for him by writing him a letter, and to change his address on his driver's license immediately.

They let him go in time for dinner.

Saigo did just as he was asked. He went to the proper bureau and filed all the necessary documents the next morning. He had to go back to the station a few times and make a statement. He wrote a letter of apology for his failure to keep up on the necessary paperwork.

His employer wrote a two-page letter to the prosecutor's office, and they dropped the charges. Saigo was relieved, but was also left in a state of almost permanent anxiety. He had more than a year to go before he could be taken off the books as a yakuza. One screw-up, one fuck-up, and he might find himself in prison.

He felt like he'd never really be free — he'd always be stuck in a crappy room in the Hotel Gokudo. There was only one way to leave — die or be killed. Inoue, The Buddha, had once said as much. He was right.

## CHAPTER THIRTY-THREE

# When everything falls apart, it falls apart at once

Yakuza and Buddhism. They don't usually go together. It was not uncommon for a disgraced yakuza boss to seek refuge by becoming a Buddhist priest, but it was not usually a genuine act. It was more of a simple exchange of an Armani suit for a priest's robes. It gave the yakuza a tax-exempt status, and allowed him to make more money. Sometimes, the robes doubled as a sort of bulletproof vest.

To become a Buddhist priest, you have to follow the ten heavy precepts. They are: do not kill, steal, engage in improper sexual conduct, lie, drink, or cloud the mind, praise self, slander others, be greedy, give way to anger, or disparage the noble path.

Takahiko Inoue was perhaps one of the only yakuza bosses to become a genuine Buddhist priest while still in the business. He said, "It's easy to give up on the delinquents of the world, but if I give up on them who will make them better people? Who will teach them discipline?"

In many ways, becoming a Buddhist priest softened him, but it also furthered his resolve in different areas. His group had given up collecting debts — one of the staples of yakuza businesses — years before. They stopped collecting protection money even when it was offered. One local bar-owner and former patron said, "Years ago, Inoue never asked for more than we gave, and he was there when we needed him."

Even before he was a priest, people called Inoue "Hotoke," which means The Buddha. Within the ranks of police enforcement, the word *hotoke* also refers to the spirits of those who have been killed or died in a tragic accident. The word was fitting for Inoue, in every way.

He died on February 20, 2013, at the age of sixty-five, under mysterious circumstances. Saigo heard about it within hours. The police determined that Inoue had fallen from the seventh storey of his office building. When the ambulance came to the scene, he told them that he was fine. He asked them to take him to the hospital, and he walked unaided into the ambulance. But he was dead by the time they reached the hospital.

Saigo was devastated. The death of Inoue was a huge blow to him. It was like losing a father, a best friend, and an older brother. The last time he had seen Inoue, he had been his usual drunk chipper self. Saigo immediately went to see Coach, and started calling associates of Inoue, including his son, to figure out what happened in more detail.

And he couldn't make sense of it. The more he asked, the more suspicious he became. In Japan, they say that even monkeys sometimes fall from trees, but it's not very often that yakuza bosses fall from their balconies. Accident, suicide, or homicide: those were the three possibilities. And not knowing which one was correct drove Saigo crazy.

Inoue had been next in line to succeed Coach as the head of the Yokosuka-Ikka. And that should have been something that made him happy. It didn't seem like a good reason to kill yourself. Not a good reason at all to die.

The "eyewitness testimony" was to the effect that Inoue had been attempting to fix the heater on the balcony, and had fallen off the ladder — but that didn't make much sense, either.

If, instead, Inoue had committed suicide, and had jumped over the balcony, shouldn't his handprints have been on the rails? Saigo had friends in the Shinjuku police department. They were happy to call the case an accident to get it off their to-do list, but privately one detective confided in Saigo. He, too, had suspicions about the death. Of course, no one really wanted to do an investigation. One less yakuza, one less problem — that was the consensus of the police's top brass.

After the funeral service, Saigo met up with Purple. They went to a Korean barbecue place near Purple's house, because Purple loved meat. As they were finishing the meal, Purple popped the question.

"*Kyodai*, what do you think really happened?"

Saigo didn't know how to answer. Instead, he gave his own eulogy for Inoue. He and Purple had different views of the man, but they had both respected him.

Inoue had saved Saigo's sorry ass countless times. Saigo was always getting into trouble, and Inoue was always pulling him out of the fire. Inoue backed his promotion as well. Without his help, Saigo would have never risen as high as he did in the organization.

Inoue understood that the yakuza world was changing for the worse and that he was an out-of-date relic of a past where *ninkyodo* was still taken seriously. Perhaps that was why he became more religious in his forties. He once told Saigo there was a world they lived in that they couldn't see. It wasn't enough to think that everything they did was okay as long as the police didn't find out. They had to uphold their precepts, or they would just be common thugs.

"We can evade the law, but we can't cheat karma."

Personally, Saigo had always thought that was a load of crap. Yet, at the same time, when looking at his life, maybe there was some truth to it. He'd climbed to the top of the mountain and been kicked off, or he'd kicked himself off. There were things he'd done that he'd never share with his son.

Saigo wasn't the only one to have climbed up the mountain to get kicked down over the years.

On May 9, 2005, Chihiro Inagawa died of multiple organ failure. He had been scheduled to visit UCLA and to get a liver transplant around 2003. The United States government denied him a visa to gain entry. Inagawa, desperate to get the best medical care possible, asked a Japanese bigwig in the Liberal Democratic Party to set up a meeting with an official at the U.S. embassy and to plead his case.

Edward Shaw, the assistant legal attaché representing the FBI in Japan, reluctantly met with Inagawa. The meeting was short. Shaw told him, "You're a member of the Japanese mafia, and that makes you undesirable in our country. If you want to make a deal, and give us everything we'd like to know upfront, we might consider giving you a visa. If you want to know why we won't, go ask Tadamasa Goto."

Chihiro Inagawa did get a liver transplant, but in Australia. There were complications. He didn't last long. No one in the Inagawa-kai understood why Tadamasa Goto had anything with the United States government refusing to let Chihiro Inagawa into the country. Another Inagawa-kai boss, Takuya Kishimoto, who was also scheduled for a liver transplant in the U.S., was similarly denied a visa.

The death of Inagawa created a huge rift in the organization, even while Saigo was still a member. The group split into two factions: the Tokyo faction and the Atami faction.

The Tokyo faction supported Yoshio Tsunoda for the fourth-generation leadership. He had gotten his start in the Yokosuka-Ikka.

He was short and fat but of solid character, and, like some tiny men, had been a ferocious fighter in his youth. He had also been the number two in the Inagawa-kai for several years and was an extremely efficient and logical leader. The Atami faction supported the son of Chihiro Inagawa, who was simply called *Waka* (the young one) by most of the Inagawa-kai. He was considered to be immature by some and not ready to rule. Kazuo Uchibori, of the Yamakawa-ikka and in the Tokyo group, had once been punched out by Waka, leaving bad feelings.

It looked as if gang war would break out between the two factions. One of Saigo's brothers (*kyodai*) was in the Atami faction; he was with the Tokyo faction, as was Coach. The two of them agreed not to kill each other, even if war did break out.

The Tokyo faction and Tsunoda got word that the Atami faction was going to hold their own succession ceremony and excommunicate Coach, Saigo, Uchibori, and everyone who didn't support Waka. Tsunoda and Coach decided to move quickly.

Tsunoda had Uchibori reach out to the Yamaguchi-gumi and requested their representative's attendance at the succession ceremony. The Yamaguchi-gumi, seeing a chance to score points with the new ruling faction of the Inagawa-kai, agreed.

On the morning of July 19, 2006, Tsunoda's men picked up Seijo Inagawa from his home and took him to the succession ceremony they were holding in Yokohama at the headquarters of the Yamakawa-ikka, the faction that Uchibori belonged to. Seijo Inagawa was already slightly senile, and the driver kept him amused by playing *enka* and traditional Japanese music while driving him to the ceremony.

The Atami faction held their own ceremony, but without the presence of the founder they had no legitimacy in the yakuza world. The war was over before it started.

Tsunoda did not last long as the head of the Inagawa-kai. He died from complications of pancreatic cancer on February 23, 2010. Jiro Kiyota, the naturalized Korean who was head of the Yamakawa-ikka, took over, and Uchibori became chairman of the board. Kiyota had suffered from throat cancer and could barely speak. Coach stayed on as the vice-chairman for a while, until a stroke forced him to more or less retire to an honorary position. He had wanted the Buddha to be his successor.

The Yamakawa-ikka appointed Kazuo Kawamoto, one of their favorite and most cooperative Yokosuka-ikka members to replace Coach when he retired. But Kawamoto was not in particularly good health, either, and had earned his nickname, The Hippo.

The Hippo died of a brain infarction on the day it was officially decided that he would be the ninth-generation leader of the Yokosuka-ikka. It was hard to find a successor for him, because it began to be rumored that Inoue's death had cursed the Yokosuka-ikka.

Bad karma.

Uchibori was the de facto ruler of the Inagawa-kai, and remains the leader of the group.

By this time, the Yamaguchi-gumi had more or less complete control of the Inagawa-kai. The new Inagawa-kai meeting facilities in the Kanagawa prefecture called the *Inagawa-kaikan* were jokingly referred to as the (Yamaguchi-gumi) Kodo-kaikan — a play on the words of Kodo-kai, the ruling Yamaguchi-gumi faction and *kaikan*, which meant meeting place.

The Saigo-gumi was dissolved after Saigo left. Mizoguchi rose up in the Inagawa-kai, gaining his own group. But, like Saigo, he couldn't make enough to pay the dues. Around the time that Jiro Kiyota became the head of the Inagawa-kai, Mizoguchi killed himself. He left a bitter note that was read by a few and then shredded.

Purple retired from the Inagawa-kai in 2014, and was miraculously making a living in Tokyo running festivals and selling items to the merchants. He sold his cars and his watch, and managed to settle his debts.

There's a saying in Japanese, "To meet the Buddha in Hell." It refers to the good fortune of finding an ally in the worst of circumstances. For Saigo, Inoue had been that person in his life. If he hadn't met Inoue, he might have very well ended up joining the Kanehara-gumi, or worse.

Saigo's son was doing well at school, but Saigo found it hard to live in the world as a civilian. It was hard driving other people around and always being short of money. It was hard seeing his friends pass away, one by one. But he had a son, a wife who put up with his short temper, and a job. And in April 2014, he finally felt that he was finally done with his yakuza life.

In April, Coach checked into a hospital complaining that he was not feeling well and having trouble eating. A few members of the Inagawa-kai came to see him, but he refused to meet anyone. And then, one day, he was gone.

The Inagawa-kai went into a panic. There was no record of him having checked out of the hospital. The hospital said that he might have just walked out.

No one saw a body, and if anyone did meet with him in the hospital before he vanished, they're not talking. Not even Saigo. The Inagawa-kai assumed he was dead and held a funeral, but rumors spread that Coach had taken a chunk of his huge wealth and skipped the country, and was now living in America or the Phillipines.

Saigo had talked to him before he vanished — whether on the phone or in person, he wouldn't say.

Coach had asked him, "Are you still doing meth?"

Saigo denied it. He'd been clean for years.

Coach said, "If that's the truth, that's good. Stay away from that stuff. You were right to leave when you did. The yakuza have no future. You do. You were always loyal to me — to the end. Thank you."

And that was the last time they spoke.

Saigo never found out what had happened to Inoue, but he had been convinced to let it go. He spoke with Inoue's son a few times after the Inoue-gumi was disbanded and one of Uchibori's hand-chosen men took over. Inoue's son wouldn't say much, but it was clear that he'd left the Inagawa-kai unwillingly. He moved back to Kumamoto, and died there of heart failure in 2015.

With his *oyabun* gone, Saigo was finished with the yakuza. He'd fulfilled his mission, and he hadn't betrayed his *oyabun*. That was something he could be proud of. The past was the past. He was didn't want to be a yakuza anymore.

# Epilogue

The life of a yakuza tends to be a short one. It's not a healthy lifestyle. The stress, the late hours, the tattoos, sexual promiscuity, drug use, chain smoking, and years spent in Japan's notoriously awful prisons take their toll. Diabetes, bad hearts, liver cancer, lung disease, and cerebral infarction are more likely to kill most of them now than being shot to death.

I understand why yakuza love dark suits; every day is another funeral.

It wasn't until I was writing an article about suicide in Japan that Saigo-san finally told me why he went to work for me and why he got himself kicked out of the organization. He explained it very casually, as we were moving books from my room upstairs into the shelves downstairs in the hallway.

I asked him if the payout for suicides in Japan was after two years or three years. I was in the process of writing an article about how the insurance industry incentivizes people in Japan to kill themselves, by not exempting suicide cases. It also encourages criminals to kill other people, disguise it as suicide, and collect the insurance money. The reason is pretty simple: only 4 percent of suspected suicides ever get autopsied. If you kill someone in Japan for their insurance money, and make it look like suicide, it's almost the perfect crime. The only people who get caught are the ones that do it two or three times.

However, many life insurance policies only pay out for suicide two or three years after the policy goes into effect. This is to discourage people from killing themselves, which seems like a good idea.

I wasn't really asking him for hard data. I was just sort of talking to myself out loud.

He thought about the question, and put down a box.

"When I met you, I had four or five months before a suicide payout was even possible. And I wanted to kill myself. I was up to my neck in debt. I was tired of the yakuza life. I was tired of everything."

I started putting the books on the shelves. *The Perfect Manual of Suicide* was already on one of the shelves.

"I thought you got kicked out of the yakuza."

"I'll confess. I wanted to be kicked out. Because it all seemed pointless. Because there was no way to be true to what I believed as a yakuza and make a living at it anymore. I could have started dealing drugs, running scams, defrauding people, but then what would I be? I'd just be a criminal. I'd be scum. I couldn't see any other way of life than being a yakuza other than being dead. But, you know, I had a family. I wanted to leave something behind for my son. So I forced them to force me out. It was the only way to leave."

"And?"

"Well, I couldn't kill myself. Because I'd leave the family with nothing but debts and the costs of my funeral."

"Okay," I was beginning to see where the conversation heading. "And so?"

"So, I figured that the yakuza boss you pissed off would kill us both. Or kill me first. And that would have been a great payout for my family. Double indemnity. And if I didn't get killed or you didn't get killed, at least I had an honest job."

I stopped putting books on the shelf. Saigo starting taking books out of another box and putting them on the shelf while I stood there, dumbfounded.

"You were hoping that you'd get killed?"

"Not really hoping, you know. But I wouldn't have minded. But, hey, it all worked out."

"You never told me that before."

"You never asked. If you don't ask, you'll never know. Is there anything else you want to ask me?"

And I couldn't think of a single thing. I could think of things I wanted to ask, but nothing new from him I wanted to know.

"*Shiranu ga hotoke.*" ("Sometimes, ignorance is the Buddha.")

And sometimes there are things you're better off not knowing.


There was one person I needed to speak with while writing this book. He had advised me to hire Saigo as a bodyguard, and I had taken his advice. I should have probably listened more closely. I wanted to thank him and to ask for a favor. He didn't come up to Tokyo often, and it was always hard to reach him. I couldn't use a cell phone, so as usual we played pay phone tag until we eventually got connected.

I had some selfish motives, and I needed to see where I stood in the underworld. Years go by. Alliances change. I don't know any reporter covering the underworld who doesn't have at least one or two yakuza contacts high up covering their ass. That's how you survive. You learn to at least give a heads-up to the opposition before you write something or do something that's going to cause them problems. That's just politeness. Even among the closest of friends — and enemies — there must be decorum. That's Japan.

It would be good to check in with the man, under any circumstances.

He picked the hotel.

I came prepared. I had something in my coat pocket that he'd want.

It had been a long time since I heard that voice. Maybe we'd spoken once since I'd asked him to vouch for Saigo. Maybe twice.

It had been over a year since I'd seen him, maybe more. His bodyguard was in the room, and there were two more outside the door.

He'd aged a lot. Time had shrunken him down, thinned him out, but when he spoke, he still had that presence. His voice still held the timbre of the New Year's Eve bell. People used to joke that he should have quit the business early on and become a newscaster for NHK. He would have been a success.

"How's Saigo-kun?"

"Good. He's eating better. His diabetes is controllable. I put him on some supplements, cinnamon, zinc — stuff that appears to work."

"You care a lot about the man. Like he was your brother."

"No," I said, "It's just that I promised I'd adopt his son if anything happened to him, and, honestly, the kid is a holy terror."

He laughed a little, wheezing slightly.

"How is the little yakuza?"

"Very good. He's like his father. Very strong-willed. A few weeks ago, Nin-kun brought his dad a book to read in English. He couldn't read it, and Nin-kun got so pissed off, he punched Saigo in the face. Gave him a black eye. He couldn't open his eye for two days."

He found the image of Saigo being punched out by a five-year-old very amusing. He laughed so hard that he coughed a little and teared-up slightly.

He said that Saigo had been lucky to get out when he had. The yakuza, as they had been, were fading fast. There were no rules anymore — pay your association dues, by any means possible. That was the alpha and omega. Anything else went.

He asked me how my kids were. I told him they were well. He still had trouble picturing Tsunami as a father. I told him that Saigo was remarkably patient and good with his kid. My contact nodded.

"He was always a good guy, so I guess he'd make a good father. He took care of his people. Guys like that don't go far these days."

"You've got a good reputation yourself, in that respect," I said.

"When people lay their lives down for the organization, you can't just disregard that. You must honor that kind of dedication. It's a matter of principle."

"I think one of your bosses would argue it's a waste of money."

"That's because he only values money. There are things that have more value than money."

I was about to quip, "Diamonds? Multi-strike Convertible Bonds? Preferred Shares?" but I didn't. Even I recognized that there's a time to shut up.

"When is he going to get out jail?"

"There's no life imprisonment in Japan. So I figure, another five years. Until then, I'll take care of his family. Or make sure someone does. That's the right thing to do, and if the law says it's not, then the law is fucked. We don't abandon our own. Not while I have any say in this organization."

There was a soccer game on the television. It was a little distracting. He wasn't really watching the game, so he turned off the television. It made the room seem very empty. But we got used to the quiet. Quiet makes some people uneasy. I don't have a problem with it.

"You don't like soccer much. You're not fond of baseball, I know."

"No, I don't. I don't like soccer or baseball very much."

"You don't like playing them, or watching them, or both?"

"I don't mind playing them. I like volleyball. I'm not much of a team player. I hate watching baseball, football — bores the hell out of me."

"Why's that?"

"Because life shouldn't be a spectator sport. Because I'm unable to see the victory of a bunch of overpaid athletes as my victory. It has nothing to do with me."

"What if you were betting a million dollars on the outcome of the game?"

"Then I'd be wearing a cheerleader outfit and screaming, 'Go team go!' over a megaphone."

He laughed.

"You might not have made a bad yakuza. In another day and time."

"What about yourself?"

"I'm the same way. There are better ways to waste our hours on this earth than watching grown men play children's games. Even when you have a stake in the game."

"You don't get any vicarious joys from the victories, the spoils of war, grabbing new territories?"

"I can see the end in sight. For decades, we've been playing a game of monopoly."

I was kind of surprised he knew Monopoly. I was expecting a Japanese Go simile. He picked up on that.

"Monopoly was huge in Japan. I loved playing that game as a kid. I figured out early that you wanted to invest in the mid-to-high-level real estate early on. Collect rent. People who banked on raking it in via Park Place and the high-end properties always lost. And there were worse things than going to jail."

"So how the did the game of Monopoly turn out?"

"We won everything, and that's why we lost. The whole board is ours, and now the game is over. The man is coming to collect the board, the properties, the investments, and everything we took, earned, or stole. Because we got too big. Japan isn't Mexico. We're not going to take over the country. A few more upgrades to the law, and we're gone. Maybe we'll exist as a cultural treasure."

"So there'll be a bunch of tattooed old men walking around in expensive suits, with some young thugs menacing people — sort of an interactive thing?"

"I don't have any tattoos. I've always been a businessman, not the illustrated man."

He was damn smart. I had to give him that. I thought I knew him completely, and here he was throwing me off by referencing Ray Bradbury. I knew he read a lot, but mostly historical fiction. Or so I thought.

"Well, you can always say the game was fun while it lasted."

"It started out as fun, but we all forgot the rules. The money was exciting for a long time, but you get to be my age, and there's not much that money can buy you anymore. It can buy you time. Maybe a new liver — if you're a coward. Maybe a new heart, possibly new lungs. Maybe it can buy you a beautiful woman who will pretend to love you and hope you die quickly, so she can inherit whatever she thinks you have. It can't buy you peace of mind, or a good night's sleep."

"JP Morgan once said, 'There's a certain amount of nirvana that comes from having money in the bank.'"

"A wise man."

"When are you going to retire?"

"They want me to take over in a few years. I don't want to."

"But isn't that the goal? You'd be one of the most powerful men in Japan, in the underworld at least."

"The real power is always the number two. The number one is a figurehead. The number three controls the money. Number four deals with all the other shit until he gets to be number three. Number five is the best place to be. You collect money from the bottom, pay a fraction to the top and you sit out the power struggles."

"It's not easy being on top, I hear. You can't smoke, and you can't drink. You're supposed to be a role model." I tapped my fingers on my chest.

He motioned for the bodyguard to leave the room. I got up and opened the window, and took a pack of Dunhills out of my pocket. I had clove cigarettes with me. I didn't want to smoke, but it would override the smell of his cigarettes.

We moved over to the balcony and stepped outside onto the patio. I opened the pack of cigarettes and gave him one, then offered him the pack, but he motioned for me to hold it. I was about to light his cigarette, like a good host, but he took the lighter from my hands and lit it himself, and then lit mine. I wasn't going to stand on ceremony.

We both looked out at the sea and inhaled deeply, and then sighed. And laughed. There was something so juvenile and intimate about the whole exchange.

"Damn. These are good. I miss smoking."

"Everything good is bad for you, you know."

He nodded.

"Maybe," I added.

"Did you ever see that movie *Ichigoichie?*"

"You mean *Forest Gump?*"

"Is that the English title?"

"Yes, *Forest Gump*. The Japanese title in English would be something like *One Meeting in One Lifetime: Forest Gump*."

"Interesting film. I saw that on a plane, and I thought to myself, *Life as a yakuza isn't a box of chocolates.*"

"What's it like then? A six-pack of beer?"

"Life is like a pack of cigarettes. It's like a fresh pack of menthol cigarettes in the Japanese summer. Someone told me that in the U.S. only fags smoke menthol cigarettes."

"Some people say that."

"Well, fuck them. Men smoke menthol cigarettes in Japan."

If there's one thing I learned as a reporter, it's that, sometimes, the best thing you can do to really understand your subject at a profound level is to just shut up and let the expert speak. Without interruption. Without asking a single question. I never forgot what he said.

"If you want them to last, you get the hard case. The box. The box is compact, solid, feels good in your hands; you light up, and the menthol makes you feel cool inside, even though it's humid and hot outside. You get a buzz, it tastes good. But that's only for the first few cigarettes. The humidity creeps in, and they go stale fast. But you keep on smoking them anyway. You begin to believe that if you smoked enough cigarettes, something magical would happen, and somewhere down the road, the last cigarette would taste as good as the first. Even if you don't get a buzz, at least it clears your head. You can think better. It's almost as good as that nicotine high.

"You wait. You smoke. You think. You work. You get tired of waiting for a buzz that doesn't come. And, finally, you throw the pack in the road carelessly and buy another.

"You know you're not supposed to smoke. Everyone knows it's bad for you. But you keep doing it.

"You gather with the other smokers. Fuck the rest of the world. If they don't like the stench, they can get the hell out of the room. If you flick your hot ash in the wind, and someone gets burned, they're unlucky. That's how it goes. You and your pals keep smoking them while you've got them. You and your friends eventually to decide to smoke the same brand — even though there's no real difference, except in the taste, the packaging, and the lethality.

"You are united in your misery and your tiny rebellion. Share a smoke, make a friend, become a blood brother, shun people not smoking your brand. That's the yakuza world. You smoke where you want to, when you want to. The whole world is your ashtray.

"When you're young, you don't know that your secondhand smoke is poisoning everyone around you. When you're older and you figure it out, you're sorry and you're a little more considerate, or you just don't care. You keep on doing this for years. Even after the first cigarettes no longer taste good, even when the cigarettes are stale right out of the pack. Quitting doesn't even occur to you as an option.

"You can change brands, buy a better quality of cigarette, but it always ends up the same. The older you get, the faster the cigarettes burn. In the end, you wind up with nothing but cancer and a trail of ashes behind you — that's your legacy.

"If you've been really successful, maybe you leave behind a gold-plated Dunhill lighter and a carton of unfinished coffin nails. And somebody else starts smoking your cigarettes."

And then, when he was done speaking, as if he'd timed it to the second, his cigarette burnt out. He took out another, and I lit it for him.

I lit one for myself.

"You know," I said a little hesitantly, "you could try quitting. It's never too late."

"You're right, but it's one of the few little pleasures I have left in life. Might as well savor it. So."

"So."

"So, did you come here because you need something?"

"I wanted to thank you for your advice all those years ago. It worked out. Not quite the way I thought it would, but it did."

"Advice is cheap. Is there anything else I can do for you?"

I explained that I had a friend in trouble. I was worried that he might do something that would put him in jail. And maybe put someone else in hospital, or in the grave.

"So what do you want me to do?"

"I want to you to handle it so no one else gets hurt."

He took a long deep breath and then said, "What exactly are you asking for?"

"I'm not asking you to do anything at all. I'm just telling you that I'm worried."

He went on.

In his own organization, there were yakuza who had bought the telephone numbers of cops, eavesdropped on their conversations, and tried to threaten the detectives by implying that they'd hurt their children or their wives. That was unheard of — that was something the mafia did. Even as a bluff, what kind of asshole threatens to hurt children? And what if they actually did? When the yakuza start menacing the police, women, and children, the police don't take that lightly.

The anti-organized crime ordinances kept gnawing away at the core business. The United States had banned transactions with the yakuza. Uchibori and the second-in-command of the Yamaguchi-gumi had their U.S. credit cards frozen. American Express? No yakuza carried it in their wallets anymore. Citibank, which had been disciplined twice by Japan's Financial Services Agency for laundering money for the yakuza — they were no longer a safe place to bank either. How was an honest thug supposed to survive without a bank account, a place to live, or a credit card? The phone companies were not renewing cell phone contracts either. A modern-day yakuza without a cell phone? Inconceivable. The police and the government were killing them off with contracts, ordinances, and inconvenience.

The organization's upper management was telling low-level yakuza to stop carrying business cards. But what fun was it being a yakuza without your *daimon*? Nobody could wear the badges anymore. The franchise was starting to fall apart.

He explained it to me in terms of a McDonald's, assuming that this was something an American would understand. Who would want to run a McDonald's if you couldn't use the golden arches or call yourself a McDonald's? The name was half the business.

There had been a code once. Not everyone kept it, but people knew what it was. The young guys coming up in the organization — they didn't know the code, and if they did know it, they didn't care. They were running elaborate frauds preying on the elderly or grandmothers estranged from their kids. They were stealing cars and exporting them overseas. Some of the brighter ones were now in the entertainment business, managing teenage girl bands, scamming idiot fans who believed they might one day be loved by the girls they obsessed over. They were making money selling child pornography and borderline child pornography. The surviving yakuza weren't engaged in any of the traditional crimes — collecting protection money, running gambling dens, simple extortion. The ones that survived were running labor-dispatch companies, dubious IT venture outfits, consumer-loan companies, and retirement funds that went bankrupt (after all the funds had been siphoned off), leaving thousands of people without a pension.

The hot-headed kamikaze type of yakuza who were good in a gang war were now useless. There were no gang wars, except in southern Japan. There was one gang that ruled them all. No need for fights. In fact, hot-headed violent members were a liability. The Japanese courts had ruled that the head of the organization bore employer liability for anything that those below him did.

Even Tsukasa Shinobu, the head of the Yamaguchi-gumi, had been sued. He'd been sued along with Goto for $2 million by the family of the real estate agent Kazuoki Nozaki.

Nozaki, as rumoured, was eventually killed, over a real estate deal in 2006. After a five-year investigation, the police and prosecution managed to put away four Goto-gumi members for the murder, and had an arrest warrant issued for one more, who was shot to death in Thailand — but they couldn't pin the crime on Goto.

Tsukasa Shinobu had been in solitary confinement at the time of the murder, and generally didn't approve of killing civilians. Goto paid the family over $1.2 million and apologised. He then fled the country — seeming to prove that you can get away with murder in Japan if you're a yakuza boss and the only underling who can testify you gave the orders is conveniently killed before he (or you) can be arrested.

Tsukasa, rightly, was able to walk away without paying damages, since he wasn't responsible.

But that was rare. As any boss could be sued for the crimes of his underlings, whether he was responsible or not, most bosses settled out of court.

If some hot-headed punk in the organization beat up a civilian or, God forbid, killed them, the family had the right to demand compensation from the bosses at the top, and increasingly they did. And so the loose cannons were let loose. The organization didn't need men with brute strength; it needed good businessmen.

There was no loyalty, no honour, no meritocracy. If you wanted to be in the upper echelon of the group, you brought a few million dollars in cash to the second-in-command, and within a few weeks you were sitting at the top. You didn't earn a position anymore; you bought it.

Even the pretense of not bothering civilians was barely heeded. Guys like Saigo, Coach, The Buddha — they were as out of date as Windows 95. Maybe some organizations tried to keep the code, but there were signs as far back as 2003 that the yakuza world was going to shit. That year, the Kudo-kai in southern Japan threw a grenade into a hostess club that wouldn't pay them protection money. They killed people with almost no compunction, and beat them up with less.

I was curious. Had things really changed that much, I asked my contact. When he looked back on it all now, had it been worth it? Did he feel like he'd lived a good life?

He took some time to mull that over. He said that there was a time when the yakuza were the only place that the *burakumin*, the Koreans, the Chinese, the dyslexic, and the outcasts of Japanese society could find a home. The yakuza would take anyone. They were the employment agency of last resort. And maybe that had been good. They gave the outcasts discipline, brotherhood, and rules to follow. Street crime was low in Japan when the yakuza were strong. That was good.

During natural disasters, the yakuza banded together and brought food, water, clothes, and supplies to stricken areas faster than the government ever did. They had no red tape; they just did it. There were ulterior motives for some of them, but not all of them. That was a public service.

He confessed something as he was speaking.

"I'm half-Chinese. My mother was from Taiwan. I'm not full-blooded Japanese. It doesn't bother me, but when I was growing up, it bothered other people. I'd have never risen this high in a Japanese company. I'd have smashed my head on the invisible ceiling."

But, for the most part, the yakuza and his group had been like every other company in Japan, all about making money, and making even more money, and controlling more of the market. It was all about business. All the gang wars in the old days, the assassinations, the fights — they were all really about mergers and acquisitions. Most of it was just about expanding the *nawabari* as far as it could go. *Giri* was something he and other yakuza had once esteemed, but for many it had lost the moral meaning of the word, the sense of reciprocity. Now it was just code for yakuza gatherings: memorials, release from prison celebrations, funerals, succession ceremonies — everything except weddings. The *daimon* — no more than a corporate symbol. The credo of the group, the lofty ideals — more or less PR. He joked about corporate governance and corporate responsibility. In that sense, in the sense that they weren't dumping toxic waste into the water supply, they had that. There were rules of conduct that had once been kept but that now no one even paid lip service to.

I didn't know if that was really the case. I asked, hadn't the gap between the yakuza as they saw themselves and how they were always been huge?

"You know, I've been in this business a very long time. And I'll tell you something. Even when I was starting, they'd be talking about 'the last true yakuza'. They'd tell us the previous generation was more honest, tougher, more patient, worked harder, kept the code. I don't know if that was ever true. It's like anything in this world. Ninety-nine percent of it is crap. There have always been, and may always be, 1 percent in the yakuza who have some sense of decency, some honor, who keep to the code. Inoue — he was one of those. Maybe he was the last yakuza."

"Well, you're still in the business."

He laughed again, very hard.

"I've done some awful things to get where I am, even worse things to stay where I am. I can say I never betrayed my own people, and that's something. I look after my people, and I pay my debts to those I owe. But I'm not a yakuza. I'm a businessman who can't retire."

He smiled, and motioned for me to give him another cigarette. As soon as I did, he put it to his lips. Without even thinking about it, I took out my lighter and lit it for him. That's the order of things.

"So, about your friend," he said, "What exactly is it you want me to do?"

"I'm not asking you to do anything," I said again. "I'm just saying I'm worried. Even if I did, I wouldn't ask."

He nodded, "And if you did, I wouldn't be able to do anything for you. So I think we understand each other. I'll take care of it."

I knew he was a man of his word. I felt a little easier.

He told me, "In your business and my business, there's always trouble. You may be a pain in the ass, but you're fair. When you wrote things that pissed everyone off, I brought their attention to that. But I won't be able to vouch for you with the regime change coming. Things aren't going to be the same."

He advised me to widen my fields of interests. I may take that advice.

We chatted about who was up and who was down in the yakuza world. And about what he would do if he was no longer with the organization.

He laughed, "I'm not in great health. Maybe I'll look for a good hospice with some gorgeous nurses. You should come visit me. Maybe I'll introduce you to one of them."

I'll probably take him up on both of those offers.

There aren't many like him left in the business — a voice of reason and diplomacy.

Like a stale cigarette himself, he's being stubbed out in the dingy ashtray of the Japanese underworld. Yes, it's a melodramatic metaphor, but one that seems most apt to me after twenty years of covering the yakuza. Whether he is put out or burns out, either way he's a year or two from becoming a pile of ashes himself. If I'm honest, in a strange way, when he dies, I'll miss him.

Hopefully, there will be somewhere he can be buried when that happens.

These days, even the funeral parlors are refusing to deal with yakuza clients, even the deceased ones.

# Afterword

I'm sorry to say that, in 2015, Saigo was given an offer he couldn't refuse, or didn't want to refuse. He was offered readmittance to the yakuza in a high-ranking position in the Yokosuka-ikka, the faction above him in the Inagawa-kai. It must have been tempting. He wasn't straight-up with me about the offer, but I knew that it was going on. Uchibori needed someone to keep the ailing faction in check and to run the group — and Saigo was a solid leader when given the chance.

I understand that it's hard to go straight. The re-employment rate for yakuza is less than 2 percent, according to Japan's foremost authority on the sociology of the yakuza, Noboru Hirosue, also known as "Professor Yakuza."

While Saigo was working for me, I encouraged him to learn new skills, but even though he could type like crazy on a cell phone, learning to type on a keyboard with only nine fingers was beyond him. And society didn't make it easy for him to rejoin. I helped him get slightly tech-savvy, which was good. His self-chosen email was inudesu (I am a dog), which is a pun on how informants are referred to in the underworld — as dogs. You can't say he didn't have a great sense of humor.

I kept him on as a driver until the summer of 2015, when he finally decided to go back to the Inagawa-kai. As a farewell present, I gave him the Mercedes-Benz I had purchased. He hadn't rejoined the yakuza at that stage; otherwise, I would have violated the laws myself. Ouch.

I didn't miss the car. Yakuza used to love those cars. They guzzle gas like crazy, but he argued furiously that no one would take him seriously if we were driving around in a Subaru. I couldn't really argue with that.

We had a bitter dispute about his decision to rejoin the yakuza, but we made our peace on October 17, 2015. He sent me a short email that was the beginning of our détente:

> Take care of yourself and live vigorously … I am glad to hear that you are well despite all that has happened. Let's meet again when the time comes.
>
> It is getting colder, but please take good care of yourself and work hard.
>
> Pardon me.

However, while he remained a friend and a source, with him back in the organization, the protocols for our contact changed quite a bit. I was politely warned by a cop who we both know that closely associating with Saigo now would probably get me named as a yakuza associate — which would mean that, just like an actual yakuza, I might lose my bank account, my phone, and even my apartment.

It was safer to let the world believe we were now bitter enemies, or not communicating at all.

He died in his home, alone, of a heart attack, during the pandemic.

He rose to the rank of director-general before passing away, and that seemed to mean a lot to him. It was Detective Lucky who broke the news to me, although Saigo's long silence before then hadn't boded well.

I had promised to do a ritual to help Saigo move onto the next incarnation if he was trapped in the lower realms of existence. There are advantages to being a Buddhist priest yourself, and The Buddha certainly wasn't around to do it.

I don't know if the prayers or the ceremony helped, but I hoped it did. I feel like everybody deserves a second chance, and sometimes maybe even a third one.

# Acknowledgments

This book took almost eight years to write, and I was delighted that it was first published by Marchialy in France in 2016. Cyril and Clemence have been wonderful editors, translators, and friends. I probably will continue to publish first in France for as long as their publishing company lives.

I'd like to thank the original editor of the manuscript, Julianne Chiaet, an accomplished writer and wonderful editor, who camped out in my house to get the book finished. I would also like to thank Amy Plambeck, who did the polishing and copyediting for the English edition. Lauren Hardie contributed marvelous copyediting here and there, although she may have forgotten she even did it.

I am also very grateful to Henry Rosenbloom, my publisher in the U.S. and in Australia and New Zealand, who painstakingly edited the English manuscript. And deep thanks to William Clark, my ever-patient literary agent, and Stephen "Steve" Breimer, who is an excellent lawyer and advocate.

And I would like to thank the yakuza who entrusted me to tell their story and who shared their lives with me. I am grateful — but don't try to shake me down. I'm grateful, but I'm not stupid. Good luck to us all.

# THE LAST YAKUZA

Jake Adelstein was born in 1969 in Columbia, Missouri. In 1988, he left to study in Japan, and for most of his college life resided in a Zen Buddhist temple in Tokyo. Upon graduation from Sophia University, he was the first foreigner to be hired by the largest Japanese newspaper, *The Yomiuri Shinbun*, to write as a regular reporter in the Japanese language. He was also the first American to be allowed into the Tokyo Metropolitan Police Press Club, giving him access to Japan's best detectives, and cementing an information network that he built up over a decade of covering crime, and primarily organized crime, in Japan.

Adelstein is considered the foremost Western expert on Japanese organized crime. He is also a member of the International Association of Asian Organized Crime Investigators, one of the only members of the organization who was not previously a law enforcement officer.

Adelstein has written for *The Daily Beast/Newsweek*, *The Independent*, *The Guardian*, and *The Atlantic*. From 2015 to 2016 he was the special correspondent for *The LA Times*. He is a regular contributor to *Asia Times*, *Zaiten* (Japan), and *Tempura* (France). He has also appeared on CNN, NPR, the BBC, and other media outlets as a commentator on yakuza-related news and Japan's nuclear industry giant, TEPCO.